The Children of Israel

The Children of Israel

READING THE BIBLE FOR THE SAKE OF OUR CHILDREN

Danna Nolan Fewell

Abingdon Press
Nashville

THE CHILDREN OF ISRAEL
READING THE BIBLE FOR THE SAKE OF OUR CHILDREN

Copyright © 2003 by Abingdon Press

This book is printed on acid-free, recycled, elemental-chlorine–free paper.

Library of Congress Cataloging-in-Publication Data

Fewell, Danna Nolan.
  The children of Israel : reading the Bible for the sake of our children / Danna Nolan Fewell.
     p. cm.
Includes bibliographical references (p.   ) and indexes.
  ISBN 0-687-08414-8 (pbk. : alk. paper)
  1. Bible—Criticism, interpretation, etc. 2. Bible stories, English. 3. Bible as literature. 4. Bible—Reading. 5. Children—Books and reading. 6. Child rearing—Biblical teaching. I. Title.

  BS511.3.F48 2003
  221.6—dc21

                                                                    2003013254

(Credits continued on page 12.)

03 04 05 06 07 08 09 10 11 12—10 9 8 7 6 5 4 3 2 1

MANUFACTURED IN THE UNITED STATES OF AMERICA

For
my daughter Aubrey Sinclair,
truly a gift,
whose presence and wisdom
inspired this book

and

For
children everywhere
who deserve more and better
from all of us

We want a world fit for children, because a world fit for us is a world fit for everyone.

–Gabriela Azurdy Arrieta, 13, speaking at the opening session of the United Nations General Assembly Special Session on Children, May 8, 2002

Let us not make children pay for our failures any more.

–Kofi Annan, Secretary-General of the United Nations

To know God is to know what must be done.

–Emmanuel Levinas

Contents

Foreword

As conscientious world citizens we are called to unpack the stories, especially the religious stories, that influence how we treat one another. Danna Nolan Fewell's book is an important and accessible work to help us fulfill that obligation. For those of us serious about the Bible and the care of our children, it is essential and invigorating reading. Lay and clergy readers of the Bible will discover new ways to read familiar texts as, through a wonderful mix of genres, Fewell plumbs the depths of stories that have formed our attitudes toward children in the church and society.

It makes me shudder even today to recall hearing as a young girl the story of Abraham taking his son Isaac up the mountain to kill him. What kind of God would require that a child be killed to prove obedience to that God? Adults' answers left me troubled and confused. This book reminds us that the Bible contains many such stories where children suffer and simply become dispensable objects in the telling of the story. So, Fewell asks, what would happen if, instead of continuing to take these stories as read, we were to begin to identify with the child Ishmael, who is sent into the wilderness, or with the parents of those children who were killed so that the story of Moses' miraculous saving can be remembered? It is our obligation to stop embracing our old assumptions, to stop ignoring the violence that is there in the text.

Such violence is also present in our own contexts as children are killed and maimed in acts of destruction and civil wars, as it is also in acts of abuse all across the world. Hearing of a young couple who beat their six-month-old boy to death and then burned him in the fireplace, I reflected on the powerful unwrapping of the text of Jeptha's daughter that Fewell gives us in this book. When exposed in this way, this text shows that the cycle of abuse and violence again rests upon the most vulnerable. One can only guess what horror these two young parents had experienced in their own lives to bring them to such a destructive point. Assumptions and realities have flip-flopped: We now often find it is at the hands of their own parents—not strangers at all—that children are abused and killed. Those of us who dream of God's kingdom must work relentlessly for nonviolent endings in the stories of each and every child's life.

Happily, this book also reminds us of the great strength of children. The Bible saves stories that honor the "least of these." Such children are heroes and heroines to their families and to their communities. They are aware of evil and remain faithful in their response.

Fewell reminds us that our own children are likewise aware of evil. We may want to think of them as innocent and untouched by the evil around them, but wishing does not make it so. They confront violence daily; and when they see it in the Bible, they recognize it. As Fewell's dramatic rendition of the story of Esther demonstrates, given the opportunities, children's insights into the ancient text can actually help them to confront the situations in their daily lives.

Increasingly our church leaders are reminding us to pay attention to our children. United Methodist bishops call the churches to be aware of children and poverty; The Children's Defense Fund calls us to "leave no child behind." From all sides we are bombarded by stories of children who are left behind and left to die. What ancient story might be fueling our inability to believe that the children are our priority? People of faith need new passion to take up the cause of the children of the world. Fewell's book is a springboard to passionate action.

This summer I spent wonderful days with three of my four grandchildren. We flew kites and rode the waves. I learned of

Rescue Heroes and they learned how to make paper airplanes. We were unaware of the wars in dozens of places in the world. We were well fed and had cool places to escape the summer heat.

At the same time I was reading this manuscript. To hold the spontaneity and contentment of my precious grandchildren alongside the pain and torture of so many other equally precious children is painful. But the greater pain comes when I acknowledge that all children, including my own grandchildren, are at risk *simply because they are children*. Only as the world is safe and caring to all children will our own children also be safe and cared for. This book calls forth a new commitment to that hope.

The depth of her commitment to all children is reflected in Danna Nolan Fewell's commitment to her own daughter, Aubrey. Fewell is a mother who is also a biblical scholar. I am grateful for scholars who allow who they are and what they care for to dictate where the energy of their scholarship gets placed. Fewell is such a scholar.

Maxine Clarke Beach, Dean
The Theological School, Drew University
August 2002

Acknowledgments

This book has been so long in the making that I fear I will forget many of the influences and encouragements that have become part of the foundation, history, and fiber of this text. Many different voices, faces, and experiences have come together to help shape this work, in many different moments, and in many different places. This book is but a small sign of our time together, of our shared commitment to the well-being of children, and of our common belief in the Bible's power to transform our thinking.

There have been many communities who have allowed portions of this work to be a starting place for their continuing education, their liturgy, and their collective ethical reflection. For their hospitality, attentive listening, and thoughtful conversation, I would like to acknowledge in particular the Candler Women's Caucus, Emory University, Atlanta, Georgia; the United Christian Fellowship at Navarro College, Corsicana, Texas; Luther Seminary, St. Paul, Minnesota; St. Andrew's College, Saskatoon, Canada; Parkin-Wesley College, Adelaide, Australia; Lake Street United Methodist Church, Eau Claire, Wisconsin; Christ Church, Summit, New Jersey; and the Adelaide, Wakefield, Murray Bridge, and Frome presbyteries of the Uniting Church of Australia. Special thanks go to the contact people and hosts for these gatherings: Beverley Elliott, George Procter-Smith, Peter Sethre, Terence Fretheim, David Jobling, Deidre Palmer, Kent Ingram, and Warren Calhoun Robertson.

Some of this material has also been presented at academic conferences. My thanks go to Athalya Brenner and George Aichele and their respective steering committees for including an earlier version of chapter 2 in a joint program of the Women in the Biblical World and the Semiotics and Exegesis sections of the Society of Biblical Literature annual meeting in Boston, 1999; to Roland Boer for including an earlier version of chapter 4 in the conference on Bible and Critical Theory, held just outside of Sydney, Australia, 1999; and to Elizabeth Castelli and her steering committee for including an earlier version of chapter 5 in the 2001 program of the Ideological Criticism Group of the Society of Biblical Literature in Denver.

Earlier versions of portions of this material have also found their way into various publications. Chapter 1 first emerged as "Changing the Subject: Retelling the Story of Hagar the Egyptian," in *Genesis: A Feminist Companion to the Bible (Series II)*, edited by Athalya Brenner (Sheffield Academic Press, 1998). Chapter 4 has appeared as "The Gift: World Alteration and Obligation in 2 Kings 4," in *A Wise and Discerning Mind: Essays in Honor of Burke O. Long*, edited by Saul Olyan and Robert Culley (Brown Judaic Studies, 2000). Chapter 2 has appeared as "The Genesis of Israelite Identity: A Narrative Speculation on Postexilic Interpretation," in *Reading Communities Reading Scripture: Essays in Honor of Daniel Patte*, edited by Gary A. Phillips and Nicole Wilkinson Duran (Trinity Press International, 2002). My thanks go to all these editors who saw fit to include my work in their volumes. The poem "Of No Account" was first published in *Gender, Power, and Promise: The Subject of the Bible's First Story*, by Danna Nolan Fewell and David M. Gunn (Abingdon Press, 1993).

Other expressions of gratitude are harder to categorize and articulate. My deep appreciation goes to all my students, past and present, who have kept the question of the Bible and children at the forefront of their critical investigation of the Bible and at the heart of their ministries; to Francis Landy for the public challenge to deal more thoughtfully with the subject; to Joan Humphreys for her David and Goliath story; to Pat Davis, whose provocative work on the spirituality of adolescent girls, even in its early stages, moved me to tackle the book of Esther and adolescent readers (thanks particularly for the haunting story of Herod's "hitman"!); to Rabbi

Nancy Kasten for several lengthy and helpful conversations about the books of Daniel, Esther, the feast of Purim, and the question of theodicy; to Evelyn Parker for using the midrash on Jephthah as a centerpiece for Dallas youth to address issues of gang violence and parental neglect and abuse; to Esther Churland for sharing her professional wisdom about children, as well as her gingered squash soup and her fascination with the artist Frank Wesley, who clearly connects redemption with children and their care; to Fred Burnett for reading and listening to earlier portions of this work, for innumerable bibliographical suggestions, and for being a most reliable source of encouragement; to Janice Virtue, who also read numerous earlier pieces of this work, for helping me think about formatting and for always reminding me of the importance and power of story; to Jane Hurwitz, Lynne Westfield, Anne Yardley, and Art Pressley for reading early drafts of the Esther play and making helpful suggestions and raising perceptive questions (If you find your comments co-opted verbatim within the script, I hope you will consider it a tribute to your critical insight.); to Gary Phillips for reading the penultimate draft of the manuscript and for many hours of conversation prior to its writing about Levinas, the ethics of reading, and what's really important in life; to the Committee on Faculty at Drew University who granted me a sabbatical in order to finish this work; to my first research assistant, Joe Monahan, for countless hours of library work; to Suzanne Sellinger, our theological librarian, and to the other staff members at the Drew library for helping to locate and to procure all the needed resources; to my second research assistant, Rob Seesengood, for both research, editorial, and clerical assistance; to Miss Leary Anna Murphy, our faculty secretary, for too many and varied tasks to even begin to keep account of; to Maxine Beach for sharing both this concern for children and this love of the Hebrew Bible and for being willing to write the foreword to this book; to Ulrike Guthrie, my editor, for her prompt and enthusiastic responses, her professional guidance, her patience with and intimate knowledge of the creative process, her passion for the well-being of children, and her unwavering commitment to the simple things in life that matter most; and finally, to my daughter Aubrey Sinclair, to whom this book is dedicated, for an uncanny wisdom, innocent, but somehow ancient and profound.

PART I

Children Between the Lines and on the Margins

Reading the Bible for the Sake of Our Children

Children in Crisis

As I write, there are approximately twenty armed conflicts going on around the world, mostly in poorer countries. Eighty to ninety percent of the casualties are civilians, mainly women and children. In the past decade, armed conflicts have killed two million children, disabled four million to five million, and left twelve million homeless. Over a million children have been either orphaned or separated from their families. And one can't even imagine the extent of the psychological damage—the official estimates are that at least ten million children have experienced some sort of war-related trauma. The U.N., in the figures released for the 2002 United Nations General Assembly Special Session on the Rights of the Child, estimates some three hundred thousand children are presently fighting in wars where they face not only the violence of combat, but also possible torture and rape. Millions of children have become refugees, and millions more are dying from war-damaged infrastructures and economic sanctions.

As I write, one hundred fifty million children in developing countries are suffering from malnutrition. This year eleven million children will die before their fifth birthday. Most of these will be from nonindustrialized countries where infant mortality soars as high as one hundred seventy-five deaths for one thousand children. (In industrialized countries, the infant mortality rate is as low as six deaths per one thousand births.) A child is dying from malaria every forty seconds—nearly six hundred thousand children a year—in countries where a few cents' worth of mosquito netting could prevent at least 35 percent of these fatalities. Two thousand children will die today, as every day, from the measles. Six hundred thousand children, mostly in Sub-Saharan Africa and South Asia, are dying this year from diphtheria, pertussis, and tetanus (DPT), diseases easily prevented with vaccines. In Uganda, Nigeria, Tanzania, and Ethiopia (combined), more than four million children under the age of fifteen are now orphaned, having lost either their mother or both parents, due to AIDS.

As I write, over one hundred twenty-five million children are not in school. A quarter of a billion work as child laborers in situations where they are enslaved, malnourished, and forced to perform labor that is physically and mentally debilitating. Millions are being sold as commodities, as a means of meeting the demands of the commercial adoption market, the global labor market, or the prostitution and pornography industries.[1] Forty million children around the world are suffering from abuse and neglect. Recent international studies report that the prevalence of sexual abuse of children ranges from 7 percent to 34 percent among girls, and from 3 percent to 29 percent among boys.

As I write, over 20 percent of children in the United States live in low-income, if not outright impoverished, families who have no health insurance. Twenty percent of the nation's two-year-olds have not been immunized. One million children in the U.S. are presently homeless. A conservative estimate of child victimization indicates that over eight hundred twenty-five thousand children in the U.S. suffer each year from physical, sexual, or psychological abuse; neglect; or medical neglect. (I say conservative because, in 1992, almost three million children were reported abused or neglected. See Edelman 1995.) In the United States a child dies from a gunshot wound every two hours, and homicide has become

---

1. See the United Nations Annual Reports of the High Commission: Report(s) of the Special Rapporteur on the Sale of Children, Child Prostitution and Child Pornography, http://www.unhchr.ch/huridocda/huridoca.nsf.

the third leading cause of mortality for children between the ages of five and fourteen.[2]

To use the now famous language of Robert Coles, *our children are in crisis*. There are many individuals, communities, organizations, even nations, in the world struggling mightily with how to address this crisis. And there are many others who seem to be indifferent to the actual lives that are at stake.

As I write a United Nations General Assembly Special Session is being held on the Rights of the Child. Officials from countries and service organizations all over the world are gathering, hoping to evaluate the world's progress in meeting the goals of the "Convention on the Rights of the Child," a document first proposed in 1989 that calls for an end to discrimination against all children, that recognizes children have the right to survive and develop in all aspects of their lives, and that asserts children's best interests must be considered first in all decisions and actions that affect them.[3] The U.N. summit is also turning its attention to setting new priorities and goals on a range of issues related to the health and education of children. At present, the United States is still vehemently opposing the addendum to the 1989 treaty. The Bush administration and conservatives in Congress are refusing to accept the terms of the document because, they claim, it impinges on parental control, it infringes upon our judicial systems' right to execute or sentence to life-imprisonment children under the age of eighteen, and it encourages the provision of sexual and reproductive health education and services to minors.[4] (Explain these objections to the millions of AIDS orphans for whom parental control is a moot point and where sexual and reproductive health education could have saved millions of lives.) As it stands now, the United States will only agree to the document if the references to reproductive health "services" is deleted (because it could be construed as a code word for providing abortions) and if a caveat is included that the U.S. is excluded from having to adhere to the directive that

---

2. The above statistics were gathered from the online sources listed at the end of the bibliography and from Edelman 1995 and Harvey 1995.

3. The entire text of this document, introduced in 1989, can be found at http://www.unicef.org.

4. See the article by Farnaz Fassihi, "U.S. Draws Heat over Kids' Rights," *The New Jersey Star-Ledger*, May 10, 2002.

children under eighteen should be exempt from either life imprisonment or the death penalty. Our government, it seems, is more interested in preserving its own right to control children—even to the point of killing them—than it is in protecting the rights, even the lives, of children.[5]

What Difference Does Reading the Bible Make?

As I, sobered to the bone, consider the staggering statistics listed above and contemplate the politics involved in even raising world consciousness regarding children, I look across my desk at a stack of Bibles, various versions and translations of the book I've spent my adult career reading and teaching and writing about. I think about the students I help to train for leadership in various kinds of religious communities. I think of the hours we've spent poring over the pages of the biblical text, being both blessed and cursed by its details, being lured into its world of wonder while simultaneously being held at arm's length by its strangeness. I think of this Book, these students, the communities they will serve. I think of the children. And I have to ask: *In a world where so many children are sick, hungry, dying, abandoned, displaced, and violated, in a world where politics take precedence over matters of life and death, what difference does reading the Bible make?*

It's obviously a vocationally driven question, downright self-indulgent some might say. But it's also a question that probes the ethical validity of (some part of) Western religious tradition, the ethical value of the academic enterprise, and the ethical possibilities of communities committed to reading the Bible with care and to responding with compassion.

---

5. Moreover, this administration's tax cuts and vastly increased spending are further manifestations of its lack of care for children. Not only will our children now be responsible for our national debt, but they are now hurt by this administration's attempts to cut the low-income, welfare-to-work childcare program, to cut state funding to prevent child abuse, to increase the interest rates of student loans, to eliminate the federal lead testing program for children in substandard housing, and to undermine the nation's clean air and clean water laws that attempt to protect the environment for our children's future. All the while, nothing is being done to check the rash of gun violence in our nation's schools.

It's related to a more universal question that Emmanuel Levinas, renowned Jewish philosopher and Talmudic scholar, asks with much more philosophical sophistication:

> Is humanity, in its indifference, going to abandon the world to useless suffering, leaving it to the political fatality—or the drifting—of the blind forces which inflict misfortune on the weak and conquered, and which spare the conquerors, whom the wicked must join? Or, incapable of adhering to an order—or to a disorder—which it continues to think diabolic, must not humanity now, in a faith more difficult than ever, in a faith without theodicy, continue Sacred History; a history which now demands even more . . . ? (1988: 164)

It's a hard question, forcing together two incongruent ideas: in the words of Levinas, "useless suffering" and "sacred history," or in my own specific conceptualization, *the useless, meaningless, suffering of children* and *the meaningfulness of a sacred book.*

For those who look to the Bible to provide answers to life's most pressing questions, there is perhaps the belief that the Bible will offer a meaning for the suffering of children. Theodicies, or theological explanations for suffering, in the Bible abound.[6] One can suffer on account of one's sin, one's parents' sins, "original sin," or one's infidelity to God. One can suffer as a trial or a test, or because God's not paying attention to what's going on. One can suffer for the sake of others or for some other greater good. One can suffer because a "larger plan" allows the forces of evil to rule temporarily in this world, but such suffering calls for justice to be served in the world to come. In the second testament, one can suffer to become more like the Christ, who is depicted as the one who has ultimately suffered for the sake of all. However, at some point, such explanations for suffering fall absurdly short. As Emil Fackenheim so insistently asks, *"What are the sufferings of the Cross compared to those of a mother whose child is slaughtered to the sound of laughter or the strains of a Viennese waltz?"*[7]

---

6. See also Levinas's more general discussion of theodicy (1988:159-64).
7. Fackenheim 1970: 75; italics mine.

As he himself admits, the "question may sound sacrilegious to Christian ears," but it haunts us nevertheless, not only in terms of the murdered children of the Holocaust, who are Fackenheim's topic of concern, but in terms of what seems to be the world's general indifference to the suffering of children and of parents who are unable to protect them. The main point is this: *There is no theodicy that makes sense of the suffering of children.* In fact, theodicy itself multiplies the pain and violence already being done to the innocent. As Emmanuel Levinas observes, "The justification of the neighbour's pain is certainly the source of all immorality" (1988: 163).

But if the Bible's explanations for suffering children at the very least no longer make sense or, at the worst, proliferate the violation, what then is the relationship between a supposedly meaningful sacred book and the useless suffering of children? *Must not humanity now, in a faith more difficult than ever, in a faith without theodicy, continue Sacred History?* asks Levinas. Must not we, as communities committed to the Bible's religious traditions, now *read the Bible for the sake of our children*? Should we not now engage the Bible with children in mind?

What would it mean to read the Bible *for the sake of our children?* I'm not proposing a study of "what the Bible (explicitly) says about children." Nor am I attempting to decipher what parts, if any, of the Bible can be described or used as children's literature.[8] Rather, I am envisioning a way of reading that allows the subject of "children" to reconfigure what is at stake in the biblical text. I am proposing an exploration of the text as a space to encounter and to contemplate the experiences and needs of children and of the adults who try to care for them.

---

8. The question of how or whether children benefit from reading the Bible (as opposed to some other kind of literature) varies too much from child to child and age to age (as well as from biblical text to biblical text) to be answered with an absolute (despite the practices of church and synagogue). We might do well to remember that the Bible was not written for children and, through the centuries, has probably done as much damage to children as it has good. When we put the Bible and young readers or hearers together, we should call upon all we know regarding child psychology and childhood development as well as upon all we can determine regarding the nature of biblical literature itself. Further exploration of this subject can be found in part 2 of this volume.

"Is it even possible?" some of us might very well ask. *Is it even possible in this secular age for a biblical vision to provide the challenge and imagination we need to care for the world's children?* Devoted readers of the Bible will of course say "Yes!" and will point to obvious passages that enjoin the care of children. "Suffer the little children to come unto me," admonishes Jesus. And didn't he, after all, raise Jairus's daughter and heal the royal official's son and—with a little coaxing—the daughter of the Syro-Phoenician woman? "Remember the widow and the orphan," is the litany of the law, the prophets, and the psalms. Then there is always the plethora of stories where the promise of God and the redemption of the people are borne by the bodies of long-awaited infants. And all of that is in addition to the Bible's general calls to mercy and compassion and the doing of justice. One can certainly find a number of biblical behaviors and attitudes toward children to emulate.[9]

But what about some of the more difficult texts? Texts where the experiences of children match those in the statistics above. Where children as victims of war, genocide, plague, and systemic abuse are depicted with disturbing theological ambiguity—or worse, certainty. Texts where children have fallen between the cracks, where their fate is not considered, erased as easily by the biblical writers as by the modern news media. Texts where children are literary and literal pawns in the stories of adults and nations and the greater plans of God, where the historical and cultural distance looms large, and the expendability of children is commonplace? How can *those texts* speak to how we might construct a world fit for our children? What would *they* demand of us as readers of the Bible and as caretakers of children? How might we read *them* in ways that help us think responsibly, critically, and creatively about how children are to be regarded, how they are to be treated, and the ways in which we, as adults, can work toward the justice and protection and well-being of children?

---

9. See, for example, the biblical rationales given in the 1996 statement by the Council of Bishops of The United Methodist Church: "Children and Poverty: An Episcopal Initiative. Biblical and Theological Foundations," and in the recent study by Pamela Couture (2000: 171-90).

The Strangeness of the Bible and the Presence of Children

The Bible is a strange book, an ancient product of an ancient culture. Its worldviews are often obsolete; its religious understandings are sometimes foreign to us. It is often at odds with itself, full of complications and contradictions, and full of stories that are as likely to be disturbing as they are to be enlightening. Yet, at the same time, it is a book that invites us into its pages to meet the people and their God who inhabit its world. The people we encounter are often faces we recognize. The struggles we witness are often struggles we know. The elusive presence of the divine is one that we ourselves have sought, sometimes found, and sometimes missed.

And the Bible tells its stories in ways that both enamor and frustrate us. It shows us a world, beautiful and flawed, both good and evil, and it rarely tells us what to think about it. Moreover, its own narrative practices are sometimes irritatingly like our own—it suppresses information that would detract from its main points; it sometimes looks away from troubling details; it often overgeneralizes; and it exhibits a tendency to be self-centered and narrowly focused on Israel and its heroes.

When it comes to children, the Bible is often no better than our own modern media. Children are either the invisible casualties, as in the stories of the Flood and the destruction of Sodom,[10] or they are casual pawns in the stories of the nation or the nation's heroes. Ishmael, for example, is a complication that sustains the suspense in the story of Abraham and the favored son Isaac. The trauma of Isaac is not even considered in the text's eagerness to tell of Abraham's obedience to God's command to sacrifice his son. The Hebrew boy babies thrown into the Nile are little more than a plot device to demonstrate the oppression of Egyptian servitude and to set up the exceptional appearance and survival of Moses. Likewise, the fated firstborn of Egypt become the collective scapegoat to

---

10. During the Persian Gulf War in the 1990s an estimated one hundred seventy thousand children died as a result of either direct military attack or health problems brought on by the bombing of the Iraqi infrastructure. Yet the dominant rhetoric of both the U.S. government and the U.S. media eclipsed these statistics by portraying the war as one between good and evil, with the primary target being the sole individual, Saddam Hussein.

illustrate the power of the God of the exodus. In a similar fashion, the male babies in the Gospel of Matthew are pawns in the Gospel's rhetoric to emphasize Jesus' divine status.[11] David and Bathsheba's first baby is sacrificed as God's punishment of David's sin. Job's children are forfeited in a wager between God and the Satan regarding Job's righteousness. Naaman's slave girl exists literarily to tell her leprous master about the prophet Elisha's healing powers. There is no concern for the children themselves, their experiences or their suffering; rather, they are there to further the stories of Israel, Abraham, Moses, David, Job, Elisha, and Jesus.

But imagine what might happen if we were to start thinking about these children who are victims of literary and theological exploitation, if we were to start looking for these children who are hidden between the lines, if children were allowed to surface and reshape the meaning of the biblical text?

We might discover that even stories that seem to exude moral certainty, where the division between right and wrong seems clear-cut, have a way of calling us back to reconsider the fate of children. If

Of No Account

Where were the children of Sodom
when the mighty destruction came?
How many cried,
how many died
midst the brimstone and the flame?

How many babies in Sodom
asleep at their mothers' breasts—
never to know
never to grow—
died with all the rest?

Of all those children in Sodom
not a daughter or a son
could raise divine pity
to save a lost city—
there wasn't a righteous one.

Such wicked children in Sodom
there surely must have been
for a whole town
to be burned to the ground
and everyone within.

How many babies in Sodom
were lost in a show of might?
How many cried,
how many died
on account of divine oversight?

—DNF

---

11. For a provocative treatment of how Matthew's "murder of the innocents" neutralizes the Jewish foundation narrative and becomes a violent template for anti-Semitic and anti-Muslim violence, see Phillips 1999.

we once believed the story of the destruction of Sodom and Gomorrah confirmed that these cities were indeed as evil as God had suspected, that not even ten righteous could be found there, if we thought that we, like Abraham, could watch such destruction from a distance (Gen 19:27-28) without involving ourselves in its causes or aftermath, the question of children forces us into the city square, where neither children nor strangers are safe at night, where violence threatens from both inside and out, and bears faces both human and divine. Once in the city square, we might begin to see all those faces the text leaves invisible. For the city of Sodom is not simply a city of violent, xenophobic, and sadistic men. There are women and children there as well, as Lot's family clearly attests. There are women and children who become hostages in contests of male power, who are not taken into account when the grand debate about the guilty and the righteous take place between God and Abraham,[12] or when military tactics are carried out by God's seconds-in-command.[13] We may find ourselves wanting to return to Abraham's attempt to intercede with God on behalf of the cities, less amazed at Abraham's audacity, and more anxious to urge him to stand his ground, to clarify the terms of the agreement, to identify specifically the parties at risk. We may find ourselves wanting to intercept the divine emissaries to offer clearer instruction. We may find ourselves at Lot's door, offering a different rhetoric of persuasion to the rapacious mob. We may find ourselves understanding differently the hesitancy of Lot to leave his home, and the reasons for his wife's fateful look backwards.[14]

---

12. The word *tsaddiqim*, usually translated "righteous ones" (masculine plural), can also mean "innocent ones." There is actually a world of difference between these two meanings. A righteous one is a person who has intentionally behaved in good and right ways. An innocent one can be blameless for several reasons: because s/he has done what is right (whether intentionally or not); because s/he has not engaged in the particular wrong behavior under question; or because s/he is not old enough to know the difference between right and wrong. While the angels' investigation might not have turned up any who were righteous, they would have found many who were innocent.

13. Throughout this story divine identity is unstable and unsettling. In Genesis 18, the text reports that "the Lord appeared" to Abraham by the oaks of Mamre in the form of three men. Later "the men" set toward Sodom while "the Lord" stays behind to converse with Abraham. The two "messengers" who go to investigate the "outcry" of Sodom actually do very little investigating. They base their judgment of the city's evil on the Sodomite men's attempted assault of them that evening at Lot's house. There is no claim in the text that the messengers are either omniscient or fair-minded. Rather, like humans, they respond with vengeance to the threat toward their persons.

14. See the discussion of this text and of feminist poetry written on this text, in Fewell and Gunn 1993: 56-67.

Reading the flood story with the children in mind produces a similar kind of reaction. Despite the fact that "Noah and the Ark" is now considered a classic children's story, despite the fact that this motif has found its way into the design of children's toys and the decorations of children's nurseries all over the United States, reading this story *for the sake of our children* makes for an unsettling experience. While we once might have fancied ourselves safe in the ark, pleased to have been found worthy of God's redemption, and enthralled with the parade of animals joining us two by two, we are now compelled to ask, what of those washed away in the deluge?[15] God and the narrator may assert all-encompassing generalities regarding the evil and violence of humanity ("all the imaginations of the [human] heart were only evil all the time" [Gen 6:5], "the earth was filled with violence" [Gen 6:11, 13], "every living body had corrupted its way upon the earth" [Gen 6:12]), but we need only peer beneath the surface of the water to find the children, the fauna, the flora, to discover the innocent victims that are erased by the text's own rhetoric. Once we imagine, as Gustave Doré has done in his famous engravings,[16] the bodies of the young and of the desperate parents trying to save them, we begin to see that *all* generalities (especially those based on binary oppositions), whether divinely sanctioned or not, do untold violence to the innocent. In this story God has responded to human violence with an overwhelming violence of his own; a violence so devastating that he, like a parent in a fit of uncontrollable rage, having resorted to the physical abuse of a child, comes to regret his action and to swear repeatedly that he will never respond in such a way again (see Gen 8:21; 9:11, 15).

What if Noah, like Abraham, had argued with God on behalf of the innocent? What if Noah, like the prophets, had attempted to get

---

15. Or, as Roemer (1995: 179) so candidly puts it: "While the plot offers us certain guarantees—the wicked will be punished and justice will prevail—stories are not finally reassuring. We identify with the hero but can hardly fail to notice that in the course of most narratives innocent bystanders like ourselves are savaged, and end up as wet spots along the road."

16. Paul Gustave Doré (1832–1883) produced two hundred forty-one wood engravings for the French folio Bible published in 1866. It is often claimed that his magnificent work turned that and subsequent such editions of the Bible into a best-seller. His images have greatly influenced the way popular Western culture has visualized biblical story.

The Deluge. (Paul Gustave Doré)

The World Destroyed by Water. (Paul Gustave Doré)

the people to change their violent behavior?[17] What if he had endeavored to protect the children? What if God had not reduced all human failure to "the same," had specified the crimes, had distinguished between the innocent and guilty? What if God had figured out other punishments more appropriate and specific to the crimes?

Interrupting the Text

Texts, says Adam Zachary Newton (1995: 57), "know that they are being read."[18]

The Flood and the destruction of Sodom are stories that know they are being read and they invite *interruption*. They leave room for it. They even imagine it. Abraham's questioning of God in Genesis 18 becomes a model for readers. As God sets his plot in motion, Abraham comes forward and asks, "Will you sweep away the innocent along with the guilty? Should not the Judge of all the earth do justice?" Abraham's questions imagine a different ending, a righter ending, an ending where a city could be spared for the sake of ten innocents. As for the Flood, God swears that next time he will interrupt himself if need be:

> "When I bring clouds over the earth and the bow appears in the clouds, I will remember my covenant that is between me and you and between every living soul that is in every living body; and the waters will never again become a flood to destroy every living body. When the bow is in the clouds, I will see it and I will remember the agelong covenant between God and every living soul in every living body upon the earth" (Gen 9:14-16).[19]

---

17. Perhaps one reason why, in later interpretation, the ancient rabbis were so critical of Noah was that they could imagine a Noah who interrupted God, who pleaded for the lives of the innocent (as did Abraham in Genesis 18), who tried to change God's mind, and who tried to do something to change the behavior of those among whom he lived. On the latter point, see Ginzberg 1998: 153-59. In general, however, the rabbis took a different tack to level out the perceived inequity, basically imagining humanity, even infants, and animals so depraved that their behavior warranted God's judgment.

18. Cf. Levinas (1998: 171):

A book is interrupted discourse catching up with its own breaks. But books have their fate; they belong to a world they do not include, but recognize by being printed, and by being prefaced and getting themselves preceded with forewords. They are interrupted, and call for other books and in the end are interpreted in a saying distinct from the said.

19. "[L]iterary texts are perfectly capable of un-saying themselves, that is being interrupted from within" (Newton 1995: 177).

As a strategy of reading, interruption is a way of stopping and questioning the text—of recognizing that, ethically, something is amiss in what we are being told. Imagine a production of Shakespeare's *Othello* in which a spectator leaps onto the stage in order to prevent Othello's murder of Desdemona. Newton's comment on such a scenario is "[L]inguistic structures *do* have worldly consequence, that art, so to speak, gives off light, that phenomenalism spills over into reference" (1995: 43). There is some kind of blurring of boundaries between the texts we watch and read and our own lives. We may be conditioned to a kind of passivity in reading (especially where the Bible is concerned). But that, in itself, bears some scrutiny. "[T]heater happens to us, we witness it, and our immobilization as spectators may therefore have something important to teach us about what it means merely to watch and do nothing" (Newton 1995: 43). Lectionary readings in congregational settings may have something in common with theater here. To watch and do nothing. To listen and do nothing. To read and do nothing. Interruption provides another, more responsible, alternative. "To read a text . . . means bearing some burden of responsibility, believing oneself addressed, and thus answerable—to the text itself, or to one's reading of it" (Newton 1995: 45).

Let me illustrate this with a story that seems to have become a common staple in Christmas Eve sermons:

> The church was putting on its annual Christmas pageant, and all the children were to be included in the production. There was one boy, Ralph, whose behavior was particularly rambunctious and unpredictable. The pageant directors were a little anxious about his participation, doubting that they could elicit his full cooperation, but they finally decided that they would let him play the part of the innkeeper. It was a small role that required only one line: "No room!" The directors reasoned that there was little damage he could do with that. The night of the pageant arrived, a full house with all the parents craning their necks to see their budding child actors. Joseph and the pillow-stuffed Mary made their way down the aisle and knocked on the make-shift door of the inn. Ralph the innkeeper opened the door and immediately announced "No room!"

33

According to script, Joseph entered his plea for accommodation, explaining their long journey and his wife's condition to which Ralph dutifully answered again, "No room!" Joseph, in a last-ditch effort, announced that his wife was due to deliver any minute and that, without somewhere to stay, the child would surely be born in the street. Ralph still stood firm. "No room!" he insisted. But as the couple turned away in despair and began to make their way back up the aisle, with Mary waddling in convincing ninth-month discomfort, Ralph's eyes suddenly filled with tears and he shouted, "Wait! You can have my room!"

For many Christian readers, hearers, and spectators, encountering the story of the nativity is a passive experience (despite the hard work of so many creative liturgists who try to make the event participatory!). As a "foundational document," it functions to inform, to remind the community of Jesus' lowly origins, giving specificity to a larger, more nebulous and often less recognized, point about the surprising ways in which God was and is present in the earthly world. Listeners and readers often simply "take the story in"—and take the story for granted. Rarely do they see the need to interrupt the text in the way that Ralph does. Ralph, having entered into the story, finds himself addressed and answerable. For him the human need presented in the story demands response, no matter who the needy family is, no matter what the larger divine plan is, no matter how the story is supposed to turn out in the end. For him the story is not primarily educational, nor is it primarily a ritual reminder of identity and belief. Rather, the story presents an ethical moment that addresses all who are capable of making room for the vulnerable, for the stranger, and who, for various reasons, do not. And ironically, Ralph's encounter with the story underscores a common biblical motif that, in being willing to interrupt one's own life to offer hospitality to a stranger, one may be welcoming the very presence of the divine.

Interruption is a strategy for both reading and living. To interrupt means to question the story being told, to imagine the story being told differently, and likewise, to question one's life and to imagine life being lived differently. This presupposes a different kind of relationship to the biblical text than many of us have had in the past. The Bible is not a text telling us directly what to think, what to do, or how to live. Rather, there is a more profound overlap between reading and living. In the language of Peter Brooks (1985: 260), "the reader is solicited not only to understand the story but to complete it: to make it fuller, richer, more powerfully ordered, and therefore more hermeneutic." In other words, there are some stories we are called upon to imitate; there are many others we are called upon to complete and, in the living of our lives, there are some we are called upon to retell, some we are called upon to rewrite, if they are to mean anything significant to us in today's world.[20]

Philosophers and theorists speak of this relationship in different ways. Levinas uses terms like "school" (1990: 138) and *espace vital*, "living space" (1989: 192; see also 210, n. 2) to describe what happens when we enter and experience the world of the Bible. Even when the text refuses to offer "a doctrine of kindness," it yet is a "school of kindness" where we encounter not figures, but *faces*, who "are entirely here and related to us" (1990: 138, 140). The Bible is a space, a "nourishing terrain" (1989: 210) that we might inhabit, where we might come to see ourselves and others in a different way. For Newton, the relationship can often exhibit more coercive tendencies: "[I]n the act of narrating, storytellers lay their hands on

---

20. Cf. Sartre (1965: 55-56):

> As for me who read[s], if I create and keep alive an unjust world, I can not help making myself responsible for it. And the author's whole art is bent on obliging me to *create* what he (sic) *discloses*, therefore to compromise myself. So both of us bear the responsibility for the universe.... However bad and hopeless the humanity which it paints may be, the work must have an air of generosity. Not, of course, that this generosity is to be expressed by means of edifying discourses and virtuous characters; it must not even be premeditated, and it is quite true that fine sentiments do not make fine books. But it must be the very warp and woof of the book, the stuff out of which the people and things are cut; whatever the subject, a sort of essential lightness must appear everywhere and remind us that the work is never a natural datum, but an *exigence* and a *gift*. And if I am given this world with its injustices, it is not so that I might contemplate them coldly, but that I might animate them with my indignation, that I might disclose them and create them with their nature as injustices, that is, as abuses to be suppressed. Thus, the writer's universe will only reveal itself in all its depth to the examination, the admiration, and the indignation of the reader; and the generous love is a promise to maintain, and the generous indignation is a promise to change, and the admiration a promise to imitate; although literature is one thing and morality a quite different one, at the heart of the aesthetic imperative we discern the moral imperative.

those they address, possibly to minister to them, possibly to do them violence (if only verbal). And those addressed, in the ways they construe or respond, perform answering actions in turn" (1995: 74). He cites, for example, the Akedah, the binding of Isaac (Genesis 22), as not only a story of child abuse,[21] but storytelling as child abuse, where storytelling itself is "binding" and violent: "Narrative forcibly yokes together lives and stories without, so to speak, G-d's blessing" (Newton 1995: 112). Newton is right in the sense that we read at our own risk. Or, to put it in Levinas's theo-philosophical terms, we continue Sacred History in a faith without theodicy. We continue to engage the biblical text even when it cannot provide easy answers and obvious meanings. Responsible reading comes with no promises of comfort. On the contrary, it comes more often with disturbance. And yet, one might argue that, even in the Akedah, God's blessing (however morally problematic) does come in the very strategy of reading and living being proposed here—through *interruption*. If, in the story world of the Bible, God from time to time interrupts his own morally questionable plots, then we can surely find the courage to interrupt the violence being done to children within, by, and beyond the biblical text.[22]

Retellings and Textual Mosaics, or What You'll Find in This Book

> The Torah, owing to its own intertextuality, is a severely gapped text, and the gaps are there to be filled by strong readers, which in this case does not mean readers fighting for originality, but readers *fighting to find what they must in the holy text.*

Thus writes Daniel Boyarin (1990: 16; italics mine) as he begins his own description of rabbinic midrash. While I do not pretend to present here anything as profound or intricate as the work of the ancient rabbis, I would nevertheless like to position the work of

---

21. On this notion, see also Delaney 1998.
22. Cf. Phillips (1999: 264):

Interruption occurs when particular innocent children disrupt the power biblical texts exercise in shaping our perceptions and informing our world. By attending to these children's faces and other innocents whose deaths rupture our critical strategies and our memory, we open ourselves to the possibility of saying "No" to all texts, biblical or otherwise, that kill children, biblical or otherwise. Short of a shaken conscience nothing is credible.

this book in the tradition of midrashic reading and to echo the sense of urgency that Boyarin captures in his language. It is time that we give up our practices of passive reading and begin "fighting to find what we must in the holy text."

Midrash seems a good place to start. As an ancient, traditional hermeneutical practice that asks questions (from the Hebrew root *drsh*, "to make inquiry") of the biblical text, *midrash* assumes that the text has multiple meanings and is relentlessly open to rereading. For the midrashic interpreter, "the multiple dimensions of the Hebrew Bible become not merely interesting, or disturbing, they provide the key for endless self-critique and renewal. They are not inconvenient complications to our finding the 'truth,' they are of *the very essence of that 'truth'*" (Magonet 1991: 23; italics mine). *Midrash* also constructs an intricate web of selected interrelated texts, allowing, inviting, forcing them into conversation and debate with one another, creating a kind of inner-biblical "endless self-critique and renewal."[23]

Moreover, *midrash* retells biblical stories in ways that address issues current in the interpreter's culture. Boyarin (1990: 14) imagines "the rabbis as readers doing the best they could to make sense of the Bible for themselves and their times and in themselves and their times—in short, as readers." Or in the words of Howard Schwartz (1998: 10-11):

> The primary purpose of the aggadic tradition [*midrashic* literature], then, was to transmit and reinterpret the past of each successive generation. This purpose has at its root a love for the past and a desire to carry it into the future, to keep it alive. The bibli-

---

23. This has come to be known in theoretical discourse as "intertextuality." Julia Kristeva, recapitulating and building on the work of Mikhail Bakhtin, coined the term *intertextuality* to describe, in spacial terms, the multidimensional intersections and interconnections among texts: "[T]he 'literary word' [is] *an intersection of textual surfaces* rather than a *point* (a fixed meaning), . . . a dialogue among several writings: that of the writer, the addressee (or the character), and the contemporary or earlier cultural context" (1980: 65); "any text is constructed as a mosaic of quotations; any text is the absorption and transformation of another" (1980: 66). This is not a characteristic that some texts have while others do not. Rather, it is a claim that "no texts . . . are organic, self-contained unities, created out of the spontaneous, freely willed act of a self-identical subject. What this means is that every text is constrained by the literary system of which it is a part and that every text is ultimately dialogical in that it cannot but record the traces of its contentions and doubling of earlier discourses" (Boyarin 1990: 14).

cal tale, once told, was found to be true for all generations; it was open to reinterpretation as well as retelling in each generation. . . . This is, by definition, what tradition is—receiving and transmitting anew what has been received. In many ways this legendary literature not only is a peculiar kind of scriptural commentary, but also considers the past from the perspective of the future, searching for oracles that have since been fulfilled and for clues that will help provide safe passage into the future.

This is not always a pleasant, or even benign, enterprise. As we discovered in our discussions of Sodom, the Flood, and Akedah, "fighting to find what we must in the holy text" sometimes leaves us disappointed in, even violated by, the text itself. As we've come more recently to recognize the cultural, gendered, ethnic biases of the Bible, we can now assert without apology that retellings often require revisions, revisions that take seriously those who are marginalized both within and by the text. But this is a process necessary to the text's own survival. As Alicia Ostriker (1993: 28) writes: "[A]ll myths central to a culture survive through a process of continual reinterpretation, satisfying the contradictory needs of individuals and society for images and narratives of both continuity and transformation. . . . [V]ital myths are paradoxically both public and private, . . . they encode both consent to and dissent from existing power structures, and . . . they have at all times a potential for being interpreted both officially and subversively."

The main point is this: "The Bible always addresses itself to the time of interpretation; one cannot understand it except by appropriating it anew" (Bruns 1986: 627-28). Thus I find myself reading the Bible and writing about it, not simply as a biblical scholar, but as a mother, a teacher of ministers, and a citizen who is both astonished by and implicated in the plight of the world's children. I read and retell, not in an effort to make the Bible more interesting or entertaining, but "fighting to find what I must in the holy text." Like a sculptor seeking to find the face calling out from the stone, the wood, or the piece of clay, I have found myself in each text presented here searching to find the faces of the children and of the parents and other adults who struggle to protect them or who ultimately abandon them. Childhood existence is precarious and fragile. We know this. The Bible knows this. The faces are screaming at us. It's time that both we and the Bible own up to this reality, come to terms with our mutual responsibilities for this reality, and find within the text, within ourselves, and within our communities, the courage to change the world for the sake of our children.

But, not surprisingly, we could use some help. Consequently, I've invited into the conversation various philosophers, theorists, literary critics, biblical critics—and children. In actuality, they all insisted on coming and I merely opened the door. (And quite honestly, I think it's time Derrida met my daughter!) And so, as you turn the pages, you'll encounter a kind of montage, or collage, of various kinds of discourse. Hopefully, this will serve as a reminder of the ways in which all of our discourses and inquiries are colored, constrained, and liberated by our cultural and personal experiences. It also dramatizes for us the dialogic nature of discourse itself.[24] When texts and interpreters come together, especially in communal settings, meaning is not static and limited, but dynamic, moving, and excessive, surpassing the bounds of the text and finding points of contact with our lives. In Peter Ochs's words,

> As the agent of a community's deep-seated rules of knowledge, Scripture engages the . . . interpreter in a tradition of meaning. Transferring agency to the interpreter, *Scripture also grants some freedom to transform the way in which that meaning will be retransmitted.* In the process, *Scripture and its interpreter are mutually transformed.* (1996: 65; italics mine)

The voices and texts in this volume are brought together to meet you the reader. The goal is a process of mutual interpretation and mutual transformation. Some of this has already transpired within the bounds of the volume; some is yet to come in the reading and discussing of this volume and the biblical texts upon which the chapters are based. What is offered here should neither settle nor limit the possible meanings to be found in biblical texts, but should be considered an invitation to further reading, moral reflection, and imagination.

The voices you will hear, the texts you will read cover a broad spectrum. Some are simple and straightforward. Others are technical and philosophical. Some readers may gravitate more toward one kind of discourse than the other. That's perfectly permissible. In

---

24. "The dialogical orientation is obviously a characteristic phenomenon of all discourse. It is the natural aim of all living discourse. Discourse comes upon the discourse of the other on all the roads that lead to its object, and it cannot but enter into intense and lively interaction with it" (Bakhtin, quoted in Todorov 1984: 62).

what has become our refrain, readers must "fight to find what they must." Some readers may also find having to deal simultaneously with multiple discourses to be distracting, even annoying. If that is the case, my advice is this: Read first the biblical text cited at the beginning of each chapter. Then read the *midrash* (which may be in the form of story, play, essay, poem, or dialogue). Then, if you have the interest and fortitude, engage the theoretical dialogue (usually found in the footnotes, but sometimes set out as quotations or as a meta-text) with the biblical text and *midrash* in mind.

Many readers may also discover that this is not a book to be read at one time, from cover to cover. The chapters vary in style, tone, subject matter, and emotional intensity. Some readings echo the Bible's own liberative themes. Others imagine the biblical text as a political and theological weapon. All the readings attempt to expose the Bible's own capacity for irony—a quality we may be less familiar or comfortable with as readers, but which demands of us a more attentive, sophisticated kind of reading. Moreover, the chapters are not meant to flow together in any kind of linear fashion. You can actually read them in any order you want. Consequently, if you find that your own reading demands "interruption"—for closer scrutiny of the biblical text, for re-reading, for further reflection, for difficult questions, for emotional respite, or for some other reason—then that's as it should be. It is simply my hope that, somewhere in this textual montage of imaginative reading and theoretical, critical, and philosophical reflection, a space is created for, an invitation is issued to both individuals and communities to begin, to continue, reading the Bible for the sake of our children and to engage in the more arduous work of repairing our world.[25]

---

25. Cf. Ochs's comments regarding reason and "postcritical" interpretation:

> The model of postcritical inquiry redescribes *reason as a relational, or dialogic, activity, assuming as many specific forms as there are contexts of suffering which call out for understanding*—or which call out for divine love. Reason is the relationality of this love: touching us most intimately in the body of those deep-seated rules of knowledge which enable us, not to know the world—for such knowing is a transient, everyday activity—but *to repair the errors that regularly arise in our everyday knowledge*. As this form of relationality, *reasoning is repairing*—an activity without which we cannot live. The tragedy of modern scholarship is that it despairs of its capacity and responsibility to participate in the work of repair. For postcritical scholars, *this is the work of exegesis and interpretation,* and they do not despair. (1996: 77; italics mine)

"Mom," asked the ten-year-old, "can anyone write a Bible?"

"Hmmm . . . that's an interesting question. Why do you ask?"

"Because I have some important things to say about God, and I think I'd like to write a Bible."

"Well, I suppose you could write one. The real question would be, would other people want to read it?"

"Why wouldn't they want to read it? I know a lot about God and the way people ought to treat each other."

"Do you think your perspective on these things would be significantly different from that of the Bible we read in church?"

"Mom, really! Just how many ten-year-olds do you think helped write that?"

CHAPTER ONE

The Other Woman and the Other Child

(Genesis 16 and 21)

There is always a castaway who scratches his name on waves or sand with his nails. Life and death fight over it in every book.

—Edmond Jabès[1]

Hagar, servant of Sarai, where have you come from and where are you going?"

She had been asking herself that over and over as she trudged through the desert night.

"Where have you come from and where are you going?"

The first question was easy enough to answer. She was coming from a house of bondage where she had been passed back and forth between Abram's bed and Sarai's kitchen, where she had suffered abuse at the hands of her mistress, while an indifferent Abram had turned his head. Despite the fact she was carrying his child.

Well, no more. She had had enough. She was running away.

---

1. Jabès 1983: 265.

It was the second question that plagued her. Where was she going? She didn't know.[2] She supposed she would go back to Egypt. But what then? How would she survive? A woman alone with no family and no way to take care of herself much less the child she was carrying inside her. Egypt was where her slavery had begun when she had been but a child herself. If she returned, destitute, would she not be enslaved again?[3] Could she bear to see her child be born into slavery?

She was filling her water skin at a spring on the way to a place called Shur when she heard the voice. "Hagar, servant of Sarai, where have you come from and where are you going?" She turned to see a man standing there. He looked like one of the gods.[4]

"That's me. Hagar. 'The displaced one.'[5] Fitting, don't you think? The woman without a home. And you? Who are you? And how do you know my name?"

The man said nothing.

"You're him, aren't you?" she said. "The god old man Abram is always talking to and talking about."

"More or less,"[6] the man replied.

"So, what do you want?" she asked.

"I want to help you."

"You want to help me? Well, where in Sheol have you been? All the times I cried for help—when I was being used by my master and mistress alike, when I was being made to produce for them a child and then being beaten for the very thing they were using me for—why couldn't you have made an appearance then? Oh, don't tell me. I know. You're the god of rich men. You make the wealthy wealthier. You promise them land and descendants—and slaves like me. How could you possibly be the god of Abram and the god of a slave woman too?"

---

2. Weems 1988 observes that Hagar's identity is so shaped by her servitude that she cannot conceive of a different future.

3. An impoverished woman without family would have had few options. She might have become a prostitute. If completely destitute, she might have little recourse but to sell herself into slavery. And, of course, there was always the danger of being kidnapped and being sold into slavery by someone else.

4. As has often been noted, the text cannot make up its mind whether the divine figure is God or a messenger (or angel) of God. Hagar obviously understands him to be a deity.

5. The play here is on *ha-ger*, "the sojourner" or "the resident alien."

6. See note 4.

"Hagar," the man repeated, "where have you come from and where are you going?"

"You know very well where I've come from. I've come from the swift and harsh hand of my mistress."

"And where are you going?"

She had no answer. She turned back to the spring to resume filling her water skin.

There was a long, heavy silence. Then the man said, "You must go back and submit to the abuse of your mistress."

Hagar whirled around angrily. "Not on your life! I'm not going back there. Why should I go back there? Am I supposed to let them beat this child out of me? Let me tell you something—if you're going to make it as a god around here, you've got a lot to learn about liberation!"

"I will greatly increase your offspring. There will be too many of them to count."

"Is this a bribe? Greatly increased offspring! That's what you've been telling Abram, too, isn't it? Is that why you want me to go back? So you can fulfill your promise to him? Just what I thought—you don't care about me. This is all about that old man who's been wandering all over the countryside acting like he owns the place."

"Don't worry about Abram. This promise is being made to you. You're carrying a son. When he is born, you shall name him Ishmael, 'God hears,' because God has heard your anguish."

"And this is what you do about it? God has heard my anguish so you send me back to suffer some more anguish? Is this the way you deities get your entertainment?"

"Your son will be a wild ass of a man—"

"Great. That's just what I need—an ass of a son." She paused. "But wild, you say? Wild, as in free?"

"His hand will be against everyone, and everyone's hand will be against him—"

"But he won't be under anyone's hand?"

"No, he won't be under anyone's hand."[7]

---

7. The recurrence of the word "hand," a euphemism for "power," retrieves and counters the theme of power and oppression symbolized by Sarai's "hand" in verse 9. Ishmael, despite a seemingly violent existence, will not have to endure the humiliation "under a hand" that Hagar has had to endure.

Hagar looked out across the desert that seemed to stretch endlessly in the morning light. She wondered how far it was to Egypt. She wondered how far it was to the next spring of water. She wondered if there would be a next spring of water. What were the chances that her baby could survive such an arduous journey? And supposing he could, then what?

She turned back to the man. "You promise, my child will grow up free?"

"I promise, he'll grow up free."

"What does Abram call you? Oh, it doesn't matter. I'm going to call you El Roi, the God of my seeing, the God seeing me, because I have seen you and you have seen me. We've seen each other face to face. We know each other's names. We each must now live up to the other's expectation. I will do what you have asked. You must do what you have promised."[8] And she named the spring "the well of the living one who sees me," and she prayed, "May it always be so."

And so Hagar returned to the household of Abram and Sarai, knowing she would pay dearly for her attempt to escape. When her baby was born, Abram named him Ishmael, "God hears," as though the boy was God's response to his own petition for a son.[9] Hagar kept her secret, pondering it in her heart, wondering from time to time whether God had really heard her anguish or whether she was just a pawn in the story of somebody more important.[10]

Most of the time it didn't really matter. She didn't mind being on the margin as long as she could see her son in the center. She didn't mind the fact that Abram completely ignored her in favor of her son. She didn't even mind that, in Sarai's eyes, she could do

---

8. This reading plays upon an obviously Levinasian image: encountering the face of the Other is ethically obligating. Compare, for example, Emmanuel Levinas's reading of Exod 33:11 (Levinas 1994) in which he equates the face-to-face encounter with God and the obligation to the other.

9. We are never told how Abram comes to name the boy Ishmael. Does Hagar tell him of her encounter at the well? Does God make a separate revelation to Abram? Does Abram simply understand the boy to be the answer to his own petition and thus names him accordingly? This particular reading tries to capture how the desires of two (and in the larger story three, maybe even four, if one includes Sarah and God) individuals run along separate but strategically intersecting paths.

10. Which is the way she is often read: a blip on the screen of salvation history. See Tamez 1986.

nothing right. She was watching her son grow up free, the first-born of a wealthy man who had been promised land and blessing by the very God who had seen her by the spring of water. She spent her days working hard for the old couple, taking care of Ishmael, and making sure she did nothing to give Abraham and Sarai cause to sell her to someone else. She couldn't bear the thought of being separated from Ishmael. He was the vision of freedom and hope that the God of Her Seeing had given her.

And then one day it happened. The miraculous conception. The withered womb of her mistress Sarah sprouted life. As Hagar watched the belly of her mistress grow, she became increasing uneasy about her son's well-being.

It was That God at work again, obviously trying to prove that there was nothing too difficult for him to do.[11]

Hagar felt very torn about Sarah's pregnancy. Sarah had always wanted a son. And because she had had none, her place in the household was really quite unstable. Twice Abraham had given Sarah to other men, claiming that her beauty was a threat to his life. Both times Abraham had been given great wealth in exchange for her.[12] That, too, was a kind of slavery, Hagar reasoned. A body sold is a body sold, whether for manual labor or sexual service. Both times, though, That God of Abraham had let Sarah go free. And Hagar wondered, somewhat bitterly, why Sarah? Why not her?

Of course Sarah could never be completely free. What woman could? She still had to go back and live with Abraham. And that was its own kind of affliction. Hagar didn't trust Abraham. He was a man of convenience. You can't trust a man who'll sell his own wife. She knew from experience that, if things got difficult for her, she would never be able to count on Abraham to help her out.

So on some days Hagar was glad for Sarah's victory. She had been treated poorly by Abraham and now That God was compensating her with a child, a child who would love her and bring her laughter in her old age. Sarah deserved this miracle of life.

But on other days Hagar was afraid. Afraid of what this miracle of life was going to mean for her son and for herself. Sarah's newly

---

11. See Gen 18:14.
12. Gen 12:16 and Gen 20:14, 16.

found security might manifest itself in personal generosity. But then, it might not. Abraham's mistreatment of her had certainly not stopped her from mistreating Hagar. Exclusion would beget exclusion, Hagar feared.[13]

And she was right. A son, named Isaac, was born to Sarah and Abraham. Everything was fine for the first couple of years. Sarah was completely preoccupied with this little child needing her milk and her care. But on the day that Isaac was weaned, everything changed. Maybe Sarah was grieving her loss of physical connection with Isaac. Maybe she was suddenly feeling old and aware that she would not always be around to protect her son's interests. Maybe she was just being an old mama bear lashing out at anything that seemed even remotely threatening to her cub. Hagar would never know for sure what generated her cruelty; but on the day Isaac was weaned, Sarah saw Ishmael playing with Isaac. She turned fiercely to Abraham and said, "Get rid of that slave woman and her son. The son of that slave shall not share an inheritance with my son Isaac!"

For all her expectant fear, Hagar still was stunned. The words fell like the blows that had often come from the back of Sarah's hand.

"Get rid of that slave woman and her son!" Sarah repeated.

"I have a name," Hagar silently screamed. "I have a name. My name is Hagar.[14] My son has a name. His name is Ishmael. God hears. God hears. God, are you listening now?" She looked at Sarah in disbelief, not daring to voice the anger and betrayal exploding inside her. "How can you do this? You forced me to have this child. 'Take my maid' you said to Abraham, 'that I may be built up through her,' you said.[15] And now, when we are no longer convenient, you throw us out? How can you do this?" She closed her eyes. "God of My Seeing, are you seeing now?"

Abraham was stunned as well. And very displeased. Not that he cared a whit about Hagar—she knew that as far as she was concerned, she was nothing more than a slave to him—but he was

---

13. See the reading of Fewell and Gunn 1993: 39-55.

14. Abraham and Sarah never refer to Hagar by name. Her name is used only by God and the narrator.

15. Note that Sarai's reasons for using Hagar as a surrogate are put not in terms of fulfilling God's promise or in terms of providing Abram an heir. Sarai's voiced concern is for her own status.

very close to Ishmael.[16] Ishmael was his firstborn. A son of his old age. But despite his obvious displeasure, he uttered not one word of protest to Sarah. Somehow Hagar was not surprised. How could he not do what Sarah asked? He owed her. He had allowed her to be taken twice into the harems of other men. Once after she was pregnant with Isaac. She could have been killed if, while in that harem, she had been found to have been pregnant with another man's child.[17] Abraham had gotten much of his wealth trading on the body of his wife. His hands were tied. His guilt obligated him.

Hagar knew he would spend the night talking to His God. She thought that maybe, just maybe, his love for Ishmael would win out. Maybe, just maybe, That God would tell him to do the right thing.[18] And maybe, just maybe, he would defy Sarah and do it.

But the next morning he arose early, summoned Hagar and Ishmael, and told them they must leave. Ishmael was confused and upset and kept clinging to his father's arm.[19] Abraham would not look Hagar in the face as he handed her some bread and water, scarcely two days' provisions, to take on their journey. She waited, thinking he would provide an animal for them to ride, or money for them to barter with. Abraham was, after all, a wealthy man.[20] Ishmael was his son. She

---

16. The text says that Abraham was displeased "on account of his son." God is the one who includes a reference to Hagar (21:12), but does so in words that perpetuate Abraham and Sarah's perspective: "Do not be distressed over the boy or your slave woman. . . ." God does not say "your son" or "your (second) wife." It seems that the character of God is fully implicated in the objectification and exploitation, though we might hope he is trying to get a rise of protest out of Abraham, such as the defense Abraham put up for Sodom and Gomorrah. Cf. Fewell and Gunn 1993: 51-53.

17. See Rashkow 1992: 66.

18. God, of course, does not insist on the "right thing" for Hagar and Ishmael. The "god of seeing" has betrayed her. See the passionate interrogation of God by Waters 1991: 200. Also, compare Fewell and Gunn 1993: 51-52.

19. The painting "The Expulsion of Hagar" by Salomon de Bray (Dutch, 1656) depicts Ishmael clinging to and kissing his father's hand.

20. Cf. Waters 1991: 200. The Dutch paintings by G. Metzu ("The Dismissal of Hagar," 1653) and Pieter Lastman ("The Banishment of Hagar," 1612) contrast starkly the wealth of Abraham and Sarah to the impoverished ostracization of Hagar and Ishmael. In Metzu's work, Abraham's dog has both a house and a bone, while Hagar and Ishmael are being ushered out of the house with no provisions. Lastman portrays Abraham as the owner of a grand estate with bird houses and feeders to provide for wild fowl, and yet he makes no provision for Hagar and Ishmael. Moreover, in the Lastman painting there is a crumbling turret on Abraham's house—an ironic deconstruction of the stability of Abraham's household. In this scene, Abraham's household is indeed coming apart. These paintings are printed in Brenner 1998.

could see his herd of donkeys beyond the tents, chewing their fodder. But she waited in vain. None was separated out and led to her. Abraham furnished them with nothing else. They were to be sent away with nothing but the clothes on their backs and those meager rations. The resentment of Sarah was in the very air they breathed. It was paralyzing Abraham and choking the life out of Hagar and Ishmael.

"What fine religious people," thought Hagar bitterly. "What a blessing they are to all the other families of the earth."

Hagar pulled Ishmael away from his father, moving mechanically as though she were caught in some bad dream. The two of them trudged from the encampment into the wilderness of Beer-Sheba, traveling slowly because Ishmael was young and tired easily.[21] By the end of the second day, they had run out of water and were suffering from exhaustion and dehydration. Ishmael kept passing in and out of consciousness, whimpering incoherently about wanting water and his father. His cries produced a sharp pain in her breast—the pain she used to feel when he was a baby, when her milk would let down to quench his hunger. She would give anything to be able to produce such milk now.[22]

Hagar was sure that this was the end. She laid her son down in the only shade she could find, that of a scrubby bush. She kissed his parched, still murmuring, lips and moved some distance away because she could not bear to watch him die.

---

21. The text is conflicted about the age of Ishmael. Gen 21:14-15 suggests that Ishmael is an infant or toddler, while the final form of the story suggests he is much older.

22. The renderings of this scene by Indian artist Frank Wesley (see Wray 1993: 201) and Italian artist Pompeo Batoni ("The Appearance of the Angel to Hagar in the Desert," 1774/1776), show Hagar with one bare breast. While Batoni seemed rather fond of painting women with one bare breast, one might deconstruct artistic convention, or even a particular artist's fetish, and allow the woman's subjectivity to determine the reading. The artist may have bared the breast to entertain the male gaze (if there is one), but the "female gaze" might instead see a woman desperately desiring to save the life of her child. The posture of the angel also supports a more "maternal" reading of Hagar's breast: As he hovers over her, one hand extends down toward her breast while the other points to a fountain of water gushing in the background. Thus, the angel himself links the mother's breast to the life-giving water. Wesley's depiction is more obviously maternal in intent, associating too Hagar's breast with a spring faintly emerging from the rocks.

She sat down in the dust, bewildered and betrayed by the unkindness of the world around her.

"What has happened to you, Hagar?"[23] she asked herself in despair. "What has happened to you?"

The only one she had ever loved, the only one who had ever loved her, the only one who had ever brought her happiness or given her hope, lay dying a bow-shot away and there was nothing she could do about it.

She covered her face with her hands and burst into sobs that evaporated without destination into the dry, empty, heat.

What has happened to you, Hagar?

The question came again.

What has happened to you?

It was as though the voice were coming from outside her, demanding that she lift her head from the cradle of her hands. She stood with a stagger. Many things had happened to her, many things over which she had had little or no control. Right now this wilderness was happening to her. It was threatening to kill her and her son. She had been threatened before. She had suffered before. But she had found the courage to leave. And then she had found even more courage to return. All on account of That God Who Saw Her, the God Who Had Heard Her Anguish. If God had seen her then, That God could see her now.

She could hear his voice again,[24] promising that her son would be free. Promising that he would become a great nation. She began to search frantically for signs of water. "God of My Seeing," she prayed. "Open my eyes." She climbed to the top of the next rise and in the valley below her the plants were greener. She ran, stumbling down the rocks and through the sage-green shrubbery, ignoring the scrapes and scratches and bruises.

And then, there it was, right in front of her. The dark opening of a cistern, mouthing its silent promise of life. She quickly filled the

---

23. Literally, "What to you, Hagar?" The usual translation "What's the matter, Hagar?" or "What troubles you, Hagar?" has the effect of trivializing Hagar's situation—as though the "god who sees" cannot see that they are dying!

24. Scholars have long noted that God is portrayed in this passage as less tangible and more distant. This God does not present himself as a visible character as in Genesis 16.

water skin and hurried back to Ishmael. She lifted the boy's head, pouring the water through his lips.

"We cannot die now, Ishmael," she murmured, stroking his forehead. "If we die now, we will have been nothing but a convenience and then a complication in the lives of Abraham and Sarah. We are more than that. God has heard you, Ishmael. God cannot give you your father, but God has given you your life."

And, lifting her son, she held him tight. He was her flesh and her blood. Her hope and her promise. She would carry him all the way to Egypt if she had to.

He was free.

And so was she.

And God was with them.[25]

---

25. The ending of the story is double-edged. On the one hand, we are told of God's presence with and protection of Ishmael and, by extension, his mother. And on the other hand, that very notice of divine presence and protection permits the reader to give no more thought to their welfare. In the next chapter we will imagine how this story might have functioned during the terms of Ezra and Nehemiah when Judean men were told to send away their foreign wives and mixed children. The obvious questions arise for both ancient Judeans and readers of every age: Where will these women and children go? How will they live? This story gives an opiate answer: Don't worry. God will take care of them. You don't even have to provide for them. After all, Abraham didn't provide anything for his foreign wife and mixed child—and God sanctioned his lack of generosity. Leave it to God. The Hagars and Ishmaels of this world will be all right. "Do not be distressed . . ." (Gen 21:12).

"Mom, I'll tell you everything I know about God," said the five-year-old.

"Everything?" asked her mother.

"Yes, everything," the daughter answered solemnly.

"Will this take long?" asked the mother.

"No."

"All right," said the mother. "Tell me everything you know about God."

"God wants us to take care of each other," said the little girl.

"Is that—everything?" asked the mother.

"Yes," said the little girl. "That's everything. Everything there is to know about God."

And she skipped off to play.

CHAPTER TWO

Other Women and Other Children Revisited

(Ezra 9–10; Nehemiah 13:23-31; Genesis 12–34)

The Context

At the end of these things, the leaders came near to me [Ezra], saying, "The people of Israel and the priests, and the Levites, have not separated themselves from the peoples of the lands, the like of their corruptions of/to the Canaanite, the Hittite, the Perizzite, the Ammonite, the Moabite, the Egyptian, and the Amorite. For they have taken from their daughters for themselves and for their sons and they have intermixed the holy seed with the peoples of the lands." (Ezra 9:1-2*a*)

And Shechaniah the son of Jehiel, of the sons of Elam, answered and said to Ezra, "We have been unfaithful in relation to our God and have taken foreign women from the peoples of the land. Yet there is hope for Israel concerning this thing. Now, let us cut a covenant with our God to expel all the women and those born from them according to the counsel of Adonai and those who tremble at the command of our God and by the law, let it be done." (Ezra 10:2-3)

Only Jonathan the son of Asahel, and Jahaziah the son of Tikvah made a stand against this. (Ezra 10:15)

The Scene

Despite the rain, the assembly was large. Under the threat of having their property confiscated and their families ostracized from the congregation, all the returning Israelites had come to Jerusalem to hear what Ezra had to say. His message was brief and to the point: "You have been unfaithful: You have brought home foreign women to compound the offense of Israel. Now confess to YHWH, God of your fathers, and do his desire: Separate yourselves from the people of the land and from the foreign women."[1]

The drenched crowd, eager to escape the rain, agreed to Ezra's demand and then dissipated to institute the new policy of ethnic purification. A few lingered behind. Jonathan son of Asahel grabbed the arm of Shechaniah son of Jehiel.

"What do you want?" asked Shechaniah.

"I want to know just what in Sheol is going on," demanded Jonathan. "You wouldn't let me speak in the assembly. You wouldn't take my questions or hear my objections. I demand to know what you think will come of all this."

"Oh, did you wish to contest this action?" asked Shechaniah. "I thought you were gesturing to show your support."[2]

Jonathan glared at him.

"What will come of all this," continued Shechaniah, ignoring the glare, "is the purification of God's people. We cannot have the holy seed of the sons of the Exile contaminated by being mixed with the people of the land."

---

1. Ezra 10:10-11.
2. The gesture reported in Ezra 10:15 is ambiguous. Cf. the JPS translation: "Only Jonathan son of Asahel and Jahzeiah son of Tikvah remained for this purpose."

"This hasn't been considered a problem before. Why all this sudden concern for purity?"

"Well, I wouldn't call it 'sudden,'" replied Shechaniah. "Foreign women have been a problem all along, according to some versions of our history."

"Are you referring to a version that you may have had a hand in writing yourself?"[3] Jonathan asked sarcastically.

"I tell the truth as I see it and as Ezra the priest sees it, I might add. The prophets have long warned us about the uncleanness of the peoples of the land."

"Says who?" Jonathan demanded.

"Says Ezra.[4] He is a priest. Do you doubt that he speaks the truth?"

"Do you think priests have cornered the market on truth?" retorted Jonathan. "The truth is that you are disrupting—no, worse—destroying lives with this new edict. You are tearing families apart. You are leaving women and children homeless with no place to go and no way to take care of themselves."

"Hard decisions sometimes have to be made," replied Shechaniah calmly. "We must now take care of our own women, the women of Judah, who have come back with us from captivity. They deserve homes and families as well.[5] Their rights must be protected and our communal identity must be kept intact and preserved from polluting influences."

"Your concern for the returning women is touching. You surely count your own sister and daughter among that number." Shechaniah's jaw tightened, but Jonathan continued. "But let me ask you this: If we were all to marry among ourselves, how in the long run would this be of any help to us as a community? If we all do this, we could very well remain landless. You know as well as I do that the so-called 'foreign' women of which you speak come from families many of whom are now in control of the land. If God

---

3. Cf. Fewell 1997; Davies 1995; Carroll 1991; and Mullen 1997. For an overview and assessment of the arguments for dating Genesis in the Persian period, see Heard 2001.

4. Ezra 9:10-12.

5. Eskenazi and Judd (1994) suggest that an imbalance in the ratio of women to men may have been part of the initial problem for the returnees. This dialogue suggests that at some point, the number of returning women increased to an adequate proportion.

has really promised us this land, if it is indeed the land of our fathers,[6] then we have a responsibility to reclaim it. If the only way we can regain possession of it peaceably is to marry back into it, so be it. There is nothing wrong with living in peace with the others who inhabit this place."[7]

Shechaniah looked disapproving. "We must have faith. If God wants to give the land back to us, then God will do it in his own good time. But it will only be done as long as the lines of inheritance are clear. He will only give it to the holy seed. Thus, we must make sure that that seed remains separate from all the peoples of the lands and uncorrupted by them and their practices. Remember our father Abraham once refused to accept property from the king of Sodom, lest anyone should say the king of Sodom made Abraham rich.[8] So, we too cannot be accepting property from the likes of the people who are now squatting here, lest we come to believe ourselves obligated to people who are different from ourselves. We must remember that the land is a gift from God."

"A gift from the Persian government is more to the point!"

"What do you mean by that?"

"Think about it. Ezra is an official of the Persian government, the government who permitted us to return to this place and who wants to keep a tight rein on what we do here. Those of us who have returned will always be obligated to the Persian government. Unless, of course, our identities as released captives somehow get

---

6. Jonathan's tentativeness reflects current theories that Jewish identity and the corresponding land claim were political constructions of the postexilic period. In addition to the work of Davies cited above, see also Hamilton 1995.

7. Using the sociological theory of *hypergamy*, Daniel Smith-Christopher (1991: 243-65) argues that the men involved were attempting to "marry up" on the social ladder. He supposes that the "foreign women" were not ethnically foreign at all, but were Jewish women who had not been in exile. He follows H. G. M. Williamson *(Ezra, Nehemiah)*, who argues that "the peoples of the land," i.e., the surrounding community that had remained in the land, controlled much of the territory and enjoyed economic and social advantages that the returned exiles did not share. Willa Mathis Johnson, exploring how Persian marriage practices play into Persian politics of land control, pushes the hypergamy theory further and argues that the "foreign women" were women from Persian noble families who were given, along with access to Persian controlled land, to some of the men of Judah who were in positions of leadership. This would keep Judahite allegiance to Persian authority strong. See her 1999 Vanderbilt dissertation on interethnic marriage in Persian Yehud; cf. Smith-Christopher 1991: 263-64.

8. Genesis 14.

confused with those who have been living here all this time. They, of course, owe no debt to the Persians, do they? In fact, one might imagine that they could come to resent the Persian government for bringing us here and complicating their lives."[9]

"That's rubbish. This is not about politics. It's about what YHWH demands of us as his people. He does not want us associating with or accepting property from the people of the land! The story of Abraham teaches us this quite clearly."

Jonathan shook his head. "Yes, well, I seem to remember Abraham associating with plenty of the 'people of the land.' He was not above compromising with them about grazing or water rights. He even purchased real estate from them.[10] And he certainly had no problem accepting property—or women either for that matter—from the pharaoh of Egypt.[11] Are you really sure God cares so much about how we reacquire the land or whether or not our seed is 'pure'? When in our history have we ever been 'pure'?"

"That's precisely the point," trumped Shechaniah smugly. "That's why we lost the land to begin with."[12]

"That's absurd," countered Jonathan. "I can't believe that God wants to put women and children at risk just for the sake of some narrow-minded view of who can or cannot be one of God's people."

"Well, you had better recall your history, brother. As you yourself just noted, our father Abraham had a foreign wife. An Egyptian. And like these women who need to be expelled, she bore him a mixed son."

"So?"

---

9. See Kenneth Hoglund's explanation of the Ezra-Nehemiah reform in which he argues that ethnic exclusivity conformed to Persian political policy (1992: 237-44).

10. Gen 21:22-33; 23:1-20.

11. Genesis 12. One might assume, as many have in the past, that Hagar was part of the property Abraham received from the king of Egypt in exchange for Sarah. Later interpreters speculated that Hagar was the pharaoh's own daughter."

12. Ezra's prayer indicates this assumption: "From the days of our fathers to this very day, we have been in great guilt. And because of our iniquities, we, our kings, and our priests have been handed over to foreign kings, to the sword, to captivity, to plunder and to disgrace to this day" (9:7).

"So, don't you see?" said Shechaniah, trying to hold his impatience in check. "In the beginning, Abraham wasn't satisfied with the woman he had brought with him from the land of the Chaldeans, either. He didn't think that Sarah could provide much of a future for him. And so he took an Egyptian woman, who came with much wealth, to provide for him a son. A strong, healthy first-born son who would, he thought, secure the promise of land and blessing that God had made to him. But his efforts to make God's promise come to pass were clearly misguided. God had a surprise for Abraham. His wife Sarah, the woman from his very own family, who had traveled with him to this land, was able to bear him a child after all."

"Well," Jonathan looked skeptical, "whether Sarah was really from Abraham's very own family has always been debatable, hasn't it? Just because he said so on occasion to save his skin, that doesn't mean it was necessarily true.[13] But, that aside, what's your point?"

"The point is that we must marry our own kind. Even if it means sending back to the land of captivity for brides from our families left behind there. Just as Rebekah was secured for Isaac, and Rachel and Leah were secured for Jacob, the sons of the exile must find appropriate brides, no matter what the cost. And if they can bring back from Chaldea property and large families to add to our diminished economy and population here, all the better."

"And all the better, too, if these women share the interests and values of the Persian government, eh, Shechaniah?[14] We certainly wouldn't want to become involved with people who might be likely to show resistance to the Persians. Isn't that what's at the heart of this?"[15]

---

13. On this point, see Miscall 1983: 23-45.

14. See Heard (2001: 179-82), who sees in the telling of the Laban stories a reflection of the hypergamy argued by Smith-Christopher. "Mesopotamian" wives would have been perceived as more geographically and politically connected to the Persian government and consequently not the same kind of threat to ethnic identity as the "people of the land."

15. Hoglund suggests that "[b]oth reformers [Ezra and Nehemiah] were sent to the Restoration community in the mid-fifth century precisely because of the need to ensure continued control over the community in the face of the challenges resulting from the Egyptian Revolt" (1992: 244). This might explain why Egyptians are explicitly named in the list of peoples with "abhorrent practices" in Ezra 9:1, whereas all the other peoples named would have been associated with territories in immediate proximity to Yehud.

"The main thing," responded Shechaniah, pointedly disregarding that last remark, "is that our sons come back here to settle the land. Only those who marry women from their own kind will be allowed to possess it. That's how Esau lost his right to the land, remember? He married women of the land and they made everyone's lives bitter. That's why Jacob inherited the family birthright and blessing."

"I seem to have heard the story differently," says Jonathan. "As I recall, didn't Jacob trick Esau out of the birthright and blessing? In fact, isn't it just possible that you're doing a similar thing now?"

"Don't be ridiculous. Isaac and Rebekah knew what was best for the family. That's why Jacob was admonished not to take a wife from among the women of the land. Remember, it was Isaac who was the son of the covenant. He was the holy seed, born of those coming from Chaldea to claim this land. Rebekah was from his very own family. He was heir to the land, and the heir after him was the son born of this perfect union who emulated his values."

"Yes, that's all very well, but the land wasn't even theirs yet. The possession of the land was still generations away."

"Yes, and perhaps that is the case for us as well. But that doesn't mean we shouldn't be attending to the purity of the holy seed who will receive it. Sarah knew that the inheritance could not be shared. That is why she insisted that the Egyptian woman and her son had to go. God saw the wisdom of this. He supported her and encouraged Abraham to do the same. That's why I say, sometimes we must make difficult decisions. God insisted that that foreign woman and her child be sent away long ago;[16] God insists that these foreign women and their children be sent away today. It's just as simple as that. God has a greater plan for us."

"Your acquiescence to this 'greater plan' wouldn't have anything to do with the fact of your own father's second marriage, would it?" Jonathan looked at Shechaniah with renewed scrutiny. "Hasn't your father taken a woman from 'the people of the land,' as you call them? And don't you have brothers who have come from that union?[17] Is that why you're so enamored with these

---

16. According to the Genesis narrative (25:1-6), Abraham also sent away the children of his third wife, Keturah. This text, too, would have supported the Ezra-Nehemiah reform.

17. See Ezra 10:26.

stories of divinely sanctioned disinheritance? Shechaniah, I would have expected better of you."

Shechaniah became indignant. "Don't try to shame me, Jonathan! I'm simply trying to follow God's will. God told Abraham to put away that Egyptian woman and her son. Abraham was obedient. It's clear from the story that we must do the same."

"But what if, unlike you, we love our families?" contended Jonathan. "We love our children. We don't want to be parted from them. We don't want to abandon them."

"No. I'm sure Abraham didn't want to be parted from Ishmael, either," Shechaniah replied with an air of cold superiority. "But he did as he was told. Abraham was willing to give up not only this mixed child, but even the child of promise when God asked him to. If our father Abraham was willing to sacrifice his children, then so must we be. Sometimes God seemingly asks us to give up our futures. We don't know why. We must simply have faith and do as he has commanded us, and trust that he will provide what he has promised."

"Yes, well, with your brothers out of the way, that will certainly provide for you, will it not?" said Jonathan sarcastically. "What about for those you're sending away? Where will these women go? How will they take care of themselves and their children? How will they live? You are insisting that we have nothing more to do with them, that we cut them off from our families, from our community, and yet you offer no provision for them."

"Well, my brother, you might certainly offer them supplies for their journey—wherever it is they are going." Shechaniah smiled indulgently. "When Abraham released the Egyptian and her son, he didn't send them away empty-handed. He made provision."

"You call a loaf of bread and a skin of water provision? Was Abraham not a man of great wealth? Do you really believe that he did all that he should have for his wife and his child?"[18]

"Well, granted, one might call his compassion somewhat conservative," conceded Shechaniah. "But the point is that the woman and her child survived without his support. God took care of them. Abraham did not have to. So you should not worry about

---

18. Cf. Waters 1991: 200.

these foreign women and their children whom we now must cast out of our own families. God will take care of them. We must take care of our own kind."

"And just who determines who 'our own kind' are?" asked Jonathan.

"Why, Ezra is putting officials in place to check the genealogies. You needn't worry. This will all be handled properly."

"No doubt," said Jonathan, shaking his head and slowly walking away. "And soon we'll believe that this has always been God's will."[19]

---

19. In 1995, fifty-three million people—1 out of every 115 people on earth—were uprooted from their homes, either displaced within their countries or became refugees across borders. Eighty percent of refugees and displaced persons are usually women and children. Up to 5 percent of refugee populations—often more in cases of panic evacuation—are children separated from their families (United Nations International Children's Emergency Fund. 2001. *UNICEF End Decade Databases*. New York: UNICEF).

⚜

"A community is made up of groups of people who are different and who like to do different things," said the seven-year-old as she studied for her first social studies exam.

"Is difference a good thing?" asked her mom.

"Oh, yes," she replied. "That's what makes us all special."

"Why is it so important that we respect others who are different from us?" her mother pressed.

"So we don't accidentally hurt them," explained the little girl, "or hurt their feelings. Or make them wish that they weren't part of this world."

The mother was quiet for a moment, dreading the next response she might hear. "Have you ever felt that way?" she finally asked. "Has someone ever made you wish that you weren't part of this world?"

"Oh, yes," answered the little girl. "Sometimes at school."

⚜

Only through suffering will we know certain faces of the world, certain events of life.

—Hélène Cixous

CHAPTER THREE

The Children from the Other Side of the River

(Judges 10–11)

> Violence is a sovereignty, but also a solitude.
> —Emmanuel Levinas[1]

All societies produce strangers; but each kind of society produces its own kind of strangers, and produces them in its own inimitable way. If the strangers are people who do not fit the cognitive, moral, or aesthetic map of the world—one of these maps, two or all three; if they, therefore, by their sheer presence, make obscure what ought to be transparent, confuse what ought to be a straightforward recipe for action, and/or prevent the satisfaction from being fully satisfying; if they pollute the joy with anxiety while making the forbidden fruit alluring; if, in other words, they befog and eclipse the boundary lines which ought to be clearly seen; if, having done all this they gestate uncertainty, which in its turn breeds the discomfort of feeling lost—then each society produces such strangers.

> —Zygmunt Bauman[2]

---

1. Levinas 1990: 9.
2. Bauman 1997: 17.

[I]n reality, murder is possible, but it is possible only when one has not looked the Other in the face.

—Emmanuel Levinas[3]

Is there no balm in Gilead?

—Jer 8:22

I desire compassion and not sacrifice, and the knowledge of God more than burnt offerings.

—Hos 6:6

Most of you know why we're here. But some of you have come for the first time and you may be wondering why we've come so far to this desolate place when our families are missing our presence and our labor at home.

We've gathered here on this mountain, like our mothers before us and their mothers before them, to commemorate the life and death of a young girl Israel has all but forgotten. Even her name has been erased from our memory and there are many in Israel who would like to see this custom halted—our gathering here four days every year to retell the story of Jephthah's daughter. They say we should not care about something that happened so long ago, we should not care about some young girl who lived across the River.[4] They say that she was not really one of us and that what happened to her is no concern of ours.[5]

---

3. Levinas 1990: 10.

4. The girl's hometown is referred to as the transjordanian "Mizpah of Gilead" (see Judg 11:29).

5. Cf. Zygmunt Bauman's statement:

What makes certain people "strangers" and therefore vexing, unnerving, off-putting and otherwise a "problem," is . . . their tendency to befog and eclipse boundary lines which ought to be clearly seen. At different times and in different social situations, different boundaries ought to be seen more clearly than others. . . . [T]he boundaries which tend to be simultaneously most strongly desired and most acutely missed are those of *a rightful and secure position in society*, of a space unquestionably one's own, where one can plan one's life with the minimum of interference. (1997: 25-26)

We can imagine this story being told in Israel, west of the Jordan, as an event or lesson of history, or as propaganda of various sorts. We sense in the transmission of this story both an ambivalence regarding strangers and societal identity as well as an ambivalent elicitation of the readers' or hearers' sympathies. By preserving their stories, the text opens the door for empathy with the plights of Jephthah and his daughter but, while remembering what the transjordanian child does, it doesn't bother to remember her name. Jephthah is claimed as an "Israelite" judge and touted as a great warrior but, as a transjordanian, a son of a prostitute, an outlaw, and a child sacrificer, he is hardly being held up as exemplary. Rather, his story might have easily been preserved in postexilic Israelite society as propaganda against outsiders, and particularly against allowing outsiders to attain places of leadership in Israelite society. The story, while luring us in, seemingly attempts to hold us at arm's length, as if to keep us from investing too much in either character.

Those of us here, however, think her story deserves to be told. We are afraid that, if we don't tell the story, no one will. If no one tells this story, someone may have to relive it. And so we tell it to you, our daughters, that you may tell your daughters and they may tell theirs.

But make no mistake—the story will never replace the child. We would rather that she had lived, grown up, grown old, and told happy stories to her own children and grandchildren. But that did not happen. She is lost to us. And our words will never compensate for that loss. They will never capture her life or the horrors of her death. They can only preserve some small trace of her that can be remembered. The story we tell can never replace the child. It can only replace the silence.[6]

The story begins long ago, before there was a king in Israel, during a time of great lawlessness and unrest in the land. The story begins not with the girl, but with her father when he was a boy.

---

6. Kristeva (1989: 43-53) argues that language starts with a negation, a loss. In mourning, we develop language that takes the place of what we've lost. We recover our loss in language and thus, through language, we negate the negation. For Kristeva, the translation of loss into language is a type of betrayal. A Levinasian perspective would argue further that any such attempt to represent the Other through language is an act of violence, an act that attempts to subsume the Other into the Same; that is, it attempts to reduce the person who has been lost into a controllable representation (see the discussion of Ziarek 1993: 62-78).

I would like to juxtapose this notion with Elaine Scarry's theory of world-making to expose a paradox that comes about in the telling of stories that mourn the loss of others. For Scarry, human artifacts, including literary artifacts, are a means of extending into the world the reality of human sentience. She writes:

> Far more than any other intentional state, work approximates the framing events of pain and the imagination, for it consists of both an extremely embodied physical act (an act which, even in nonphysical labor, engages the whole psyche) and of an object that was not previously in the world, a fishing net or piece of lace where there had been none, or a mended net or repaired lace curtain where there had been only a torn approximation, or a sentence or a paragraph or a poem where there had been silence. Work and its "work" (or work and its object, its artifact) are names that are given to the phenomena of pain and the imagination as they begin to move from being a self-contained loop within the body to becoming the equivalent loop now projected into the external world. It is through this movement out into the world that the extreme privacy of the occurrence (both pain and imagining are invisible to anyone outside the boundaries of the person's body) begins to be sharable, that sentience becomes social and thus acquires its distinctly human form. (1985: 170)

Though such a gesture to make sentience sharable risks the loss of alterity, at the same time, it can be a way of keeping some dimension of alterity alive and, in the case of the story of Jephthah and his daughter, disturbing (cf. Levinas's description of the "trace" in 1986: 354-59).

You see, this isn't a story about one child, but a story about two children. Two abused and neglected children—Jephthah and his daughter.

Jephthah grew up in Gilead—a place across the River, a place that is part of Israel and yet not of Israel. He grew up during a time when the people among whom he lived had turned away from the face of their God. They turned away from God's face in the same way they turned away from the faces of their children. It's a curious thing, how the face of God and the faces of children are often abandoned in the same moment.[7]

Jephthah's mother, more than likely once a damaged child herself, had been forced to become a prostitute. Prostitution was the only way she could take care of herself, and then later, of her son. Jephthah's father could have been, for all either of them knew, anyone in the territory of Gilead.[8] No man took responsibility for him. With no father to claim him, he had no property and no hope of inheritance. He and his mother lived in poverty. He was a nobody. He learned to take care of himself. He grew up tough and, before he was very old, he had learned how to fight his way—or talk his way—out of any scrape. He wasn't afraid of anything because he had nothing to lose.

The people of Gilead were afraid of him, though. For that very reason, Jephthah had nothing to lose.[9] It made him reckless. It made him dangerous. His presence threatened the very people who had made sure that he had nothing to lose, the very men who engaged the prostitute but who then turned the prostitute's son into an outcast.[10] The

---

7. Levinas writes: "[T]hrough my relation to the Other, I am in touch with God" (1990: 17). Further on, in the same essay, he writes:

> The Justice rendered to the Other, my neighbour, gives me an unsurpassable proximity to God. It is as intimate as the prayer and the liturgy which, without justice, are nothing. God can receive nothing from hands which have committed violence. (1990: 18)

8. Hence the enigmatic "Gilead sired Jephthah" (Judg 11:1). Cf. the comments of Burney 1970: 308; Boling 1975: 197; and Trible 1984: 94.

9. "The early mention of his prowess (1a) . . . hints that fear of domination may have been the unexpressed motive behind his expulsion" (Webb 1987: 51). Cf. also Gray 1967: 332.

10. In Bauman's terms, Jephthah doesn't fit the "cognitive" or "moral map" of Gilead. Not only does his presence confuse what ought to be straightforward lines of familial descent and property inheritance, it also prevents the forbidden fruit of the prostitute from being fully satisfying because it exposes an immoral secret, a crack in the welfare system of ancient Israel into which poverty-stricken women are pushed and into which their children fall behind them.

whole town sired him, then neglected him; and when they saw what their neglect had turned him into, they kicked him, bodily, out of the community. "You do not belong among fine, upstanding citizens. You have no right to make demands on us. You own no property and we'll make sure you never do! Your mother is a prostitute. You're not one of us. You are not welcome here."[11]

The young man Jephthah, now without father, mother,[12] or home, wandered aimlessly for a while. He lived out, away from civilization. He made acquaintances with other young men like himself—young men without families or homes or futures—

---

11. Bauman borrows two of Lévi-Strauss's concepts to describe how societies deal with strangers. The first strategy is anthropophagic: "annihilating the strangers by devouring them and then metabolically transforming into a tissue indistinguishable from one's own. This was the strategy of *assimilation*." The second strategy is *anthropoemic*: "*vomiting* the strangers, banishing them from the limits of the orderly world and barring them from all communication with those inside. This was the strategy of *exclusion* . . . 'cleansing'—expelling the strangers beyond the frontiers of the managed and manageable territory." When neither strategy works, societies resort to "destroying the strangers physically" (1997: 18). Bauman's subject is post/modern Western society, and yet his observations and categories for analysis pertain remarkably to this ancient text. Gilead vomits out Jephthah, expelling him "beyond the frontiers" of their "managed and manageable territory."

In psychoanalytic terms, as the son of a prostitute whose paternity is in question, Jephthah's presence exposes the hypocrisy of the male members of community and creates an anxiety about their identity and their security. "Anxiety is the unease of indeterminateness" (McAfee 1993: 122, also 120). Jephthah's presence reminds the men of Gilead that they have desired what is forbidden (Jephthah's mother) and have kept her marginalized and economically oppressed. Moreover, the men don't know who they are in relation to Jephthah. They fear paternity, fraternity, and the corresponding obligations. Following Kristeva, McAfee writes:

> Before the foreigner, the native recalls her own incompleteness; she becomes anxious. The body that becomes anxious is both the personal body of the native and the political body of the nation. The foreigner threatens the borders of the symbolic—and national—order. (1993: 123)

12. Kristeva writes:

> Eventually, though, the time of orphanhood comes about. Like any bitter consciousness, this one has its source in others. When others convey to you that you are of no account because your parents are of no account, that, as they are invisible, they do not exist, you are suddenly aware that you are an orphan, and sometimes, accountable for being so. (1991: 21)

"empty men"[13] who had nowhere to go, no place to be, and nothing to lose.[14] They formed an outlaw band. They raided villages and caravans and hired themselves out as mercenaries. They earned the reputation of being the meanest, most ferocious fighters the territory had ever known.[15]

One day, after Jephthah had grown up, the citizens of Gilead found themselves on the brink of war. The Ammonites were threatening to overrun their borders. The people of Gilead were in danger of losing all they had worked so hard for—their lands, their homes, their freedom, even their very lives. The people

---

13. A literal translation of the Hebrew expression *'anashim reykim*. Cf. Kristeva's comments on the foreigner:

> Free of ties with his own people, the foreigner feels "completely free." Nevertheless, the consummate name of such a freedom is solitude. Useless or limitless, it amounts to boredom or supreme availability. Deprived of others, free solitude, like the astronauts' weightless state, dilapidates muscles, bones, and blood. Available, freed of everything, the foreigner has nothing, he is nothing. But he is ready for the absolute, if an absolute could choose him. (1991: 12)

14. Bauman discusses tourists and vagabonds as metaphors of postmodern life. While tourism might be an anachronistic concept to apply to the Bible, one might still profitably contrast a figure such as Abraham whose travels are the result of the call of his (divinely inspired) dreams and whose economic autonomy allows him to go wherever he needs or wants to go, with the figure of Jephthah who has no choice but to wander.

> [N]ot all wanderers are on the move because they prefer being on the move to staying put. Many would perhaps refuse to embark on a life of wandering were they asked, but they had not been asked in the first place. If they are on the move, it is because they have been pushed from behind—having been first uprooted by a force too powerful, and often too mysterious, to resist. They see their plight as anything but the manifestation of freedom. Freedom, autonomy, independence—if they appear in their vocabulary at all—invariably come in the future tense. For them, to be free means *not to have to* wander around. To have a home and to be allowed to stay inside. These are the *vagabonds*. (1997: 92)

15. The relationship between poverty and criminal behavior in the contemporary world is well documented and continues to be a serious problem in many societies across the globe. See, for example, the analysis of the relationship of poverty and violence in the United States by Harris 1996: 146-93; the collected studies of child poverty in various countries in Cornia and Danziger 1997; and the scathing critique of the ideology of the "economically correct" in Great Britain and the United States by Bauman 1997: 35-45.
We might compare Jephthah to the son of a single, welfare mother who, uncared for by the community, falls through the net. He has no skills, no assets, no education, and no investment in a community that would like to deny his very existence. We shouldn't be surprised at his turn to crime. What other options does he have?

implored God to save them from this crisis, but God, perhaps feeling like an outcast himself, was tired of only being sought out as a matter of convenience, and he refused to reassure them of his presence. With each passing day, invasion appeared to be more eminent. The officials of Gilead cast about for someone to command their troops against the Ammonites, but no one from their midst stepped forward. Each man there felt that he had too much to lose.[16]

Then someone had a brilliant idea. Why not call Jephthah home? He was the fiercest fighter imaginable. He could lead the troops to victory. He might even bring his own fighters with him, and fewer of the Gilead troops would need to be deployed. Yes, they all agreed. Let's bring Jephthah back. We'll make him the captain of our army. And if anything should happen to him in battle, well, it won't really matter. He is nothing to us.[17]

And, just as the people had called on the God they had once rejected, so the officials of Gilead summoned Jephthah from the badlands,[18] hoping that Jephthah would be easier to mollify than God had been. "Come, be our army commander so that we may fight the Ammonites!" they said to him.

Jephthah, understandably, was wary of their overtures. "Are you not the very ones who treated me like filth? The ones who ran me off because you could not stand to live with the likes of me? Why do you come to me now when you are in trouble?"[19]

---

16. Cf. Boling (1975: 195):

> The trouble with the captains of the force [translated "officials" above] was that none of them wanted to go. The implication is that the high office of judge is here regarded as a protection against the erosion of the good life enjoyed by the captains. The judge would "start the fighting" (vs. 18) and perhaps finish it.
> This final narrative form balances the bumbling approach of the people in the face of the Ammonite threat (vss. 10-16) with the self-serving stance of their captains.

17. The Gileadites have a particular goal in mind and, because of this, the acceptance of Jephthah into their community is only temporary. In the words of Bauman (on modern society): "A permanent coexistence with the stranger and the strange, and the pragmatics of living with strangers, did not need to be faced point-blank as a serious prospect" (1997: 19). To return to Bauman's use of the images of Lévi-Strauss, the officials of Gilead only mean to hold Jephthah temporarily in their mouths before spitting him out again.

18. Ironically called *the land of Tov* ("good") in the Hebrew text. Tov may have traditionally been allied with the Ammonites. See 2 Sam 10:6-8.

19. Compare this interchange with that between the people and God in 10:6-16, particularly verses 13-16. Both God and Jephthah are rejected and then summoned back when crisis strikes. They respond in similar ways.

The officials skirted his interrogation. "Nevertheless," they replied, "we have turned back to you so that you may go with us and fight the Ammonites." Jephthah was unmoved. The elders knew they would have to raise the stakes: "Look, we know you like to fight. You could fight the Ammonites and become our leader—not just over our army—but over all the citizens of Gilead."

Jephthah should have turned them down flat. He should have laughed in their faces after the way they had treated him as a boy. But deep down inside he wanted so desperately to be somebody. He wanted to prove himself to the community that had never valued him. He wanted to have all of those things that that community had taught him to desire: a home, possessions, a place of belonging. More than that, he wanted to rise above the citizens of Gilead. He wanted to have those who had driven him away treat him with respect, with deference. He wanted to rule over them. He wanted the satisfaction of having them feel indebted to him.[20]

"Very well," he said. "If you bring me back to fight the Ammonites and God grants me victory over them, then I will become your leader."

Jephthah and the officials of Gilead swore to this agreement before God at Mizpah. Jephthah became commander of the army with the understanding that, if he defeated the Ammonites, he would become leader over all of Gilead. The officials, of course, were secretly hoping that something rather fatal would happen to Jephthah once the Ammonites were driven back.[21]

---

20. In sociological terms, Jephthah is being offered the opportunity to discontinue his life as a nomad or vagabond and to become a *parvenu*, someone with a newly acquired position but with, of course, none of the respect, acceptance, or social qualifications that might come with it. Of parvenus of the modern era, Bauman writes:

> Definitions are *born with*; identities are *made*. Definitions tell you who you are, identities allure you by what you are not yet but may yet become. Parvenus were people in frantic search of identities. They chased identities because, from the start, they *had been denied* definitions. (1997: 73)

21. Compare Bauman's description:

> Wherever they come and dearly wish to stay, the nomads find themselves to be parvenus. Parvenu, *arriviste*; someone already *in*, but not quite *of*, the place; an aspiring resident without a residence permit. Someone reminding the older tenants of the past which they want to forget and the future they would rather wish away; someone who makes the older tenants run for shelter in hastily erected permit-issuing offices. . . . The parvenu's stay must be declared temporary, so that the stay of all the others may feel eternal.
>
> The older tenants hate the parvenus for awaking the memories and premonitions they struggle hard to put to sleep. (1997: 72)

Jephthah's first act was to send emissaries to the king of Ammon to make a gesture toward negotiating peace. It was not successful. But there are those who say it was never meant to be. Jephthah was very pretentious: "What is there between you and me," he said to the king of Ammon, "that you should come to me to make war against my land?" The bewildered king of Ammon didn't have a clue as to who Jephthah was. He stated his claim to the land in question, to which Jephthah responded with a long-winded, blustering recitation of Israelite history (told, of course, from an Israelite point of view!). If that weren't enough to kill the negotiations outright, Jephthah called the Ammonite god by the wrong name, compared the Ammonites to the Moabites, and claimed that the Ammonite king had sinned against him, Jephthah, by making war on him. The negotiations came to a screeching halt.

One could say that Jephthah's training as an outlaw had never included the art of diplomacy. Some thought his bumbling attempt to negotiate was a sure sign of his lack of political sophistication. But looking back on it now, that interpretation is not so certain. After all, what did Jephthah have to gain by making peace? Nothing. If he were to negotiate peace, he wouldn't be needed as commander of the army. And he would never become leader of Gilead. His political position was contingent on his defeat of the Ammonites. He could not defeat them if he did not fight them.[22]

Once it became clear that war was inevitable, Jephthah felt a mighty rush of spirit come upon him. Some have said it was the spirit of the Lord that had come on Jephthah. Others say that it was nothing more than what soldiers normally feel before going into battle. Still others have wondered if it weren't the manifestation of his frantic desire to succeed and be accepted. Perhaps there's no way to distinguish among all these. But whatever the source, whatever the reason, Jephthah became a whirlwind of activity, so they say. He rallied troops from all the areas across the River. Then he rendezvoused back in Mizpah before confronting the Ammonites. He was fiercely determined to win this war and he

---

22. In the words of Barry Webb, "The tone [of Jephthah's speech] is not conciliatory, and these are not the words of a man who is desperate for peace" (1987: 54-55). He continues: "Jephthah has gone on the diplomatic offensive—a very bold move in the circumstances! . . . His message ends . . . with a virtual declaration of war (v. 27*b*)" (p. 58).

demonstrated that determination to his troops by making a most outrageous vow.[23]

Thus he spoke before the Lord at Mizpah: "If you deliver the Ammonites into my hands, then whoever comes out of the doors of my house to meet me when I return will be the Lord's, to be offered up by me as a burnt offering." Jephthah wanted everyone to know that he meant business. But the content of the vow was very telling. On the one hand the vow appeared to be reckless. It was as though Jephthah still behaved as if he had nothing to lose. But on the other hand, the vow had an air of desperation—as though he now had everything to lose. Centered completely on Jephthah himself, the vow was not about the nation's victory; it was about his own: "If you deliver the Ammonites into my hands," he had said. If you will do this for me, personally, I will give something personal in exchange, something from my own house. Even in the midst of a military initiative, Jephthah could not stop being the loner, the deal-cutter, the one who, in self-defense, had to be fiercely dedicated to his own personal survival and success.[24]

As you all know, the Ammonites were soundly defeated. As the news of Jephthah's victory spread, the land of Gilead was filled with ambivalence. On the one hand, everyone was joyous and relieved that the Ammonites had been driven away. But on the other

---

23. While many interpreters assume that this is a private vow "from the trenches," private piety seems somewhat anachronistic in this case. Rather, it makes more sense to attend to how such vows would function as part of military rhetoric. Compare Saul's vow in 1 Sam 14:24-46 and a similar type of "oath" sworn by David in 2 Sam 23:13-17.

24. This negotiation with God echoes the personal nature of both this negotiation with the elders of Gilead and his exchange with the king of Ammon. My thanks to my student Sergei Petrov for pressing me to see this aspect of Jephthah's character and behavior. Compare the reading of Webb:

> Publicly and officially (Episode III) Jephthah has spoken only of the interests of Israel; privately his mind works on his own interests. Publicly he has argued that Israel is the innocent party and expressed confidence that Yahweh's judgment will be in Israel's favour; privately he remembers that he himself has been the innocent party in a dispute (11.1-3) and found his rights disregarded by those who should have protected them (11:7). The emphatic infinitive (*naton*—if you will *indeed* give) expresses his insecurity—will Yahweh, after all, reject him too? Jephthah has everything to lose if the battle goes against him, not least his life (see 12.3), but also his position in his clan and tribe, and that clearly means a great deal to him. Formerly an outcast, he is now "head and commander of all the inhabitants of Gilead." But if he loses the war the whole cycle of rejection will begin again. If Yahweh rejects Jephthah now, so too will Jephthah's people—again. (1987: 63-64)

hand, they were now stuck with Jephthah, the outcast, as their leader. Moreover, he had made this ridiculous vow to sacrifice the first one coming to greet him on his triumphant return. The people became more and more curious as to what would happen next. All in all, the turn of events did not bode well for Gilead's future under Jephthah's leadership. He had certainly shown himself to be a good soldier, but he had also indicated through his vow that people were expendable. The people realized that Jephthah would treat them the way they had treated him. He would not know to do any differently. They had all seen to that in their neglect of him and his mother, and in their violence against him as a young boy.[25]

When Jephthah came home to Mizpah, the town was unusually quiet—except for one lone figure who made her way down the empty street to greet him. It was his daughter—his only child— playing her timbrel, dancing and singing a victory song as women have been known to do for generations. Who would have thought that Jephthah had a daughter? Most of the people of Gilead didn't know. Most of the people didn't want to know. To recognize the existence of Jephthah's daughter would be to implicate themselves further in the extent of their abuse of Jephthah; it would be to own up to the fact that the effects of their violence had had no end.

How did she come to be there? Where was her mother?[26] Who had been taking care of her while Jephthah had been off fighting Gilead's battles? No one knows now because no one bothered to know then.

---

25. Abjection, according to Kristeva, is the state in which the border between the self and other blurs, disintegrates.

> The abject has only one quality of the object—that of being opposed to *I*. If the object, however, through its opposition, settles me within the fragile texture of a desire for meaning, which, as a matter of fact, makes me ceaselessly and infinitely homologous to it, what is *abject*, on the contrary, the jettisoned object, is radically excluded and draws me toward the place where meaning collapses. A certain "ego" that merged with its master, a superego, has flatly driven it away. It lies outside, beyond the set, and does not seem to agree to the latter's rules of the game. And yet, from its place of banishment, the abject does not cease challenging its master. (1982: 1-2)

Jephthah, the abject, has not "ceased to challenge" the identity of Gilead. His behavior mirrors how the people of Gilead have treated him (and God. See Judg 10:6-16).

26. The story's repression of the presence of the girl's mother, like its repression of the fate of Jephthah's mother, is evidence of the story's attempt to efface maternal alterity. On maternal abjection, see Kristeva 1995. If a mother had been present in the story, could the story have continued as it stands? Or would a mother, as in the case of the Shunammite woman, have averted the death of the child and thus have rewritten the story? Instead, the confrontation with the father has overruled the protective sanctuary of the mother's house.

Alone she danced in a street silent except for her thin child's voice and the tinkling of her timbrels. Alone she danced in a town where God's presence was sought out and where people came to make public vows of responsibility. Alone she danced in a community that did not want her and that could not be relied upon to offer her sanctuary. Alone she danced through the town square toward the gates where justice was dispensed daily—except for that day. Alone she danced, while behind her—far behind her—the people of Mizpah stepped timidly from their houses and followed her through the street.

No one seems to know what was in that child's mind when she stepped out of the house that day. Some say she didn't know any better, that she didn't know about the vow, that she was only doing what she thought might please her father. She was simply in the wrong place at the wrong time.[27] Others say that she did know— that everybody knew—and that her act was deliberate.[28] They say that she must have known how the people of Gilead felt about her father and was determined that someone would honor his homecoming. Still others say that there was more to it than that.

They say that when Jephthah saw his daughter, he was distraught. He tore his clothes—some say in anger, others say in anguish. "Oh, no, my daughter," he said. "You have brought me very low. You have become one of my troublers! I have made a vow to the Lord and I cannot take it back!"[29]

Clearly, he had not expected her to be the first one coming out, but no one could ever be certain as to whom he thought he would see. An animal? A servant? A soldier who had been left behind to protect the girl? One of the elders of Gilead perhaps? Had he even

---

27. See the readings of Trible (1984: 100-103) and Fuchs (1993: 116-30; esp. 120-21), who sees the daughter's ignorance as a patriarchal construction designed to minimize Jephthah's responsibility. "The daughter dooms herself—unknowingly. She is responsible for her death just as much as her father is, if not more" (Fuchs 1993: 121).

28. Fewell 1992: 71.

29. Several recent commentators have noticed that Jephthah's rhetoric blames his daughter. Trible writes:

Repeatedly, Jephthah's language triumphs; blame overwhelms the victim. At the moment of recognition and disclosure, Jephthah thinks of himself and indicts his daughter for the predicament. (1984: 102)

See also Fuchs 1993: 121-24.

thought about it at all? A man with nothing to lose seldom thinks of consequences. He was grief-stricken and angry, and he blamed her. "You have become one of my troublers!" he said.

The girl then made a curious response to her father's accusation. "My father," she said. "You have indeed made a vow to the Lord. Do to me what you have vowed. After all, the Lord has given you vengeance against your enemies, the Ammonites."

Now there have been many in Israel who have praised her for being submissive and obedient,[30] but there are also those who say that her words to her father were hard words. Many who were present that day noticed that she didn't have to ask what he had vowed. She knew.[31] She knew that someone would die that day because of his reckless and desperate vow. Perhaps she also knew that no one else's death would make him stop and realize that his disregard for innocent life made him no better than the Gileadites who had treated him like garbage to be discarded.

"After all," she had said, "the Lord has given you vengeance against your enemies, the Ammonites." With the tone of her voice, Jephthah's vengeance against the Ammonites was reduced to an absurdity. The Ammonites were Jephthah's enemy only because he had been paid to make them his enemy.[32] He had chosen vengeance against them as a way of elevating himself in the community—in the community that had been his real enemy, his real troubler from the time he was born.

Some say the girl betrayed her father by doing what she did,

---

30. Fuchs argues that the daughter is constructed as submissive in order to serve patriarchal interests:

> The narrator could not be more effective in constructing the perfect filial role model. Jephthah's daughter is the supreme image of the perfect daughter, whose loyalty and submissiveness to her father knows no limits. (1993: 126)

In a similar vein, Cheryl Exum (1993: 137) speaks of the storyteller using

> the young woman's own words against her. How does Jephthah's daughter speak against herself? By neither questioning the man who consigned her to death nor holding him accountable.

31. Fewell 1992: 71.

32. See note 18. Jephthah may have even been residing previously in territory associated with the Ammonites.

that, in the end, she had turned against him as everyone else had done. Others say she was trying to redeem him, trying to make him see that his violent struggle for recognition was not the answer to anything and that it certainly was not worth the cost to him or the people around him, no matter how callous and calculating they had been. Some say that what she did was simply inevitable—that the violence that had been visited upon her father was bound to come to rest on her, that her father's past grievance against Gilead was bound to be taken out on her. She simply had decided the moment.

No one can be sure what she really meant to achieve. No one can be sure what, if anything, Jephthah learned from this. If the girl had dared to hope that he would put aside the pain of his childhood and his adult ambition and recant his vow, if she had hoped that, in seeing her face, he would be moved to rethink what his obligations to God truly were, she was tragically disappointed. It was as though he never saw her face at all, because he simply could not see beyond the wall of Gilead.[33]

Whatever her reasons, whatever her intentions, whatever her expectations, she made a gesture to her father that neither he nor the community around him would ever be able to appreciate. She risked her life to meet him, dancing determinedly toward a world that would forever resist her song. She never looked back.[34]

---

33. Levinas writes:

> Only the vision of the face in which the "You shall not kill" is articulated does not allow itself to fall back into an ensuing complacency or become the experience of an insuperable obstacle, offering itself up to our power. In reality, murder is possible, but it is possible only when one has not looked the Other in the face. The impossibility of killing is not real, but moral. The fact that the vision of the face is not an *experience*, but a moving out of oneself, a contact with another being and not simply a sensation of self, is attested to by the "purely moral" character of this impossibility. A moral view [*regard*] measures, in the face, the uncrossable infinite in which all murderous intent is immersed and submerged. . . . The infinite is given only to the moral view [*regard*]: it is not *known*, but is in *society* with us. The commerce with beings which begins with "You shall not kill" does not conform to the scheme of our normal relations with the words, in which the subject knows or absorbs its object like a nourishment, the satisfaction of a need. It does not return to its point of departure to become self-contentment, self-enjoyment, or self-knowledge. It inaugurates the spiritual journey of man. (1990: 10)

The tragedy for Jephthah is that there will be no spiritual journey beyond who he has become.

34. Despite the ambiguity of her character and the various ways she has been read—an unwitting victim, a scapegoat, an androcentric caricature, a self-sacrificing

When it became clear to her that her father could not bring himself to recant his vow, she didn't weep. Not there. She wasn't about to weep for herself or for her father in front of the people of Gilead. She would save her weeping for later. Rather, in that moment she summoned all her dignity and made a public request of her father. She asked to spend two months in these mountains with her friends—friends who would be present to her during her last remaining days, and who would miss her and mourn her when she was gone, friends who would tell her story and preserve her memory and her courage in a world that would go on without her. It was only a small group of young women—not nearly as many as are here today—but they stood in stark contrast to the adult citizens of Gilead who made no move to save her or comfort her. The young women accompanied her into the hills. They grieved together over her coming fate. They grieved about being young women in a world where the young were expendable, where adult ambition and position and possessions eclipsed care and responsibility for children.

In the meantime her father, caught in the web of his fear of failure and rejection, continued to fight as a means of defending his honor and his position.[35]

At the end of the two months, the girl returned to her father. The whole community was waiting to see what he would do. The officials were hoping that he would renege, not because they cared about him or his daughter—quite the contrary—but because they thought he would thereby discredit himself and they would be

---

subject—all of which are problematic to some extent, I would like to envision her action along the ethical lines described by Levinas. The girl makes a movement toward the Other (her father and secondarily the community of Gilead) knowing that she can never return to the point of her departure. Her action, in Levinasian terms, is indifferent to her death. It is aimed at a world without her, a time beyond the horizon of her time. She exemplifies the ability "to-be-for-death in order to be for-what-is-after-me" (1986: 349; see further his discussion of the necessity of ingratitude on the part of the other and the problem of reciprocity). This is not self-sacrifice simply as a gesture of obedience, but a risking of self in the hopes of inaugurating a "spiritual journey" in the Other.

35. The episode in chapter 12 is a flashback, occurring after the war with Ammon and before the fulfilling of the vow (see Gunn and Fewell 1993: 117-18). It continues the themes and motifs of the events narrated here: violence, honor, and identity; insiders, outsiders, boundaries, borders, and belonging; words that bring death; and the destruction of family ("house"). It shows Jephthah irrevocably caught up in the world of personal survival and success.

able to take his position of leadership away. They weren't about to tell him that there were ways to be redeemed from such vows. They, of course, had such privileged knowledge, while, he, being an outcast from their society, would have no way of knowing that.[36] They wanted him to feel trapped by his own recklessness. He must have felt the predatory scrutiny and, playing the role of a man who now had too much to lose, he carried out his vow. He did to his daughter what the community had long ago done to him— he got rid of the child whose presence would threaten his security and position.

No one intervened. No angel appeared to stay his hand. No ram appeared as a substitute.[37] Not one person in all of Gilead stepped forward to put a stop to this senseless violence.[38] The people said nothing at all. They watched in silence and, when the burning was over, and with the smell of the smoke still on their clothes, they all went to their homes and to their inheritances and they washed their hands and they ate their evening meals and they went to bed that night saying to themselves, "Well, she wasn't our daughter."[39]

The people did not speak up for the girl or for her father. They did nothing to set their world right. That is why those of us on this hillside must speak up now. For all the children across the river whose lives are seemingly expendable and who, perhaps until today, had nothing to do with us.

---

36. See, for example, Lev 5:4-13; 27:1-8.
37. Cf. Genesis 22.
38. Cf. 1 Sam 14:45.
39. The strange, the abject, helps us to define ourselves as subjects. As Kristeva puts it, "The border has become an object. How can I be without border?" (1982: 4). In their encounter with the Other, the people of Gilead, like Ulysses in Levinas's analysis, return to the point of their departure. An ethical encounter with such an Other, on the other hand, would have been a movement without return. It would have created, as I hope this retelling does for those who read it, an "irremissible disturbance," an "unrightness" that calls the subject to responsibility. "The relationship with another puts me into question, empties me of myself" (Levinas 1986: 350).

The elderly woman sat alone at a table in the airport cafe.

"May I join you?" asked the traveler.

"Certainly," said the woman, moving her things to make room. "I'm waiting for my plane and would appreciate the company."

"What brings you to Orlando?" asked the traveler.

"I'm a social worker," she said. "I was here teaching a course to other social workers and to emergency room physicians on how to recognize the physical and emotional signs of child abuse."

"That's very important and difficult work," said the traveler.

"Yes," she replied. "Seventy-three children died last year in the state of Florida as a result of child abuse. They're predicting that the numbers will be even higher this year. Unfortunately, fewer and fewer people are going into this area of social work. It's just too difficult. I suppose we'd all rather pretend that the problem just doesn't exist. No one wants to believe that so many families are killing their own children."

CHAPTER FOUR

The Gift

(2 Kings 4:8-37)

He will have obligated.

—Jacques Derrida[1]

Reciprocity is a structure founded on an original inequality. For equality to make its entry into the world, beings must be able to demand more of themselves than of the Other, feel responsibilities on which the fate of humanity hangs."

—Emmanuel Levinas[2]

S he had not asked for the child.
  In her mind the child was a gift that she had neither requested nor expected. Every day with that child had been a gift.
Now he was dead.
The woman[3] spurred her donkey on toward Mount Carmel. She

---

1. Derrida 1991: 11.

2. Levinas 1990: 22.

3. The woman is not given a name in the story and, while it has become a common practice in feminist criticism to name unnamed women characters, I find such naming usually reduces the characters to only one particular character trait or to a social or familial connection or to an event that may have happened to them. Rather than trying to correct what is usually seen to be an androcentric narrative strategy, I would like to honor what Adam Zachary Newton (following Iris Murdoch) calls "contextual privacy." By not restricting her signification to a name, the woman is granted "an interior and unrepresentable space" (1995: 157, 316 n. 45) which opens up rather than closes down possibilities of interpretation. (For a

was on a singular quest to find the man of God.[4] He was the one responsible for all of this. He was the only one who could do anything about it.

She had met the man of God long ago. He had wandered through her village and she had insisted[5] that he share a meal in her home. He did not tell her he was a man of God, but she sensed that it was so, and she always made an effort to provide him with food whenever he passed through. He passed through quite often. At one point she had suggested to her husband that they build an additional room onto their house to accommodate this traveler. He could have been homeless for all she knew. She supervised the house-

---

different understanding of the narrative functions of the anonymity of the Shunammite woman, see Reinhartz 1994.)

One might also compare this phenomenon of namelessness with Derrida's observations on pseudonymity (in reference to Kierkegaard):

> This pseudonym . . . reminds us that a meditation linking the question of secrecy to that of responsibility immediately raises the question of the name and of the signature. One often thinks that responsibility consists of acting and signing *in one's name*. A responsible reflection on responsibility is interested in advance in whatever happens to the name in the event of pseudonymity, metonymy, homonymy, in the matter of what constitutes *a real name*. Sometimes one says or wishes it more effectively, more authentically, in the secret name by which *one calls oneself*, that *one gives oneself or affects to give oneself*, the name that is more *naming* and *named* in the pseudonym than in the official legality of the public patronym. (1995: 58)

The woman of Shunem is, of course, not the author (pseudonymically or otherwise) of her own story, but this particular secrecy, this "contextual privacy," suggests that her determined attempt to save her son's life is spontaneous, uncalculated, and not motivated by a concern for recognition. She acts, not in her own name, but on behalf of her son. She acts before she thinks (cf. Levinas) about her own identity, her subjectivity, or about whether or not her action is reasonable in the eyes of others.

She is, in the words of Edmond Jabès describing Jewish identity, a "maze of signs," and his poetic dialogue (1983: 249) could easily apply to her:

> "What is your name?"
> "Look at my face."
>
> "What is your name?"
> "Look at my hands."
>
> "What is your name?"
> "Look at the road."

4. While the man of God is named (Elisha) in the narrative, the woman herself never calls him by this name. She refers to him and perceives him only as "the man of God." He refers to her as "the Shunammite."

5. The Hebrew root used here *(ḥzq)* suggests a kind of overpowering: she "prevailed upon him."

hold addition herself: it was a second-floor chamber with everything he might need—a bed, a chair, a table, a lampstand. She quite enjoyed constructing this space for him—it was something she could afford to do (and no one else in her village could) and it gave the man a place to rest and recover his strength in the midst of his wanderings.[6] She rather liked the idea of making room in her home, making room in her life for this traveler. The very materiality of the newly created space—the cool stones in the walls, the warm wood on the lintels and in the furniture—made her feel as though she had made a difference in the world.[7] The

---

6. The woman's construction hints at the depth of her perception and empathy. The structure is from beginning to end designed to protect the man and to alleviate his discomfort: the walls recognize physical vulnerability in face of the natural elements, the bed and chair mitigate the weight of a fatigued body; the table provides the place for sustenance; and the lampstand fights off the darkness (cf. Scarry 1985: 288).

> If one imagines . . . one human being perceiving in another discomfort and in the same moment wishing the other to be relieved of the discomfort, something in that fraction of a second is occurring inside the first person's brain . . . , not just a perception of an actuality (the second person's pain) but an alteration of that actuality (for embedded in the perception is the sorrow that it is so, the wish that it were otherwise). Though this interior event must be expressed as a conjunctive duality, "seeing the pain and wishing it gone," it is a single percipient event in which the reality of pain and unreality of imagining are already conflated. Neither can occur without the other: if the person does not perceive the distress, neither will he wish it gone; conversely, if he does not wish it gone, he cannot have perceived the pain itself. . . . If this complex, mysterious, invisible percipient event, happening somewhere between the eyes and the brain and engaging the entire psyche, could be made visible, could be lifted out of the body and endowed with an external shape, that shape would be the shape of a chair. (1985: 289-90)

Or, in the case of our story, the shape of a room or a bed or a table.

The Shunammite's concern for the protection and sustenance of the body is contrasted to the man of God's lack of concern for either the woman's body (manifested by his blithe assignment of a pregnancy) or her son's (manifested by his obliviousness to the child's welfare).

7. The woman's gesture involves imagination, work, and artifice, the significance of which is often overlooked. Scarry writes:

> While imagining may entail a revolution of the entire order of things, the eclipse of the given by a *total reinvention of the world,* an artifact (a relocated piece of coal, a sentence, a cup, a piece of lace) is *a fragment of world alteration.* Imagining a city, the human being "makes" a house; imagining a political utopia, he or she instead helps to build a country; imagining the elimination of suffering from the world, the person instead nurses a friend back to health. Although, however, artifice is more modest and fragmentary than imagining, its objects have the immense advantage over imagined objects of being real, and because real, sharable; and because the objects are sharable, in the end artifice has a scale as large as that in imagining because its outcome is for the first time collective. (1985:171)

We don't know if the woman of Shunem was inspired by a larger vision of change, but her ability to see and to transform her imagining into artifice allows the man of God to share in the benefits of her world-altering act and encourages

room was her gift, her gift to God and to the man she believed spoke on behalf of God.[8]

The man of God began to stay there whenever he passed her way. She imagined that room might give him some sense of place, of belonging, some sense of connectedness to a home and to a family. Somehow a man of God who knew of such things would be, in her mind, better able to do what he had been called to do.

One day when the man of God was there, his servant summoned her to the second-floor chamber. As she entered the room, the man of God was lying on his back staring at the ceiling. Not turning to look at her, he spoke to his servant. "Say to the woman," he said, "'You have gone to all this trouble for us.[9] You have rearranged your life for us. What can I do for you? Shall I speak to the king on your behalf perhaps? Or to the commander of the army?'"

She had been amused at the time at the man's self-importance. She never would have taken him to be such a political name-dropper. And why he couldn't even look her in the face or speak to her directly, she didn't know.[10] She hadn't waited for the servant to repeat the speech to her. (She didn't take to such games of pretentious mediation.) "I'm quite content," she had replied as she

---

him to live a different kind of life (namely, one more connected to the people around him) and to enter into a different kind of relationship with her. "The making of an artifact is a social act," continues Scarry (175), "for the object (whether an art work or instead an object of everyday use) is intended as something that will both enter into and itself elicit human responsiveness."

8. Contrast the motivation assigned by John Gray: Elisha did "not actually need the Shunammite lady's hospitality," but she pressed him "observing the ancient Semitic convention of hospitality to sustain her own credit and bringing herself within the range of the 'blessing' which a man of God enjoyed" (1964/1970: 495).

9. The Hebrew word *harad* (often translated "to tremble") connotes here a pronounced disturbance, an intense attentiveness.

10. Burke Long argues that this protocol that separates the woman from the man of God is designed to amplify the importance of Elisha, but the fact that, in the course of the story, the protocol breaks down invites a double reading of the tale.

> [F]rom the beginning the Shunammite seems to have refused the agendas set by others. It was her initiative that established the wayside room for Elisha; she asked nothing when it was confidently suggested by the men that she must have some sort of need; and she pursued justice against thoughtless obstacles of convention thrown in her path by her husband and the prophets.
>
> On the other hand, throughout the narrative Elisha is a man of power. This is his and the narrator's view, at least most of the time. Yet on this occasion Elisha is left without second sight, resists a moral claim, and finally turns the magic trick without confessing any shortcoming to his public. The reader shares a private knowledge of

turned to go back downstairs, "right where I am, living among my own people. There's nothing I need from you or the king or the commander of the army."

She had returned to her work frustrated by the man's words. The man of God clearly wanted to pay her back for the room and for her hospitality. But this was not a matter of economic exchange, and she was somewhat offended that her gift had been reduced to that.[11] It

---

the prophet's vulnerability and thus perceives matters in ways that subvert other tendencies in the narration. (1988: 174)

However, the double-edged nature of the tale that Long exposes so expertly, makes it difficult to claim that only one reading represents "the narrator's view" (even qualified with "at least most of the time"). Rather, it seems that the story is rife with irony regarding the prophet's sense of self-importance. Cf. the reading of Mary E. Shields and her final assessment:

[I]n this text we find a unique blend of the two perspectives—neither canceling the other out. . . . The fact that the patriarchal gender roles are restored at the end does not negate the fact that a woman is elevated at the expense of the man of God. . . . [I]t is no accident that a woman . . . does the subverting. The subversion is all the more effective because it is one whose gender would normally marginalize her who challenges the structure of sacred authority. If the patriarchal or androcentric view wins out in the end, there is nevertheless a gynocentric emphasis that cannot be completely hidden. (1993: 68)

Long later returns to this text to examine more critically the tradition of "Elisha-centered" interpretation and issues a call for more "honest" reading:

I would like to see the day when biblical scholars practice a form of criticism that goes against the grain of such a constructed consensus. By long cultural habit such agreed upon interpretation may seem naturally true, even harmless, but that for those excluded from its protection, can be destructive. . . .

Multiple strategies diminish [the Shunammite's] place in the tale. The writer encloses her with protocols that protect a lionized Elisha. The editor of Kings includes her as a minor character in a larger collection of stories about the prophet Elisha that reinforce expectations about Elisha's greatness and miracle working. A long procession of commentators read each other's works, but more importantly, share a socially formed way of reading that fixes on Elisha and diminishes the Shunammite.

On the other hand, one may refuse the premises that lead to this regime and, like the Shunammite, break with protocol. She can be a model of sorts for readers in a new world. The great lady from Shunem might inspire us to counteract the weight of consensus interpretation, but in a way that does not deny Elisha's place or the voice of commentators who guard a privilege for Elisha. This might be a way that allows both Elisha and the Shunammite power and independence in the story. It might even provide for new religious insights. (1991: 42)

11. On the problem of the gift, Derrida writes:

The moment the gift, however generous it be, is infected with the slightest hint of calculation, the moment it takes account of knowledge [*connaissance*] or recognition [*reconnaissance*], it falls within the ambit of an economy; it exchanges, in short it gives counterfeit money, since it gives in exchange for payment. Even if it gives "true" money, the alteration of the gift into a form of calculation immediately destroys the value of the very thing that is given; it destroys it as if from the inside. (1995: 112)

was, in her mind, just that, a gift. She had chosen to rearrange her life to accommodate this man. Whatever "trouble" she had gone to was her business, not his.

It wasn't long before she was summoned upstairs again. This time she didn't bother to enter the room. She stood in the doorway unwilling to be pulled into this silly conversation about compensation. This time the man spoke directly to her. "This time next year," he said, "you will be holding a son in your arms."

The abrupt announcement had caught the woman off guard and had greatly annoyed her. The thought of two men, guests in her own home, making reproductive plans for her was quite maddening. They hadn't asked her if she wanted a child. They had merely assumed. They assumed that was what every woman wanted, what every woman needed to make her life complete.[12] They assumed that a child would more than repay for their frequent lodging. And they assumed that bringing a child into the world required no careful thought, no preparation, no responsibility on their parts. They assumed that she would be delighted.

She was not.

"No," she said to the man of God. "Do not toy with me."[13] She turned and left the room.

She had spent the rest of the day distracted and irritable. Children were not to be taken so lightly. They were not to be plopped thoughtlessly into the world for any reason. Certainly not simply as symbols of a prophet's miracle-working virility. Certainly not simply as some sort of reimbursement to keep him from feeling obligated. It was this last thing that irritated her the most. The offer of a child was really more about him and his feeling of indebtedness than it was about her, her desires, or the quality of her life.

Her brusque retort had not deterred the man of God, however. The woman became pregnant in the course of that year. And while the child had grown inside her, she lived every day torn between hope and fear. She had had to reorient her thinking completely.

---

12. In her critique of how a patriarchal perspective has dominated traditional commentary on this story, Shields writes, "No one thinks to ask whether a child is really the woman of Shunem's greatest desire" (1993: 67). Cf. also Fuchs 1985.

13. The root of the verb here is *kzb*, usually translated "to lie" or "to deceive." I'm pressing for the more basic understanding of "to say something which has no substance or basis in reality."

After many years of marriage without children, she had no longer expected ever to be a mother. Not only did she have to reenvision herself and her responsibilities, she had to think realistically about providing for this child. Her husband was much older. She had to prepare herself to be, at some point, her child's only parent. But she also had to prepare for the possibility that her husband, old as he was, might turn out to be her child's only parent. And, of course, she constantly worried that her child would grow up without parents at all. She had watched many of her friends die while giving birth and she knew that her own age was a complicating factor.[14]

She often thought that any other woman would rely on the man of God's promise and would trust that everything would work out fine, but the fact that the child had been promised by the man of God never gave her any sense of security—not even for a moment. She was convinced that the man of God never really understood the magnitude of his impulsive offer.[15] To him, the child existed only as a word on his lips. Its presence in the world would make no difference to him. It was simply a way of canceling his debt.

For her, however, the presence of the child was making all the difference in the world. It was changing her body; it was changing her perception of everything—including herself.[16] Its transforming

---

14. In the ancient world, one in every four pregnancies ended in death for either the mother or the child or both (see Meyers 1988: 112-13). With that kind of mortality rate, the dangers of giving birth would be uppermost on any woman's mind.

15. Shields writes:

Perhaps the gift he offered her was one he had no right to offer except when instructed by YHWH. In this case, the reference to YHWH's hiding knowledge from Elisha (and Elisha's preliminary failure as well) could be YHWH's judgment on the prophet's hubris, which the woman sensed in some way when she resisted the gift. (1993: 65-66)

This is not the first time that Elisha has abused his power as a man of God in relation to children. In 2 Kgs 2:23-24 he curses in the name of YHWH a group of children who mock him. On account of his curse, forty-two children are mangled by bears.

16. Scarry writes: "[T]o be barren is not just to be without child but to be unalterable, unable to change from the state of without child to with child: barrenness is absolute because it means 'unalterable' except by the most radical means, unalterable except by divine intervention. . . . God in changing the body from barren to fertile is not simply changing it from being unpregnant to pregnant but changing it from being 'unchangeable' to both changed and pregnant" (1985: 194).

power exceeded the protective walls of any room. It could not be contained in any kind of simple economy of exchange. She knew that nothing would ever be the same again, and she found herself rearranging her life (as she had done for the man of God), making room for, accommodating the fragile body who, in the course of time, came to dwell in her home. The child was not, could not be, a payment for anything. He was a gift—an extraordinary gift from an Imagination far greater than that of the man of God. He was a gift who deserved more love and care and attention than even she could possibly give him.

Every day with her son was a gift. He taught her things she had never known. She had never known she could love so much. She had never known how differently the world looks through the eyes of a child. She had never known such fear, such delight, such hope.

And until today she had never known such pain or such rage.

The servant had brought her son to her this morning from the fields where he had been helping his father. The child, clearly in terrible pain, was complaining about his head. She had held him all morning, trying to comfort him as best she could, applying cool cloths and caressing his forehead. She had no idea what was wrong, and she had never felt so helpless in all her life. At midday he died in her arms.

At first, her pain was almost paralyzing. She sat there unable to breathe, unable to move. She looked at her lifeless son there in her lap and she remembered the words of the man of God, "This time next year you will be holding a son in your arms." Suddenly she was so angry she could hardly see. She made her way with the boy up to the room she had prepared for the man of God, the room designed to sustain and protect and provide comfort. She laid her son on the bed and closed the door.

She sent a message to her husband, telling him to send a servant and donkey, telling him that she was going to find the man of God. She said nothing to him about the boy.

"Why are you going to see the man of God today?" her husband had demanded to know. "It is neither New Moon nor Sabbath."

"Shalom. Good-bye" was her curt response.[17]

She saddled the donkey herself.[18] The servant was too slow. She set out at such a pace, the servant could hardly keep up.

"This time next year you will be holding a son in your arms." The prophet's words echoed in her head, crescendoing into a scream. The promise had become a cruel joke. The arrogant attempt to "fulfill" her and to repay her had become a wound that throbbed with every breath she took.

"How could you know," she asked the absent man of God, "what it means to hold a son in your arms? How could you possibly know what this entails?"

She prodded the donkey again. "Children are such fragile gifts. How could you possibly know what it means to hold in your arms such a fragile gift and to know that your arms cannot ultimately protect it?"

She thought of all the children she had known who had not lived to see adulthood. She thought of their parents. She thought of a story she had heard once about Abraham and Sarah and Isaac,

---

17. Her response, "shalom," is loaded as is evidenced by the various ways it has been translated and interpreted: "Peace;" "good-bye;" "it will be well," "it is well." This response and the interchange with the Gehazi that follows in which she repeats "shalom" in response to all his questions is parallel to a similar interchange in the Jehu story (2 Kgs 9:15-28). In that story, as Jehu rides madly toward Jezreel to seize the throne, he is repeatedly asked, "Is it peace?" Clearly, peace is the last thing on Jehu's mind. So, too, for the Shunammite woman: Her mission is not one of "peace" toward the man of God. She is anything but at "peace."

On the other hand, the response "peace" allows the Shunammite woman both to follow and to break through the protocol that separates her from the man of God. One might also see here a comparison with Abraham's response to Isaac in Genesis 22. When Isaac asks, "Where is the lamb for the burnt offering?" Abraham's response is "God will provide." On this passage Derrida (in dialogue with Kierkegaard) explains, "Abraham thus keeps his secret at the same time as he replies to Isaac." "He speaks in order not to say anything about the essential thing that he must keep secret. . . . He says something that is not a non-truth, something moreover that, although *he doesn't know it yet*, will turn out to be true" (1995: 59). The Shunammite woman uses "peace" when formality requires that she speak, and although she doesn't know it yet, "peace" will be the outcome of her passionate determination.

18. Despite the attempts of some translations to make use of the servant's presence (e.g., the Tanakh's rendering "she had the ass saddled"; NEB: "When the ass was saddled"), the text clearly says that she saddles ("binds" or "bridles") the donkey herself. Rather than understanding this to indicate her urgency, Gray assumes this indicates her size: "The 'great lady' of Shunem personally harnesses the ass. She is a substantial peasant" (1964/70: 498).

the child of promise. Abraham and Sarah had waited so long for Isaac, they had almost given up hope. But finally he came, a gift from God. Then one day Abraham began to hear voices, the voice of God he believed, demanding Isaac back. Abraham was willing to let his son die. How could that be, the woman wondered incredulously. Sarah would surely not have been so willing. How could anyone receive such a gift and not be willing to take care of him, to fight for him, to ensure that he lived no matter what the cost?[19]

She could see Mount Carmel.[20] She thought again of Mount Moriah, of Abraham keeping his secret about what he was going to do. Abraham had to keep the secret. Otherwise, someone would have stopped him. Anyone would have thought he was crazy, trying to sacrifice his son.[21] (And he had to have been, as far as she

---

19. Derrida, too, wonders what might have happened if Sarah had been included in this story:

> It is difficult not to be struck by the absence of woman. . . . It is the story of father and son, of masculine figures, of hierarchies among men (God the father, Abraham, Isaac; the woman, Sarah is she to whom nothing is said . . .). Would the logic of sacrificial responsibility within the implacable universality of the law, of its law, be altered, inflected, attenuated, or displaced, if a woman were to intervene in some consequential manner? Does the system of this sacrificial responsibility of the double "gift of death" imply at its very basis an exclusion or sacrifice of woman? A woman's sacrifice or a sacrifice of woman, according to one sense of the genitive or the other? Let us leave the question in suspense. (1995: 75-76)

Later, Derrida quotes Hegel's identification of woman as "the eternal irony of the community." One might say that the story of the Shunammite woman is a case in which "the logic of sacrificial responsibility" is clearly "altered," perhaps even "displaced." Her action on behalf of her son renders ironic the traditional honoring of Abraham's repeated willingness to sacrifice members of his family.

20. The distance from Shunem to Mount Carmel is thought to be about fifteen miles.

21. Derrida writes of Abraham's secret in Genesis 22:

> Kierkegaard reflects on this double secret: that between God and Abraham but also that between the latter and his family. Abraham doesn't speak of what God has ordered him alone to do, he doesn't speak of it to Sarah, or to Eliezer, or to Isaac. He must keep the secret (that is his duty), but it is also a secret that he *must* keep as a double necessity because in the end he *can only* keep it: he doesn't know it, he is unaware of its ultimate rhyme and reason. He is sworn to secrecy because he is in secret.
>
> Because, in this way, he doesn't speak, Abraham transgresses the ethical order. According to Kierkegaard, the highest expression of the ethical is in terms of what binds us to our own and to our fellows (that can be the family but also the actual community of friends or the nation). By keeping the secret, Abraham betrays ethics. His silence, or at least the fact that he doesn't divulge the secret of the sacrifice he has been asked to make, is certainly not designed to save Isaac. (1995: 59)

By contrast, the Shunammite's secret betrays rationality. She has ethical expectations beyond what is normally considered to be reasonable. And her silence is most certainly designed to save her son.

was concerned.) She, too, was keeping a secret for much the same reason. How could she explain what she was doing? Who would possibly understand? If she were to speak the truth, she would surely be deterred from her mission.[22] No one was going to tell her she was crazy for thinking she might save a child who was already dead. In spite of the shared secrecy, however, she was no Abraham. She would not give up such a gift so easily.[23]

She saw a figure coming to meet her. It was the man of God's servant. He greeted her. "My master saw you in the distance. He sent me to ask you, 'Are you well?'"

"Shalom. I'm fine," she said, not slowing her pace. She was not about to disclose her secret to some surrogate.

"Is your husband well?" he asked, stepping in the donkey's path.

"Shalom. He's fine," she said, reining the animal around him.

"Is the boy well?" he persisted.

---

22. Derrida writes:

> To the extent that, in not saying the essential thing, namely, the secret between God and him, Abraham doesn't speak, he assumes the responsibility that consists in always being alone, entrenched in one's own singularity at the moment of decision. . . . But as soon as one speaks, as soon as one enters the medium of language, one loses that very singularity. One therefore loses the possibility of deciding or the right to decide. Thus every decision would, fundamentally, remain at the same time solitary, secret, and silent. Speaking relieves us, Kierkegaard notes, for it "translates" into the general. . . .
>
> The first effect or first destination of language therefore involves depriving me of, or delivering me from, my singularity. By suspending my absolute singularity in speaking, I renounce at the same time my liberty and my responsibility. Once I speak I am never and no longer myself, alone and unique. It is a very strange contract— both paradoxical and terrifying—that binds infinite responsibility to silence and secrecy. (1995: 59-60)

23. The figure of the Shunammite woman represents the way in which Kierkegaard's apology for Abraham's responsibility to the Wholly Other has been countered by Levinas. Derrida points out the implication of Kierkegaard's argument: "God, as the wholly other, is to be found everywhere there is something of the wholly other" and cites Levinas's counter-reading (1995: 78 n. 6):

> In evoking Abraham [Kierkegaard] describes the meeting with God as occurring where subjectivity is raised to the level of the religious, that is to say above ethics. But one can posit the contrary: the attention Abraham pays to the voice that brings him back to the ethical order by forbidding him to carry out the human sacrifice, is the most intense moment of the drama. . . . It is there, in the ethical, that there is an appeal to the uniqueness of the subject and sense is given to life in defiance of death. (Levinas 1976: 113)

(On this reading of Genesis 22, cf. Fewell and Gunn 1993: 53-55.) The Shunammite woman, in contrast to Abraham, is moved by the wholly otherness of her son and demands "life in defiance of death."

"Shalom. He's fine. Now get out of my way!" *Prophetic protocol be damned!* she thought.

The woman continued the relentless pace until she came to the man of God. She dismounted, ran to him, and clutched his feet. His servant who, by that time, had caught up with her, tried to push her away, but she was immovable.

"Let her alone," said the man of God. "Can't you see how upset she is?[24] Something is wrong and God has hidden it from me."[25]

Yes, the woman thought bitterly, *God has hidden a lot of things from you. If you had been present to the child you so glibly pronounced into being, you would know much more than you know now.* She found her voice.

"Did I ask you for a son? Did I not say to you, 'Don't treat me thoughtlessly'?"

The man of God could not sustain her glare. He turned to his servant.

"Here. Take my staff.[26] Hurry to the boy. Don't stop for anything. Place my staff on the face of the boy."

---

24. The Hebrew phrase *napšâ marâ lâ* would translate literally, "her soul is bitter within her."

25. The woman's secret is hidden from the man of God who, by virtue of who he is, should be privy to knowledge of God. But the man of God cannot graciously accept a gift—how can he be trusted with a secret? As in the case of the gift, the man of God has, in the language of Levinas, failed "to identify the particular interhuman events that open towards transcendence and reveal the traces where God has passed" (Levinas and Kearney 1986: 32).
Derrida writes:

> [God] is made manifest, he manifests his nonmanifestation when, in the structures of the living or the entity, there appears in the course of phylo- and ontogenetic history, the possibility of secrecy, however differentiated, complex, plural, and overdetermined it be; that is, when there appears the desire and power to render absolutely invisible and to constitute within oneself a witness of that invisibility. That is the history of God and of the name of God as the history of secrecy, a history that is at the same time secret and without any secrets. (1995: 109)

To return to the issue of the woman's namelessness, or as we might at this point say, secret identity, we have here an invitation to view differently the woman's anonymity. The secrecy that surrounds her reveals "traces where God has passed."

26. Fokkelien van Dijk-Hemmes (1994: 227) has noticed the phallic significance of the staff. The man of God, as far as the symbolism of the narrative is concerned, is the "father" of the child. The (impotent) phallus-like staff meant to bring the child back to life, is the male counterpart to the womblike room provided by the woman. The balance of the created and creative artifacts suggests that the woman has helped/is helping to create/construct the man of God in a way that is parallel to the man of God's bringing the child into being.

96

The servant hurried away, but the woman refused to let go of the man.

"Don't think for one minute that a substitute will do," she said. "You brought this boy into the world. You are responsible for his well-being.[27] I swear by God and by your very life, I am not leaving here without you!"[28]

There was nothing the man of God could say. He followed her back in silence. On the way they met his servant returning.

"I did as you said," he reported. "The boy will not wake up."

When the man of God arrived, he went upstairs into the room where the boy was lying and he closed the door, leaving the servant to stand as sentry. The woman could hear the muffled tones of the man of God's prayer.

"It will take more than prayer," she said, even though he could not hear. "It's not like speaking to the king in exchange for a room. It takes more than prayer to make a child live and grow. It takes your presence and your proximity.[29] And sometimes"—she felt the ache of watching her child die in her arms—"sometimes, even that is not enough."

---

27. On paternity Levinas writes:

The fact of seeing the possibilities of the other as your own possibilities, of being able to escape the closure of your identity and what is bestowed on you, toward something which is not bestowed on you and which nevertheless is yours—this is paternity. This future beyond my own being, this dimension constitutive of time, takes on a concrete content in paternity. It is not necessary that those who have no children see in this fact any depreciation whatever; biological filiality is only the first shape filiality takes; but one can very well conceive filiality as a relationship between human beings without the tie of biological kinship. One can have a paternal attitude with regard to the Other. To consider the Other as a son is precisely to establish with him those relations I call "beyond the possible." (1985: 70-71)

The Shunammite woman is urging the man of God to establish with her son relations "beyond the possible."

28. Concerning this interchange van Dijk-Hemmes observes:

Only after the woman says to him (v. 30) the words he himself has spoken three times to Elijah (2 Kings 2:2, 4, 6),

As YHWH lives, and as your soul lives, I will not leave you,

does Elisha recall his vocation, recognize that he cannot shake off his responsibilities any longer, and follow her. . . . Thanks to the persistence and actions of the "Great Woman," Elisha proves to be a man of God and the child is brought back to life. (1994: 229)

29. In describing "proximity" Levinas says:

The tie with the Other is knotted only as responsibility, this moreover, whether accepted or refused, whether knowing or not knowing how to assume it, whether

She heard other noises through the door—the creaking of the bed, footsteps pacing back and forth. She peered through a crack in the boards of the door. She saw the man of God lying on top of her son, trying to warm his lifeless body. Face-to-face, hand-to-hand, the man of God breathed into his mouth again and again. After some time—she had almost given up hope—she heard the boy exhale and gasp for breath again. The door opened.

"Call the Shunammite," the man of God was saying as she pushed past him to reach her son. His eyes were open. He was alive. She put her cheek against his, feeling his breath against her ear, feeling as though she, too, had just come back to life.

"Pick up your son," said the man of God.

She bowed in gratitude and relief that her persistence had not been in vain, that the man of God had indeed been capable of doing what needed to be done, that her son had been returned to life, to her. She picked up her son, holding him in her arms gently yet tightly—as if he were the most precious, fragile gift in the world—and she took him away to care for him, leaving the man of God standing there, alone, in the room she had built for him to stay in whenever he passed through.

---

able or unable to do something concrete for the Other. To say: here I am [*me voice*: the French translation of the Hebrew *hineni*, an allusion to Genesis 22 and Isaiah 6]. To do something for the Other. To give. To be human spirit, that's it. The incarnation of human subjectivity guarantees its spirituality. . . . I analyze the inter-human relationship as if, in proximity with the Other—beyond the image I myself make of the other man (sic)—his face, the expressive in the Other (and the whole human body is in this sense more or less face), were what ordains me to serve him. . . . The face orders and ordains me. (1985: 97)

⁓

"Valentine's Day is my favorite holiday," announced the ten-year-old.

"Oh?" said the mom. "Why is that?"

"Because it's the only day when it's OK to give something to **everyone.** On any other day people would just think you're weird. Or after something."

⁓

PART II

Heroes of Their Own Lives, Redeemers of Their Own Worlds

"Did you enjoy the puppet show?" the mother asked.

"Oh, yes!" said the little girl.

"What was it about?"

"You wouldn't believe it, Mom. It was about this really big bad guy who was mean to everybody. I mean he was really big. He was bigger than you," explained the little girl, her enthusiasm mounting. "He was bigger than our car. He was bigger than our house. He was probably even bigger than God!"

"My goodness!" said the mom. "Well, what happened?"

"Well . . . there was this little boy with a swishy thing—"

"A swishy thing?"

"Yeah, he had this thing with a rock in it that he swished around and around and around. Then, all of a sudden, he let it go, and the rock flew out and hit the big bad guy right between the eyes and it knocked him down dead!"

"Hmmm" mused the mom, now somewhat worried about the impact of the story's violence. "What did you think about that?"

The little girl pondered the question. Finally she said, "Can we change that little boy into a little girl?"

Children of the Book

Herod's Hit Man

The year [Nilla] was in sixth grade, she and her parents decided that it would be a good thing for her to be in the church Christmas Eve pageant being organized by the new pastor's wife. Being sensitive to avoid leaving anyone out, or casting people in roles they didn't want, the pastor's wife was determined to allow the children to choose their own parts. She assigned Mary and Joseph to two older children, then gathered all the others and began slowly to read the familiar story of Jesus' birth. As she read, the children called out the characters they wanted to play; angels, shepherds, kings, lambs, donkeys, camels all claimed their roles. At the end of the story, Nilla hadn't found a role to suit her.

Mrs. Alexander, the costume manager, tried to coax Nilla into being a king or a shepherd, to no avail. Nilla finally asked if she could have the Bible. She took it off to read by herself. For fifteen or twenty minutes she was hardly noticed, reading intently, amid all the confusion of trying to find wings and crowns for all the angels, kings, and beasts.

After awhile she returned. "Mrs. Alexander, I've found my role."

"Yes, Nilla—who are you going to be?"

"A hit man."

Mrs. Alexander swallowed hard, noticing the upward glance of the minister's wife. "There are no hit men in this story, honey."

"Right here: 'Rise, take the child and his mother, and flee to Egypt, and remain there till I tell you; for Herod is about to search for the child, to destroy him.' I want to be Herod's hit man."

"What would a hit man wear?"

"All black—to hide—and he'd carry a sword."

"You're sure that's what you want?"

"Yes, ma'am."

"Okay, Nilla. That's you."

On that Christmas Eve night—thanks to Mrs. Alexander and Nilla—their Methodist church saw and heard a fuller version of the story of Christ's birth, with both the wonder and the horror intact. In this church the wise men traveled to King Herod before they arrived in Bethlehem; they were accompanied by a shadowy figure on their way to the stable. Outside the stable, a hit man lurked as Mary cherished the baby and angels sang. On that Christmas Eve, Nilla's church may have been the only church in Christendom to remember Christ's birth in this more complete narrative, including not only the beauty and glory but also the fear, the evil, the grief, and the hit man.[1]

Thus we return to the nativity for yet another example of the extraordinary willingness of young people to expose the moral ambiguity of the biblical text. While adults in the church community are often content with re-rendering this foundational story in "nice," heart-warming, traditionally acceptable, and nonprovocative ways, young people like Ralph (see introduction to part 1) and Nilla, when left to their own reading and interpretive devices, are compelled to see disturbing aspects of the story.

Moral Intelligence and the Reality of Evil

Of all the things I learned from reading Pat Davis's new book, *Beyond Nice: The Spiritual Wisdom of Adolescent Girls* (and there were many!), what struck me the hardest were the keen perceptions that adolescents have of evil in the real world and the ways in which the church is failing to help them deal with those percep-

---

1. Excerpted from Davis 2001: 46-47.

tions.[2] Davis's study suggests that, in many cases, the church doesn't seem to recognize and to respect the moral intelligence[3] of children or their astute observations and their critical, sometimes painful, experiences of the "wrongs" of society. There is often the attitude that young people are, or should be, innocent and untouched by the multiple complications and corruptions and violences of everyday life (because, I think, that's what adults *want* to believe!). Consequently, there's little move to address the difficulties these children perceive in themselves and in the world around them.

The church's predilection for the second testament and, as the story of Herod's "hitman" illustrates, its usual habit of benign, naïve reading, exacerbates this problem. If the church's habit of reading scripture is to steer clear of texts that present moral and theological difficulty, then its children are left with nothing textual and tangible to help them articulate their experiences, concerns, and fears, or to help them grapple with their own development as moral beings.

> A reflecting and self-reflecting mind at some point gives way to a "performing self": the moral imagination affirmed, realized, developed, trained to grow stronger by daily decisions, small and large, deeds enacted, then considered and reconsidered. Character is ultimately who we are expressed in action, in how we live, in what we do, and so the children around us know: they absorb and take stock of what they observe, namely, us—we

---

2. My sense is that synagogues do not face quite the same problem, due to the history of anti-Semitic oppression and the nature of the primary scriptures of Judaism that recognize the reality of evil and that focus on ethical behavior. Christianity's predilection for the second testament and its focus on "grace" and a kind of interior spirituality often offers tempting paths away from having to deal with issues of evil and justice.

3. "Moral intelligence" is a term I've borrowed from Robert Coles:

> "Moral intelligence" isn't acquired only by memorization of rules and regulations, by dint of abstract classroom discussion or kitchen compliance. We grow morally as a consequence of learning how to be with others, how to behave in this world, a learning prompted by taking to heart what we have seen and heard. The child is a witness; the child is an ever-attentive witness of grown-up morality—or lack thereof; the child looks and looks for cues as to how one ought to behave, and finds them galore as we parents and teachers go about our lives, making choices, addressing people, showing in action our rock-bottom assumptions, desires, and values, and thereby telling those young observers much more than we may realize. (1997: 5)

adults living and doing things in a certain spirit, getting on with one another in our various ways. Our children add up, imitate, file away what they've observed and so very often later fall in line with the particular moral counsel we wittingly or quite unself-consciously have offered them. (Coles 1997:7)

What this means in terms of reading scripture is this: If children don't see their religious tradition, their religious community, confronting and wrestling with difficult texts or the hard parts of life, they "will absorb and take stock of what they observe." First, they will conclude that the religious tradition in which they have been raised has nothing significant to do with the real life they live.[4] Second, and consequently, they will not perceive their religious community as a "safe place" where true thoughts, experiences, and anxieties can be expressed or honest questions can be raised. In short, their religious community will not be a place where they can be themselves and, like any place in society that requires a façade, it will eventually become an unsatisfying place to be. Third, they will surmise that if religious institutions, whose purposes are to bring redemption and healing to the world, ignore the world's evils then, as individuals, they are free to do the same. "Interior" spiritual insight, so promoted in most Christian communities, is thus divorced from a sense of ethical responsibility.

Children Reading the Book

I realize that, to a large extent, I'm skirting the question of younger children reading the Bible. My mixed feelings about this issue have long been known by my family, friends, students, and

---

4. And irrelevance may be the very least of the problem. Cf. Bettelheim's psychoanalytical assessment of the importance of the disturbing content of fairy tales:

There is a widespread refusal to let children know that the source of much that goes wrong in life is due to our very own natures—the propensity of all men (sic) for acting aggressively, asocially, selfishly, out of anger and anxiety. Instead, we want our children to believe that, inherently, all men are good. But children know that *they* are not always good; and often, even when they are, they would prefer not to be. This contradicts what they are told by their parents, and therefore the child becomes a monster in his own eyes. (1976: 7)

colleagues in the discipline.[5] I still hold that much of the Bible, when taken at face value, is not appropriate for the eyes and ears of young children. However, once a child starts to become aware of the complexities of life, the Bible can represent a "truer, more real world" that "speaks to our condition" (Josipovici 1988: 28 quoted by Landy 1997: 162). As Francis Landy (1997: 164) points out, the teaching of the Bible to children has been something of a catch-22:

> Children's Bibles and Sunday schools select and emphasize those stories and texts which they think will be pleasing and edifying to children. Their work of censorship and repression is necessarily partial, since elimination of all unwanted properties will result in a text denuded of its most important meanings and, not least, pleasures. Few Children's Bibles omit the stories of the Garden of Eden, the Flood, and the Exodus, troubling as they may be. Some of the gratifications of the text may be contrary to conventional ethical values. Tales of violence and derring-do are among the enduring attractions of the Bible, making the Old Testament more exciting than the New. The antinomy of poetry and ethics is one aspect of this, the indulgence in illicit pleasure at one remove. The Bible, moreover, as an ethical document is essentially concerned with the violence and horror of the world, which is, in its terms, the knowledge of good and evil. In this respect, it is no different from the literature of the world, including children's literature.

Landy goes on to insist that "[c]hildren will focus on those aspects of the text that are of most interest to them, and exclude others." With that wisdom in mind, I would like to explore a few of the aspects of the Bible that children might find to be of interest—namely, stories about children.

Landy is certainly correct in his assertion that the Bible, with its essential concern for "the violence and horror of the world," is no different from children's literature throughout the world. Traditional fairy tales and folk tales are notoriously stocked with evil characters and forces, unfortunate mishaps to children, and parents and other authority figures who are unreliable, even

---

5. See Fewell and Gunn 1993 and Francis Landy's insightful rejoinder (1997) to our question there of whether we want our children to read the Bible.

treacherous. It is not at all uncommon for child protagonists in fairy tales to be orphaned. Otherwise, parental authority and familial constraints would keep the child from the very activities and behaviors that make the story interesting. These literary threats of abandonment, betrayal, and even death make the stories an imaginative space where children can learn to cope with what is bewildering and frightening about life.[6]

Children in the Book

In the Bible there are few stories in which a child is the main protagonist. However, those that exist, like the fairy tales described above, also include the theme of orphanhood of one sort or another. The child Daniel, we're led to assume, is made an orphan as a result of the Babylonian siege of Jerusalem. Esther, too, is introduced as an orphan who has been adopted by her cousin Mordecai. Joseph, Moses, and Samuel are also children separated for various reasons from their families.[7] In all of these stories, some type of violence (social, national, or familial) initiates the plot or, at the very least, colors the background of the story world.

Moreover, all of these young people experience and learn to deal with some kind of *interruption* in their lives. For some, like Daniel and Moses, interruption initiates their stories. For others, like Esther and Samuel, interruption marks a significant turning point in their lives. For the longer stories, like those of Moses, Joseph, and the extended stories of Daniel, interruption becomes a way of life. As soon as one complication is overcome, another presents itself.

Daniel and his friends are captured as prisoners of war. Their childhoods are interrupted as they are torn from both their families and their homes. In the story of Daniel 1, we witness a moment of moral and political awakening, in which a child must learn how to preserve his integrity and still survive in spite of the violent upheaval in his life and as he negotiates the oppressive social structure in which he now resides.

---

6. See Bettelheim 1976; but see also critiques of his work, especially Dundes 1991 and Zipes 1979.

7. I'm including a brief description of the stories of Joseph and Moses in this initial catalog of stories of children, but the following chapters will only deal with Daniel 1, the book of Esther, and 1 Samuel 1–3.

Esther's life, too, is disrupted by the summons to the king's harem. We never learn her feelings regarding this turn of events. Rather, she soon is decisively tucked away as the king's favorite, seemingly untouched by the unpredictable and volatile palace culture around her. But her peaceful and privileged existence is interrupted when political resistance and personal survival come into conflict with one another. When authority figures prove to be unreliable and her people are threatened with extermination, she must break out of her prescribed role and find a way both to protect herself and to save her people.

For Joseph, the violence is domestic. His own brothers, jealous of their father's favoritism, and fed up with Joseph's conceited dreams and tattletaling tendencies, ambush him and conspire first to kill him and then to sell him into slavery—an interruption indeed of his advantaged childhood. For young readers, the themes of sibling rivalry, parental partiality, and familial violence may seem particularly relevant, as well as the story's refusal to shy away from the issue of child's own culpability in how she or he is treated. Moreover, for children who've been the victims and survivors of domestic abuse and who are struggling with issues of forgiveness, the story of Joseph may offer a significant model of psychological and emotional interruption. For although Joseph claims when the brothers are at last reconciled that, though they meant their actions for evil, God used them for good, Joseph is still careful to forgive his brothers only after he is in a position of power, removed from any further abuse at their hands.[8]

Moses is born into political violence. The Pharaoh's genocidal decree against the Hebrew male babies provides the backdrop for a series of acts of resistance, first on the parts of the "midwives to the Hebrews," then on the parts of Moses' own mother, his sister, and the daughter of the pharaoh himself. The baby is delivered and taken care of but then given up out of necessity. He comes to live—as does Daniel, Joseph, and Esther—in the court of the foreign king. He benefits from the very regime that tried to kill him and that supposedly succeeded in killing a multitude of others. His privileged life is interrupted one day as he witnesses Hebrew slaves being beaten. As he oscillates between courage and

---

8. My thanks to Pat Davis for making this observation in sermon delivered in a chapel service at Perkins School of Theology.

cowardice, he eventually comes to terms with the hybridity of his origins and upbringing. It is perhaps this very hybridity that provides Moses with the two main qualities that enable him to free his people: his confidence to confront Pharaoh in the royal court, and his moral solidarity with the Hebrew slaves.

Samuel, too, as we shall see, is born into both an era of intertribal conflict, a time when "there was no king in Israel and all the people did what was right in their own eyes," and a household where inequity and verbal abuse abounds. Before he is ever conceived, his desperately unhappy mother vows to give him to God and, when he is weaned, hands him over to Eli, the priest of Shiloh. Thus Samuel, too, is brought into the midst of one of the very institutions oppressing Israel, or at the very least leading Israel astray. The priesthood is corrupt (1 Sam 2:12-17, 22-25) and spiritually and morally bankrupt (1 Sam 2:27-36; 3:1-18). While Samuel both serves and benefits from the priesthood at Shiloh, his sleep one night is interrupted by a call from God. After that time, he repeatedly stands over against the corruption that is cancerously eating away at the house of Eli. In childlike innocence he utters prophecies of judgment against Eli and his sons. He is the conduit of God's word to Israel and, in contrast to Eli's sons, becomes known to Israel as a trustworthy prophet of God. He will inaugurate an era where many of the elements of his mother's vision (1 Sam 2:1-10) will start to become manifest.

One can find in all of these stories the crucial psychological message to children that has been imputed to traditional fairy tales: "that a struggle against severe difficulties in life is unavoidable, is an intrinsic part of human existence—but that if one does not shy away, but steadfastly meets unexpected and often unjust hardships, one masters all obstacles and at the end emerges victorious" (Bettelheim 1976: 8). This is no small realization for children of any era and culture.

But one also finds in the Bible *something more*: namely, that children, too, can be not only heroes of their own lives, but redeemers of their own communities (even saviors of the world!). In the Bible children become part of something larger than themselves and their personal development. They become obligated to a larger community, both within their story world and beyond it. They play their part to "continue Sacred History" (if we allow them to) as interrupters of our mundane and sometimes oblivious ways of living. And what's most redemptive about this portrayal of child redeemers is that all of these characters are flawed, compromised, and compromising. Daniel comes to live a life of political concession with his own dreams of grandeur and vengeance. Esther gets caught in the web of escalating violence. Joseph is himself partially responsible for his brothers' hostility. In saving the nation of Egypt, he winds up enslaving it and, in saving his family, is not above toying with the lives of his brothers. Moses has trouble controlling his temper and comes to put himself in the same category as God. Samuel falls into the same trap of wanting a priestly dynasty as did Eli. In short, all of these biblical children are human, a mixture of good and evil, living in worlds that are both good and evil. But when faced with *interruption*, they make choices that change their lives and alter their worlds. It is *this* vision of moral courage in morally compromised contexts that our children most need to see and to hear and that we as adults most need to take to heart.

"I am a cat," said the seven-year-old.

"Is that so?" asked Mom.

"Yes," she nodded. "And I'm teaching my friends to be cats, too."

"How, exactly, does one become a cat?"

"You learn to act like a cat. Cats are very smart. There are lots of dogs in the world, you know, and there are a lot of things you need to know if you want to escape them."

"Oh? What sorts of things?"

"Well, I made up a list of rules to follow if you want to be a strong cat. Do you want to hear them?"

"Sure," said Mom. "Tell me these rules."

"Well," said the little girl, "first, you have to face your enemies. Always look them straight in the eye. Whatever you do, don't run away.

"Second, if they try to hurt you, just move out of the way. You've got to be quick. And if they start to circle you, you circle them, too.

"Third, always look where you're going. (Dogs will set traps for you and you don't want to step in them.)

"Fourth, learn to make deals, because sometimes you have to.

"Fifth, learn to fight back, because sometimes you have to.

"Sixth, if you're doing something really important—even if it's really hard—don't give up. Keep trying as hard as you can.

"And seventh, if you have to look for your own food and all you can find is bugs, it's OK to eat them because a lot of people in other cultures eat them—except flies. Never eat flies. They're really gross."

CHAPTER FIVE

Resisting Daniel

(Daniel 1; the Book of Lamentations)

A Document of Resistance

The book of Daniel may be the Bible's foremost book of resistance against political domination. Its triumphalist stories and visions of overturned power structures have given voice and form to the fantasies and hopes of subjugated people throughout the centuries. A mighty statue of dominance and oppression crashes to the ground, its debris scattering to the winds. Young Israelites defy Babylonian rule even at the risk of death by burning. An arrogant monarch goes mad, trading his kingly existence for a bestial one. Ominous handwriting on the wall signals the end of a defiling king's reign. Monstrous beasts and talking horns are judged by God. Battles with evil are won by heavenly forces. It's hardly any wonder that this literature has galvanized the hopes and courage of countless oppressed communities. The book has functioned again and again, in the terminology of James C. Scott, as a *hidden transcript*,[1] articulating a counterorder in the face of real and present persecution.

The book even repeatedly claims for itself the role of hidden transcript: The vision of defeated kings "is true," insists the angel Gabriel in 8:26; "but you," he says to Daniel, "close up the vision, for it is for many days hence." At the end of the book, the archangel Michael issues a similar command: "You, Daniel, close up the words and seal the book until the time of the end" (12:4). When Daniel delays and questions, he admonishes again: "Go, Daniel, for the words are closed up and sealed until the time of the end" (12:9). The book is the hidden transcript that repeatedly exposes the precarious state of those who dominate: Their arrogance masks their anxiety; their power is no match for the power of God; their downfall is but a matter of time.

But somewhere before the mysterious sealing of the book, before the miraculous deliveries from fiery furnaces and lions' dens, before the cosmic court sits in judgment against the devouring beasts—a more modest script is written, a more modest drama is performed that indicates why a hidden transcript is needed to begin with. Within the story's own world, a child named Daniel learns how to survive in the midst of an oppressive social system. Captured and pressed into Babylonian service, Daniel is, by all indication and for all practicality, an orphan in a foreign land. He is forced to take a foreign name and speak a foreign language, forced to adopt a new history and literature, forced into a position of obligation to his captors. We know that, by the end, he rises above his social constraints. He becomes a successful courtier, the king's own confidante, and a wise visionary who is privy to future events that will end present oppression. But long before the promise of deliverance, before Daniel's climb up the ladder of courtly influence, there is first a lesson about living with oppression, a simpler story of survival[2] in which the child Daniel comes to discover that truth-

---

1. Scott uses the term to describe the discourse of a subordinate group "that takes place 'offstage,' beyond direct observation by powerholders" (1990: 4). "[T]he hidden transcript is specific to a given social site and to a particular set of actors. . . . Each hidden transcript, then, is actually elaborated among a restricted 'public' that excludes—that is hidden—certain specified others" (1990: 14).

2. It's not surprising that form critical studies often have difficulty categorizing this story, often relegating it to a later "introduction" to the stories that follow. It is neither clearly a story of "court conflict" or "court contest," and resists the label of "mantic wisdom" that is often associated with the other stories in Daniel.

telling is vastly overvalued and that survival often depends upon mimicking a *public transcript*[3] while living a hidden one.

Constructing the Public Transcript

> Identity was to be erected systematically, level by level and brick by brick, following a blueprint completed before the work started. The construction called for a clear vision of the final shape, careful calculation of the steps leading towards it, long-term planning and seeing through the consequences of every move.
>
> —Zygmunt Bauman[4]

Zygmunt Bauman, in his provocative essay "The Making and Unmaking of Strangers" (1997: 17-34) borrows a concept from Lévi-Strauss to describe one of the ways in which an order-building society deals with strangers. This *anthropophagic* strategy is described as

> annihilating the strangers by *devouring* them and then metabolically transforming [them] into a tissue indistinguishable from one's own. This was the strategy of *assimilation*: making the different similar; smothering of cultural or linguistic distinctions; forbidding all traditions and loyalties except those meant to feed the conformity to the new and all-embracing order; promoting and enforcing one and only one measure of conformity.[5]

While Bauman's topic is postmodern society, his description fits well the situation of Daniel 1's exposition. Nebuchadnezzar, king of Babylon has captured Jerusalem and has seized, along with the city's material treasures, the "children" (rendered variously in Hebrew as "sons," "seed," and "male children" [*yaladim*]). These are the children of the Judean royalty and nobility. He commands his chief eunuch to select from among the captives children "without blemish" who are "good of appearance" and who demonstrate intellectual potential. In the phrase "without blemish" we hear the

---

3. Scott uses the term "public transcript" to describe "the open interaction between subordinates and those who dominate" (1990: 2).

4. Bauman 1997: 20.

5. Bauman 1997: 18; see also 26.

bleating of Levitical sheep (Lev 21:16-24; 22:17-25) designated for sacrifice. We have here Bauman's concept of assimilation, only in ancient cultic linguistic garb. Sheep to be herded into conformity, sheep to be sacrificed and devoured by the Babylonian new world order.

And indeed this is the plan: The children are to be trained "to stand in the king's palace." They are to learn "the language and literature of the Chaldeans." They are to eat the food from the Babylonian king's table. They are to be given Babylonian names. At the end of three years of this special preparation, they are to stand before the king and, if found fit (read: "suitably assimilated"), they are to enter the king's service.

Unblemished Judean sheep being reconstructed as unblemished Babylonian sheep.[6] Palimpsest identities[7] where the new script is inscribed over the old, where, in the learning of the new, the old is to be forgotten; where forgetting the old script may be as important for survival as learning the new is for success.

Learning to Wear the Mask

> The builders of a better world . . . are enclosing and walling up our sons like the living bricks of biblical Egypt spoken of by the Talmud; and in these uniform bricks, . . . we can see a strange germination in such a homogeneous matter. That germination is *Difference*, within which we find the stirrings of a stubborn and difficult freedom.
>
> —Emmanuel Levinas[8]

In the story of Daniel, the builders of the Babylonian world are literally "enclosing and walling up" the sons of Judah, placing them in relative seclusion, reducing them all to the Same. They endure the same experiences; they live in the same place; they are taught the same language; they learn the same subject matter; they eat the same food—all with the same goal in mind: to stand before

---

6. The fact that this attempt to transform the captives follows a typical rite of passage also supports this notion of conformity. The Judean boys are undifferentiated initiates, colorless in the characterization, uniform in their description, undergoing the liminal phase of the rite. See Fewell 1991: 17.

7. Bauman 1997: 25.

8. Levinas 1990: 272.

the king at the end of their ordeal, "metabolically transformed" into the king's own tissue.

It is in the midst of this forced transformation that we see the "strange germination in such a homogeneous matter." As the chief eunuch is *determining, setting (yasem)* for them, their new Babylonian names, the child Daniel *determines, sets (yasem)* his heart upon not defiling himself with the king's food and wine. As the chief eunuch makes a gesture toward redefining Daniel's public identity—how he will be known, how he will be signified—as he attempts to bring Daniel into conformity with Babylonian culture and expectation, Daniel internally resolves to protect himself against change. He *sets his heart upon not being defiled.* Where does such resolve come from? And what is at stake in this gesture of resistance? Are his motives rooted in some sense of cultic piety? His language of defilement would certainly suggest this and many traditional interpretations assume this to be the case.[9] Is his resolve politically motivated? Invitations to eat at (or from) the royal table have long been recognized as more than mere offerings of hospitality: Political allegiance and obligation are the usual cost of the plate.[10] Can religious and political concerns be clearly separated from one another? Do both of these concerns become intertwined with a need to preserve some semblance of individual identity, to claim some modicum of control over one's circumstances? Do we have here "the stirrings of a stubborn and difficult freedom" that honors older allegiances, memories, and ways of being in the world?

Whatever its source, the strength of Daniel's stubbornness is matched only by his political naiveté. He seeks out the chief eunuch and, with childlike innocence, requests outright that he not be made to defile himself. He acts as though he actually has such autonomy, as though his captors will seriously listen to him, even respect his request, as though there's no need to censor such insulting language. This behavior not only marks him as truly a child of

---

9. See, for example, Ginsberg 1954: 256 and Porteous 1965: 29-31.

10. See 1 Sam 20:30-34; 2 Sam 9:9-13; 2 Kgs 25:27-29; cf. Dan 11:26, where the rebellion against the king of the south is unexpected and extreme because the rebels eat the king's *patbag.* See Baldwin 1978: 82-83; Davies 1985: 90-91; and Fewell 1991: 16-19.

the noble class who is used to saying what he pleases and getting what he wants, but it also indicates how deeply unaware he is of the nature of his subjugation.

As we ponder the potential impact on his superior of such audacity and such emotive language, the narrator quickly offers an aside: "Now God extended to Daniel kindness and mercy in the presence of the chief eunuch" (1:9). We are left to conclude that, if it were not for such divine mercy, the outcome of Daniel's request would have turned out quite differently. The chief eunuch might not have responded to Daniel at all or Daniel could have easily received a stinging reprimand, if not something far worse. Instead, the chief eunuch gives Daniel some pointed, if understated, tutoring in palace politics: "I fear my lord the king who appointed your food and drink. If he should perceive your faces to be more discontent[11] than the other boys of your circle, you would incriminate me in the eyes of the king."[12]

Whatever the nature of Daniel's request, be it religious, political, or personal, the chief eunuch immediately perceives the political ramifications of it. To refuse to eat the king's food symbolizes political dissent. Such dissent is bound to manifest itself eventually in more overt expressions of discontent. Then, the chief eunuch himself would be implicated for not stifling defiance from the start; in other words, if he were to honor Daniel's request, he would be forfeiting his own head.

The interchange is rich with lessons for the boy Daniel. He learns that small personal gestures can have significant political effects—for others as well as for himself. He learns that it doesn't necessarily pay to speak the truth about oneself and one's desires. He learns that he must be careful in how he publicly interprets the commands and actions of the king. He learns that the king is not interested in seeing real faces, especially if they are discontent; the king wants only to see masks that all look alike. (And, we might add, it is the last time we will see Daniel publicly exposing his face, to use the language of Levinas, "in all its nudity.") From this episode, Daniel learns that, in order to get what he wants, he must employ a certain kind of subterfuge.

---

11. The Hebrew word *za‘aph* connotes a raging anger that leads to violence.
12. More literally, "inculpate/indict my head to the king."

And that is exactly what he does. The chief eunuch's answer is no. So Daniel turns instead to the next in command, the guard who oversees the welfare of Daniel and his closest friends. "Please test your servants for ten days, giving us vegetables to eat and water to drink. Then compare our appearances with those of the boys who eat the king's food and deal with your servants according to what you observe." He makes overtures to someone closer to his own rank in the political system. He changes his approach and his language considerably. He is polite ("please") and self-effacing ("your servants"). He says nothing about "defilement." He proposes the altered menu as a test, with healthy appearance (and not political dissent) being the only thing at stake. And the guard need never tell anyone about this arrangement; he can keep the king's fare himself and dispense with it as he pleases. And since this is only a test, the guard has nothing to lose. Daniel has indeed learned the difference between the public and the hidden transcripts.

He has learned that, in a world that affords no privacy and no public gestures of independence, he must construct a world of secrecy. He must conceal personal behaviors and opinions that would be considered threatening to the powers that be.[13] He must mimic the public transcript, appear to be no different from the others, or at least express his difference only in his superior skills used in service to the king when at last he is called "to stand in the king's palace." And the double life of Daniel and his associates is held before the reader in the narrator's continued use of the boys' Hebrew names. Whoever they appear to be and whatever they are called in the king's court within the story world, for the storyteller and audience, they are still sons of Israel who have set it upon their hearts not to be defiled.

---

13. Social theorists distinguish privacy from secrecy. "Privacy . . . protects behavior that is either morally neutral or valued by society as well as by the perpetrators" (Warren and Laslett 1980: 26). Secrecy conceals behavior that would be considered immoral, illegitimate, or threatening to the order of society at large.

> Secrecy [as opposed to simple "privacy"] would be most likely where persons are morally stigmatized or where they have inadequate financial or other resources to provide themselves with privacy. We would thus expect that secrecy would be utilized more by lower than higher status persons, by children and the institutionalized elderly rather than adults, by the mentally and physically ill more than the healthy, and by the morally stigmatized more than the "normal." (Warren and Laslett 1980: 31)

The Story's Hidden Transcript

[A] mask presupposes a face.
    —Emmanuel Levinas[14]

To be deprived of parents—is that where freedom starts?
    —Julia Kristeva[15]

And thus the story is not unlike hundreds of other folk and fairy tales we may have heard or read: An orphaned child embarks on an adventure or endures a test eventually to rise to a high status in the royal court. In fact, in most cases, the child must be orphaned (especially if a girl) or at the very least separated from or abandoned by parents, for the story to work at all.[16] Parental authority must be dispensed with; otherwise the protagonist would not be in a position to be at liberty to adventure into foreign contexts, to face the dangers that make the story exciting, to become an independent and autonomous character.[17] In this case we have the clever orphan who tricks the system and rises to success in what many commentators believe to be the editor's introduction to the stories that follow. Daniel 1 puts the appropriate characters in their necessary place and, through a simple plot, introduces the courtly and mantic wisdom that Daniel and his friends will successfully display again and again in the chapters to come.[18]

But while the text relays with familiar tropes the story of its juvenile hero, it suppresses by its very style, the traumatic character of Daniel's predicament. It is as though the narrative of Daniel 1 (as well as of those that follow), with its emotionally understated, folktale-like tone, is exercising its own resistance against the horror of the events that gave rise to the story to begin with.

---

14. Levinas 1986: 355.
15. Kristeva 1991: 21.
16. See Amiran 1992.
17. Unlike many modern children's stories that avoid discussing unpleasant topics like death, disease, and aging, the traditional fairy tale, according to Bettelheim (1976: 8) confronts children "squarely with the basic human predicaments. . . . [M]any fairy stories begin with the death of a mother or father; in these tales the death of the parent creates the most agonizing problems, as it (or the fear of it) does in real life."
18. See, for example, Nicholsburg 1981: 20, 38; and Müller 1972: 279.

Life doesn't begin for Daniel in the Babylonian palace:[19] It begins with a family in Jerusalem, a family that is disrupted, perhaps even destroyed, by war. The story alludes to the downfall of Jerusalem quite matter-of-factly, avoiding the details of the siege, and portraying the event in rather benign terms.

> In the third year of the reign of Jehoiakim king of Judah, Nebuchadnezzar king of Babylon came to Jerusalem and besieged it. And Adonai gave into his hand Jehoiakim king of Judah along with the vessels of the house of God. He carried them to the land of Shinar, to the house of his god and he deposited the vessels in the treasury of his god. (Dan 1:1-2)

The description, unconcerned with historical accuracy[20] or causes, reads as though it were a simple relaying of gifts: Adonai gives the king and the temple vessels to Nebuchadnezzar, who in turn gives the gifts to his own god. Senseless acts of violent generosity. No reason is given for Nebuchadnezzar's attack of the city. No reason is given for Adonai giving him the city. We enter a story where there is no "why,"[21] and we are expected simply to accept that fact. The reference to Adonai, though a rationalization without reason, is most certainly part of the story's hidden transcript: It marks the belief that despite what appears to be the case, despite the propaganda of the conquerors, the god of the captives is indeed in control. And this might be the very reason why many of the gruesome details are left out. We are not told any of the particulars of the siege, the capture, the destruction of Jerusalem. We see

---

19. In speaking of traditional plots, Roemer writes:

The story begins when something goes wrong, when the social order is disturbed. In myth, this disruption is often caused by a supernatural force or figure, like the plague or sphinx. But even when the source of the trouble is human, it tends to come from a realm beyond our control. . . . The outcome of the story is known but its origin is shrouded in mist. No story begins at the beginning. The roots of the action extend back into uncertainty, and the known is determined by the unknown and unknowable. (1995: 42)

20. According to 2 Kings 25, the Judean king is Jehoiachin, not Jehoiakim.
21. Compare James Hatley's discussion of the concentration camps as places where there is no "why" (Hatley 2000). While not wanting to collapse the biblical treatment of the Babylonian Exile with the experiences of the Holocaust, I am indebted to Hatley for many observations that seem to "open up" also the text of Daniel.

no soldiers; we hear no weapons or battle-cries; we smell no smoke; we witness no violence; we sense no sorrow or panic. We do not see the train of prisoners making their weary way to Babylon. We do not hear Rachel weeping for her children, refusing to be comforted, because they are no more (Jer 31:15).

Daniel 1 intentionally looks away from what the book of Lamentations forces us to confront:

> Alas!
> How she sits alone—the city once great with people!
> The one great among nations has become like a widow
>
> . . . .
>
> Her children have gone away, captives before the enemy.
> Gone from daughter Zion are all that were her glory;
> Her leaders are like stags that find no pasture;
> They without strength walk before the pursuer.
>
> . . . .
>
> Remember, O LORD, what has happened to us;
> Behold, and see our disgrace!
> Our heritage has passed to strangers, our homes to foreigners.
> We have become orphans, fatherless; our mothers are like widows.
>
> . . . .
>
> They have raped women in Zion,
> Innocent young women in the cities of Judah.
> Princes have been hanged by their hand.
> No respect has been shown to the elders.
>
> Panic and pitfall have come upon us,
> Desolation and destruction. (Lam 1:1, 5-6; 5:1-3, 11-12; 3:47)

Lamentations over a fallen people are all but drowned out by the emotionally distant telling of Daniel 1. And yet, those who are present in the text cannot help but point to those who are absent. In the gaps, in the silences between the words, remnants of lamentations continue to echo. Traces of sorrow and suffering and loss yet remain.[22]

---

22. Drawing upon the works of Emmanuel Levinas, Susan Handelman, and Krzysztof Ziarek, Hatley describes this textual phenomenon (in relation to Holocaust literature) accordingly:

> Because textual indeterminacy arises from the intertwining of singular, transcendent voices, of nodes of address, the issue of how a text registers the various responses of a plurality of speakers becomes its preoccupation. This registering, in which the text is inflected in the other's voice, as well as all the other others' voices, is a rendering

The words of the story tell us of captive children. The silences fill in the features of their faces: *children captives before the enemy*, children *whose homes have passed to strangers, who have become orphans, their mothers like widows*. The words of the story place the children in the Babylonian palace. The silences point to what they have seen and experienced before that moment: *women raped in the streets of Jerusalem, princes hanged, elders dishonored, leaders walking feebly before the pursuer, panic and pitfall, desolation and destruction*.

What has happened to these children's families, we can only imagine. But it is clear that, whatever their particular lot, they are lost to the children of Daniel 1. Cut off from their families, their homes, their past lives, the "unblemished" children are taken into the Babylonian palace. And another absence suddenly emerges: What becomes of the "blemished" children? What happens to those not chosen, those about whom no stories were written? Daniel 1 offers no answer, and we may very well shudder to think of their fate.

And what of the "unblemished" children themselves? Clearly, they are "privileged prisoners." The first criterion of their selection: the accident of their birth. The second: good looks. With status and appearance, they have an opportunity to rise above the fate of forced labor that would have awaited many of the other captives. Consequently, we can be assured that their chances of survival are good and that they may even spend their remaining days in some measure of physical and social comfort. But are these not the very children Isaiah foresees in his indictment of Hezekiah's short-sighted dealings with the Babylonians over a hundred years prior (Isa 39:5*b*-7)?

> "Hear the word of the LORD of Hosts: 'Behold the days are coming when everything that is in your house, even what your fathers have treasured up until this day, will be carried to Babylon. Nothing will be left,' says the LORD. 'And some of your sons, your own issue whom you will have sired, will be taken and will become eunuchs in the palace of the king of Babylon.'"

---

traumatic of the text. The text carries more than can be said, because the saying of multiple voices intervene in every said. The instability of the traumatized text is not so much hermeneutical, in which one thinks of the inexhaustible variety of interpretations it elicits, as it is ethical, in which one is confronted with a plurality of addresses, of other expressions, that dispossess the subject of its own intentions and meanings and breaks open any possible closure of the text. (2000: 124-25)

What, exactly, are the conditions of their captivity? We witness these boys undergoing a cultural and emotional emasculation. Are they physically emasculated as well? Would the Babylonian king really want to see the royalty of an enemy nation breed more royalty? The story looks away, protecting the modesty of its characters, yet making us aware that eunuchs populate the Babylonian court and avoiding any mention of Daniel ever having a wife or children of his own. So the question lingers, Have these children lost not only their parents, their pasts, but also their own children, their futures? Is it on account of children like Daniel that the Isaianic prophet of the restoration declares to eunuchs that they are now welcome into the house of God and assures them they have futures despite their lack of children?[23]

We have here, in the now-famous phrase of Eric Auerbach, "a story fraught with background," in which the economy of narration represses a world too painful to consider in detail. And yet it is this background that forces us to reread the story of Daniel's resolve, to consider more fully its implications. Consider where Daniel has been. Consider what Daniel has seen. Consider what Daniel has lost. Consider that Daniel is a child.

A child being herded toward Babylonian service, being metabolized into Babylonian tissue, being forced to become part of what has just destroyed his home and family, being educated to serve a king who will besiege other cities, lay waste to more communities, destroy more families, capture and devour more children. *Daniel set his heart upon not being defiled.* The Babylonian system is set up to "defile" him, to turn him into a part of what has ruptured his life. To force him to help perpetuate the evil of which he is a victim.

Daniel set his heart upon not being defiled. How would he know to do this? How would he know what this means? Whether his concern is for cultic purity or whether he knows the connection between hospitality and obligation, his knowing has come from some past moment, some past person or set of persons in his life.

---

23. "Let not the eunuch say, 'Behold, I am a dried up tree.' For so says the LORD to the eunuchs who keep my Sabbaths and choose the things I desire and take hold of my covenant: 'In my house and within my walls, I will give even to them a share and a name better than sons or daughters. I will give them an everlasting name which shall not be cut off' (Isa 56:3*b*-5).

He *remembers* something, someone; he remembers a teaching that he refuses to have erased. He will not be completely written over. His resolve honors a past, preserves glimpses of the faces, of the home, that have been taken away from him, safeguarding them for those who come after. By safeguarding *this something* for those who come after, he keeps them as well as himself from being metabolized completely into Babylonian tissue.

When read as a text "fraught with background," Daniel 1 becomes more than a simple story about a clever boy who exhibits courtly wisdom. It does more than simply entertain us. It does more than comfort the subjugated. It does more than provide a model for living in the Diaspora. It does more than teach us the wisdom of knowing how to enact the public transcript. Rather, Daniel's behavior becomes a more profound gesture of resistance, a gesture of remembrance and obligation to the Other, the very other that the text itself cannot bring itself to name. *"The daily fidelity to the ritual gesture,"* writes Emmanuel Levinas, *"demands a courage that is calmer, nobler and greater than that of the warrior"* (1990: 19; italics mine). For a child to show such courage in such circumstances raises all kinds of ethical questions about our own responses to systems of domination, about our obligations as parents to "teach our children well," about our obligations as children to our own parents who have taught us well, about our own participation in social forces that press people into conformity and treat them as commodities.

But, of course, the story still stands as is, its very tone mocking this attempt to foreground loss and trauma and risk, this move to accentuate the ethical response of both Daniel and his readers. God protects Daniel (1:9), gives Daniel wisdom and skill (1:17), grants Daniel success, just as God gave him into captivity for no apparent reason. The tone of the story presupposes other readers in another time, readers who perhaps could only bear to hear this one thing: that God is in control despite how things may appear. For such an audience, explicit descriptions of the devastation of God's own people would be more than they could stand. For how could such accounts stand easily next to the affirmation of God's presence and power? If "Adonai" is in control of present circumstances, the depth of Daniel's loss would put God's justice and compassion into question. The story serves as "hidden transcript" for the oppressed, assuring them that God, not an evil conqueror, is sovereign.

However, the story's function as "transcript" takes an ironic turn: It also serves as "public transcript" for a particular theological party line. It affirms a system of power, namely that of God's sovereignty, that is not self-evident in the lives of ordinary people living under political domination. In so doing, it not only muffles the voices of those who didn't survive at all, but it even reduces the suffering of children like Daniel, minimizing their moral courage, erasing the intensity of their loss. It covers their faces with masks, forcing them to conform to a theological assertion in much the same way the children in the story are forced to conform to the Babylonian order.

What are we to do with such a lighthearted treatment of such a heavyhearted subject? We are implicated in its very reading and torn by its parallel gestures of hope and betrayal. For, having imagined the story as it has been told to us, we have allowed ourselves to become part of a world that can be explained by a folktale mentality. A world that can easily tolerate irrational violence and repress suffering, a world in which children are thoughtlessly captured, reduced, and devoured for the sake of a particular construction of society, a world in which an individual's success is all that matters—even if that success is serving a system that is bent on conquest, destruction, and exploitation. A world perhaps not so very far removed from the one in which we live.

We find ourselves in a quandary, wanting desperately to be comforted by assurances of divine control, but unable to quell the lamentations that emanate from the text's own silences. And unlike the later Daniel, we cannot simply close the book and seal it up. We have opened it and we are responsible for it[24]—for it and all the faces that its stories and visions try to mask.

For we judge the angels to be mistaken: this book, this story, is not for the time of the end.

---

24. "You are perfectly free to leave that book on the table. But if you open it, you assume responsibility for it" (Sartre 1965: 42).

Awww, not **this** church!" exclaimed the little girl, as the car turned into the church parking lot.

"What do you mean, 'not this church'?" asked the mother. "This is the church we go to."

"I don't want to go to this church. I want to go to that other church we went to last time."

"What other church?"

"The one we went to at night. Where all the children were dressed in costumes."

"Oh . . . you mean the synagogue."

"Yeah, where everybody brought groceries for people who didn't have any food. And they had a play about that girl named Esther. Remember? All the boys were girls and the girls were boys. And we got to make a lot of noise every time they said the bad guy's name. Don't you remember? We made so much noise, we frightened the bad guy away. I want to go back to that church, where we can frighten the bad guy away."

Nice Girls Do[1]

(The Book of Esther)

The more unspeakable the truth, the more it must be camouflaged by artifice.
—Michael Roemer[2]

Dramatis personae:

RABBI DEBORAH ROSEN, a young associate rabbi at the local Reformed synagogue

---

1. Because the book of Esther is *carnivalesque*, or *carnivalized* literature (see the descriptions and discussions in the notes below), the genre of this chapter attempts to mirror the carnivalesque quality of Esther. Bakhtin, the foremost theorist on the carnivalesque, offers the following as one of the characteristics of carnivalized literature:

> The prime characteristic of all the serio-comic genres is their new relationship to reality: their object or—what is more important—their starting point for understanding, evaluating and formulating reality is the *present*, often the topicality of the immediate present. For the first time in ancient literature the object of a *serious* (though at the same time comical) representation is presented without epical or tragical distance, presented not in the absolute past of myth and legend, but on the contemporary level, in direct and even crudely familiar contact with living contemporaries. In these genres mythical heroes and historical figures out of the past are deliberately and emphatically contemporized, and they act and speak in familiar contact with the unfinalized present. (1973: 88)

2. Roemer 1995: 193.

Girls from the synagogue:
SOPHIE (age 13-14)
NINA (age 15-16)
ADELA (age 16-17)

REVEREND JULIE SPRINGER, a young associate minister at a local, ethnically diverse, congregationalist church

Girls from the church:
ANNIE (age 13-14)
JESSICA (age 16-17)
VENESIA (age 14-15)
MARLENA (age 13-14)

REVEREND RICHARDS, the senior pastor at JULIE's church

ACT 1

Scene 1

Setting: the front of a dimly lit synagogue.

RABBI ROSEN comes in, followed by SOPHIE, NINA, and ADELA, who are talking and laughing.

SOPHIE: Ooo! It's dark in here!

R. ROSEN: Just a minute. I'll get the lights. (*She goes up to the back of the bima and reaches behind a panel and turns on the lights.*)

SOPHIE: That's better!

ADELA (*sarcastically*): Gee, and I thought it might be cool to do the play in the dark.

R. ROSEN: In a way, you might say that we are.

SOPHIE: What do you mean?

R. ROSEN: Well, not only is this the first time in our congregation that this age group has taken charge of the Purimspiel, but it's definitely the first time we're inviting Christian friends to join us in the production. An all-girl, but not all-Jewish cast—a real first. And, we don't even have a script yet. So I'd say we're doing this in the dark.

NINA: An ecumenical Purim celebration? Whoever heard of such a thing? If we're going to do something with a church in the area, why Purim?

R. ROSEN: That's the same question our senior rabbi is asking. Why Purim? Why not introduce our friends to some other, more serious, Jewish holiday, like Yom Kippur or Rosh Hashanah? Purim, he says, hardly represents the best Judaism has to offer and is easily misunderstood by non-Jews.

SOPHIE: Oh, I love Purim. It's a big party. We all have so much fun.

NINA: But it *is* sort of *silly*. Why *are* we getting together with Christian girls for Purim?

R. ROSEN: Well . . . it's actually an idea that my friend Julie and I cooked up. Julie is the new youth minister at the church across the street. We were talking the other day about young people from different traditions reading the Bible, especially girls reading the Bible, and it just occurred to us that the book of Esther might be an interesting text for you girls to read together.

(*There's a commotion at the back of the synagogue and another group of girls enter, whispering and looking around them, led by JULIE.*)

R. ROSEN: There they are now! (*She moves forward to greet them.*) Hello! You made it! (*She gives JULIE a hug and gestures for the girls to join them up front. She turns to the new girls.*) Hi, I'm Deborah Rosen, an associate rabbi here at Temple Shalom. You girls know each other from school, right? (*The girls nod and greet each other. To her girls:*) This is Rev. Julie Springer. (*Turning back to JULIE*) Julie, this is Sophie, Nina, and Adela, the leaders of our youth group here at the synagogue.

JULIE: And this is Jessica, Annie, Venesia, and our quiet one, Marlena.

R. ROSEN: Welcome! I was just explaining to my girls how this whole enterprise got started.

JULIE: By all means, continue. My girls are curious as well.

ADELA: (*dryly*) Inquiring minds want to know.
(*They all laugh.*)

R. ROSEN: Well, first, make yourselves comfortable. (*The girls sit on the steps of the bima.*) As I was saying, Julie and I were thinking that, since it's one of the few biblical stories that involves a young girl, the book of Esther might be a fun book of the Bible for you girls to read and talk about. And, Purim's coming up soon on the Jewish calendar. We thought, what better way to get into the text than dramatizing it?

ADELA: So, drama queens, unite!
(*They all laugh again.*)

JESSICA: I didn't know there was any such thing as a "*fun* book of the Bible."
(*Others agree.*)

JULIE: OK, OK, give it a chance. How many of you have ever read the book of Esther? (*SOPHIE, NINA, and ADELA raise their hands. JULIE looks at the girls who came with her.*)

ANNIE: Well, you *did* tell us to read it before we came here.

JULIE: And did you?

ANNIE: *I* did.

JESSICA (*shrugging*): I didn't have time. I had cheer leader practice before this.
(*Some of the other girls roll their eyes.*)

VENESIA: I read it. My preacher from my old church even preached on it one time. He said Esther was just like Moses. She saved her people from oppression and that's what we're all called to do.

(*MARLENA, sitting next to VENESIA, nods in agreement.*)

R. ROSEN: That's a good start. Our goal here is to do a play based on the story of Esther. In the synagogue we do this every year at Purim. But, in Jewish tradition, we read the text a lot of different ways. We can play it straight or camp it up. Since there's a kind of carnival atmosphere[3] at Purim, we usually allow ourselves to have fun with it.

JULIE: Tonight we thought we would start reading through the text, float some ideas about how we could stage the story, and assign parts.

SOPHIE: How are we going to assign parts? We don't have any boys. There are a lot of boys in the story of Esther. More boys that girls.

R. ROSEN: Well, unfortunately, that's a problem with most of the stories in the Bible. There are *always* more boys than girls. However, there's no reason why we should be content with that. One of the ways we can have fun with the story is to do a little gender-bending—some of *you* can play the boys.

ADELA: From drama queens to drag queens!

JULIE (*gently, but with a slight grimace*): Perhaps we should avoid using disparaging labels.

NINA: Yeah, besides, we'd be drag kings, you know! (*Julie rolls her eyes and shakes her head.*)

---

3. On the carnivalesque quality of the book of Esther and celebrations of Purim, see Craig 1995, who correlates both the text and the holiday with the theories on carnival and carnivalesque literature developed by Mikhail Bakhtin.

(*MARLENA nudges and whispers something to VENESIA, who then speaks up.*)

VENESIA: Marlena wants a small part where she doesn't have to say very much.

R. ROSEN (*turning to MARLENA*): Is that true, Marlena? (*MARLENA nods.*)

VENESIA: Marlena doesn't like to talk in front of a lot of people. (*MARLENA nods again.*)

R. ROSEN: Well, there are a lot of messengers and attendants in the story. Would you like to be one of those? (*MARLENA nods.*) OK, that's easy enough. But if you change your mind, let us know. (*MARLENA nods.*) What about some of the larger roles? Adela, you're one of the older ones here. Would you like to play the part of Esther?

ADELA (*looking skeptical*): You're kidding, right?

R. ROSEN: No, why would I be kidding? It *is* the "starring role."

ADELA: The girl who runs around pleasing everybody, doing as she's told, making everybody happy? No, thank you. I'd rather play Vashti.

SOPHIE: Why Vashti? She doesn't even have any lines!

ADELA: She gets to say no!

JESSICA: Big deal. One word.

ADELA: Well, it *is* a big deal if your alternative is to be the only girl at an all-boy party and *you're* supposed to be the entertainment. Thanks, but no thanks. I don't need that kind of male attention.

JESSICA (*tossing her head*): I kind of like it when the boys all notice me.

ADELA: Fine. You be Esther then. You can make *all* the boys happy.

NINA: Well, except for Haman. By the end of the story, Esther doesn't make him too happy.

JESSICA: Why? What happens to him?

ADELA: If you'd read the story, you'd know.

VENESIA (*interrupting*): I'll be Esther. I like her. She's just like Moses, saving her people. Except there's no burning bush or anything. That makes her even braver than Moses, don't you think?

JULIE: Hmmm, perhaps you're right. OK, Venesia, you play Esther. What about some of the rest of you?

NINA: I'll take the role of Mordecai. (*with admiration:*) He's an in-your-face kind of guy.

ADELA: Sort of like Vashti.

NINA: Yeah, I suppose. Except he gets out of his trouble. She doesn't.

ADELA: The old double standard. They both disobey an order. She gets canned. He winds up Prime Minister. There's no justice in this world.

R. ROSEN: OK, we need a Haman and a Zeresh.

ANNIE: Who's Zeresh?

R. ROSEN: That's Haman's wife.

SOPHIE: I'll play her. I don't want to be a boy. Boys are gross.

JESSICA: You'll be changing your tune in a year or two! Who's this Haman?

ADELA: If you'd read the story, you'd know.

JULIE: Haman is the villain, who tries to destroy the Jewish people in order to get back at Mordecai.

NINA: Every good story needs a villain![4]

JESSICA: Does he wear black? I look good in black.

R. ROSEN: I suppose he could . . .

VENESIA: How come black always has to be the color villains wear? I'm sick of that. Black isn't evil. And every time we put those two things together, we make life hard for a whole lot of folks who just-so-happen not to be white!

R. ROSEN: Point well taken.

JESSICA: OK, how about red? That's a wicked sexy color. I look good in red, too.

ADELA: Do you look good impaled on a stake? Because that's what happens to Haman in the end. No pun intended!

EVERYONE (*groaning with disgust*): Oh, gross! Yuk!

JULIE: That part should take place off stage. There's only so much reality we can stand!

NINA: Well, if you ask me, the book of Esther is not about reality at all!

SOPHIE: What do you mean?

---

4. Michael Roemer (1995: 281-82) writes:

[W]ithout a destructive threat—whether it be divine or human—there is no story. Most narratives begin when something goes wrong, and evil is often the energy that drives it forward. Moreover, we don't come to story—even popular story—just to see good people doing well but to make contact with the negative qualities in ourselves.

NINA: It's a farce! There's nothing real about it. The story goes overboard with everything.[5]

JESSICA: Like what?

ADELA: If you'd read the story, you'd know . . .

NINA: Like the king's six-month-long stag party. Can you imagine a king drinking for six months with his administrators?

JESSICA: Not without girls there! How in the world could they be having any fun without girls?

NINA: More important, who'd be running the kingdom? I mean, geez, the man can't make any decisions on his own. He takes the suggestions of anybody who's around. And he never thinks about anybody but himself. What kind of king is that?

ADELA: Oh, I don't know—he reminds me of some of our elected officials . . .

JULIE (*laughing*): OK, let's not go there!

R. ROSEN: Nina's point is well taken. There is a farcical quality to the story of Esther. It's a story that's making fun of a lot of people and things that we usually take quite seriously—like government

---

5. Although certainly not the only one to address the issue of Esther's genre, Celina Spiegel (1994: 193) describes well the peculiarities of Esther:

> Although critics have tended to concede isolated moments of farce and invention, the Book of Esther is filled with historical improbabilities, exaggerations, coincidences, and neat ironies that point to a reading of Esther as satire, expertly structured to mock the established order while empowering the Jews.
>
> Though it plays with history, subverts and challenges it, satire is the most antihistorical of literary genres. It is not just an imagined vision of the world but, in Aristophanes's words, a vision of the "world remade," the British Empire reduced to Lilliputian size or the Russian Revolution led by pigs. Its spirit is a carnival one, rooted in the ancient saturnalian tradition, which can be characterized by the well-known words of the Book of Esther itself—"*ve-nahafokh hu*," "it was turned upside down." The story playfully, yet willfully, takes the familiar world and turns it on its head, exposing its underside for all to see.
>
> That satire is born of tragedy is evident throughout Esther, where the loftiest and most crucial issues of identity and survival are in constant tension with a farcical lightness and comic exaggeration.

officials, community leaders, law and even problematic things, like bigotry and violence.[6] That's why in Purim celebrations, the story usually gets hammed up.

ADELA: The only kind of ham Jews tolerate!
(*Everybody boos and hisses for the lame joke.*)

R. ROSEN: Adela's joke is right on target—the celebration of Purim and Esther's story is a way of making fun of ourselves as Jews, of not taking ourselves too seriously. And it's also a way of dealing with painful things in a way we can manage.[7]

---

6. Cf. Bakhtin's description (1973: 101): "The laws, prohibitions and restrictions which determine the system and order of normal, i.e. non-carnival, life are for the period of carnival suspended; above all the hierarchical system and all the connected forms of fear, awe, piety, etiquette, etc. are suspended, i.e. everything that is determined by social-hierarchical inequality among people, or any other form of inequality, including age." Familiarization is another quality of carnival: "The unfettered familiar attitude encompasses everything: all values, thoughts, phenomena and things. . . . Carnival brings together, unites, weds and combines the sacred with the profane, the lofty with the lowly, the great with the insignificant, the wise with the stupid, etc."

Moreover, as Craig (1995: 106) points out, the feasts in the story of Esther and the feast/festival of Purim have much in common with the medieval carnival feasts studied by Bakhtin. In medieval times, while the government or the church may have sanctioned the celebration, the celebration itself often ridiculed the very institution that made the festival possible. According to Bakhtin (1984: 81),

> The medieval feast had, as it were, the two faces of Janus. Its official, ecclesiastical face was turned to the past and sanctioned the existing order, but the face of the people of the marketplace looked into the future and laughed, attending the funeral of the past and present.

7. Roemer writes:

> All comedy permits us to face our limitations, including those imposed on us by chance and circumstance. Jesters and clowns have always made the truth bearable by telling it playfully and within a safe arena. They effectively use our limitations to liberate us. By making us face and laugh at our own helplessness, they free the energy we must use in daily life to repress the truth. In comedy, as in jokes, we can confront our worst fears: death, dismemberment, deformity, hunger, abject poverty, raw sexuality, aggression, violence, stupidity, and failure. We can even face the evil in ourselves and recognize that it is often critical to our survival. (1995: 289)

VENESIA: My daddy says, sometimes in life you have to laugh to keep from crying.[8]

JULIE: Your daddy is quite wise. That's the kind of wisdom that makes a story like Esther work.

ANNIE: So, you mean that the story of Esther didn't really happen? In history, I mean?

R. ROSEN: Well, no, certainly not the way it was written. We don't know if there ever was an actual Queen Esther or a prime minister named Mordecai in the Persian government. And the events are a little too contrived to reflect the way the real world works.

ANNIE: What do you mean?

JULIE (*jumping in*): Well, the way everything gets turned upside down in the story. Everything turns out the opposite of what is expected. For example, when Mordecai saves the king's life, we expect him to be promoted as a reward. Instead, the king promotes Haman, someone no one's ever heard of. Later, when Haman thinks he's about to be honored by the king, it turns out that the king has his enemy Mordecai in mind. On the day Haman's cronies are supposed to destroy the Jews, the Jews destroy their enemies. The story's reversals are just a little too neat. The real world isn't like that.[9]

---

8. Cf. Michael Fox (1991: 253):

> The book's incongruous humor is one of its strange hallmarks. It mixes laughter with fear in telling about a near-tragedy that is chillingly reminiscent of actual tragedies. We laugh at the confused sexual politicians, the quirky emperor, and, above all, the ludicrous, self-glorifying, self-destructive villain. This is almost literally gallows humor, except that the gallows are finally used on the hangman.
>
> Humor, especially the humor of ridicule, is a device for defusing fear. The author teaches us to make fun of the very forces that once threatened—and will again threaten—our existence, and thereby makes us recognize their triviality as well as their power. "If I laugh at any mortal thing," said Byron [in *Don Juan*], "t'is that I may not weep."

9. Cf. Bakhtin (1973: 103-104):

> All of the images of carnival are two-in-one images, they unite within themselves both poles of change and crisis: birth and death . . . , benediction and damnation . . . , praise and condemnation, youth and age, top and bottom, face and backside, stupidity and wisdom. Paired images, chosen for contrast (high and low, fat and thin, etc.) and for similarity (doubles and twins) are characteristic of the carnival mode of thinking.

NINA: And *everything* gets exaggerated. Like a tall tale. Six-month parties. Year-long beauty treatments. Gallows a zillion feet high.

SOPHIE (*puzzled*): If the book of Esther isn't *true*, then why are we reading it? Why is it even in the Bible?

VENESIA (*vehemently*): But it *is* true. Maybe there wasn't a real queen Esther, but there are a lot of real Hamans out there who threaten people every day. Especially in my neighborhood. Even in school. Hamans come after you all the time. For all kinds of reasons: who you are, who you're not, where you live, what you look like. Not because of anything you've done. Just because you're not like they are.[10]

(*The girls have all turned to look at VENESIA. MARLENA whispers to VENESIA.*)

VENESIA (*giving voice to MARLENA*): Yeah, and not all the Hamans are boys, either.

R. ROSEN (*gently*): And what do you do when that happens— when the Hamans come after you?

VENESIA: Most of the time there's not much you *can* do, not directly. But sometimes we do like you say—when we're on our own, we poke fun at the people who think they're better than us, who try to make us afraid, who try to keep us down. We mimic the way they walk, the way they talk. We make them look stupid. And we imagine a day when the shoe will be on the other foot.[11]

---

10. "Perhaps you will say to me, 'Are you sure that this legend is a true one?' What does it matter what the reality which exists outside myself may be, if it has helped me to live, to feel that I am and what I am?" (Charles Baudelaire, "Windows;" cited in Newton 1995: 125).

11. Peripety, or reversals of circumstance, are characteristic of carnival and the literature of carnival. Bakhtin writes:

Carnival celebrates the destruction of the old and the birth of the new world—the new year, the new spring, the new kingdom. The old world that has been destroyed is offered together with the new world and is represented with it as the dying part of the dual body. This is why in carnivalesque images there is so much turnabout, so many opposite faces and intentionally upset proportions. (1984: 410; cited in Craig 1995: 81)

R. ROSEN: Our community understands the story in a similar way, Venesia. The story has truth even if it isn't factual. And it provides a coping mechanism. The book of Esther gives us permission to ridicule the enemies and the social institutions that have endangered our lives. There have been many Hamans who have threatened to wipe out the Jews.[12]

ADELA: Not the least of whom was Hitler. Next to him, Haman looks like a nice guy. But, somehow, it's a little hard to spoof the Holocaust.

R. ROSEN: It's difficult to say anything about the Holocaust that makes any sense of it.[13]

SOPHIE: I certainly don't understand the Holocaust. How could people be so mean? And how could God let so many people die?[14]

R. ROSEN: That's the question many people ask. About the Holocaust and about all kinds of human suffering.

NINA: It's as though God just steps out of the picture. He's nowhere to be found when he's needed.[15]

---

12. Cf. Newton:

Fiction does not demarcate art from life by announcing: this close but no closer—in fiction we stand as spectators but life is where we participate. Rather it offers up *for encounter—not simply for contemplation*—hard facts of distance, separation, and alterity which seem familiar as "facts of life," but which gain extra pathos and piquancy when framed by the special boundaries of art—a proscenium arch, the rootedness of painting and sculpture, the closed covers of a book. (1995: 129; emphasis mine)

13. In the words of Emil Fackenheim (1970:70), the Nazi murder of Jews was "annihilation for the sake of annihilation, murder for the sake of murder, evil for the sake of evil."

14. "In faithfulness to the victims we must refuse comfort; and in faithfulness to Judaism we must refuse to disconnect God from the holocaust" (Fackenheim 1970:76).

15. Levinas (1988:162) writes:

[T]he Holocaust of the Jewish people under the reign of Hitler seems to us the paradigm of gratuitous human suffering, where evil appears in its diabolical horror. This is perhaps not a subjective feeling. The disproportion between suffering and every theodicy was shown at Auschwitz with a glaring, obvious clarity. Its possibility puts into question the multi-millennial traditional faith. Did not the word of Nietzsche on the death of God take on, in the extermination camps, the signification of a quasi-empirical fact?

ADELA: In that sense, then, the book of Esther seems truer than ever. God doesn't seem to be present in that story either.[16]

VENESIA: But at least there was Esther.

NINA: Yeah, just too bad there was no Esther in Nazi Germany to rally the Jews to fight back.

JESSICA: That's something I've never understood. Why *didn't* the Jews fight back? During the Holocaust I mean.

ADELA: Pu-lease! Let's blame the Jews one more time for being killed! How rude of them to be gassed like that!

R. ROSEN: Some of the Jews did fight back. They simply weren't strong enough to defeat that kind of evil.

ADELA (*to JESSICA, with some degree of anger*): There's something *I've* never understood: Why didn't the Christians help the Jews?

JESSICA (*defensively*): How do I know? I wasn't there.

JULIE (*intervening*): Some of them did. But there were too few to make a difference. The rest were afraid.

ANNIE: "Dumfounded." That's the word the story of Esther uses. When the people of Persia are told to destroy the Jews, it says they are "dumfounded."

R. ROSEN: Moreover, many people in Europe believed what they were told, that Jews were responsible for Germany's poor economy. The political propaganda in that time and place was much like that reflected in Haman's indictment of the Jews: a "certain people" subverting authority and causing a disruption. People are often willing to blame others for their problems.

---

16. For a profound exploration of human suffering and divine silence in a space where the book of Esther, the celebration of Purim, and the devastation of the Holocaust meet, see Wiesel 1997.

JULIE: When you consider all these questions and parallels, there's all the more reason for Jews to continue celebrating Purim, even after the Holocaust.[17]

R. ROSEN: Indeed. Despite the fact that it's harder these days to believe in tidy endings. And speaking of celebrating Purim, we still need someone to play the part of the king, our obtuse and frequently inebriated leader.

ANNIE: I guess that leaves me. I can play the king. I know how drunk and stupid people act.

NINA (*teasing*): Yeah, right! Like you hang out with a lot of boozers.

ANNIE (*Quietly*): Well, I hang out with at least one. (*They all turn to look at her.*) My dad's an alcoholic. (*MARLENA comes over to ANNIE and puts her arm around her.*) It's OK. He's sober now. But I remember how he used to be. And worry sometimes that he'll be that way again.

JULIE: Maybe we should take a break. Take five everyone. When we come back, we'll read through the text and brainstorm about how we can act it out.

(*The girls scatter. JULIE walks out with ANNIE, the two of them speaking in low tones.*)

---

17. In applying Bakhtin's theory of the carnivalesque to the book of Esther, Craig writes,

> Death offers the greatest challenge to celebration, but it also becomes the necessitating force, the driving force *for* celebration. Always ambiguous, death is what is most celebrated against. It is for this reason that festivity, in literature such as the Esther story, plays such an important role in highlighting the carnivalesque concept of death as renewal. Triumph over death requires a recognition of its power and inevitability, but a larger sense of life emerges when the community affirms itself against individual mortality. (1995: 121)

Scene 2

The girls drift back in twos and threes. R. ROSEN takes a Bible and opens it.

R. ROSEN: OK, I'll read some of the text and you girls be thinking about how we might stage this. I'm going to skip some parts in the interest of time. You all know about the six-month drinking party. I'll start at the point when the king summons Queen Vashti: "On the last day when the king was merry with wine . . ."

JESSICA: You mean he's—smashed?

NINA: Completely pickled.
(*ANNIE lowers her eyes at this.*)

JULIE: Annie, are you sure you want to play the part of the king?

ANNIE: Yeah, I'll be OK. Like Venesia says, sometimes you gotta laugh to keep from crying.

R. ROSEN: "On the last day when the king was merry with wine, he ordered his seven eunuchs to bring Queen Vashti before him wearing her royal crown, to display her beauty to the peoples and the officials for she was a beautiful woman."

SOPHIE: What's a eunuch?

JULIE (*quickly*): A servant. An attendant.

(*The older girls, ADELA, NINA, and JESSICA, snicker.*)

JESSICA: There's a little more to it than that . . .

ADELA: A little *less*, you mean.
(*The older girls giggle again.*)

SOPHIE (*pleading*): Come on, tell me—what's a eunuch?

NINA: A eunuch is a guy who is, let's say, missing some of the parts that make him a guy.

SOPHIE: What happened to him?

(*ADELA makes her fingers into a pair of scissors and mimics snipping.*)

R. ROSEN (*jumping in*): In the ancient world, children were often captured by enemy armies and enslaved. And sometimes poor families gave their children into the service of noble families or, as in this story, the king himself. It was a common practice to do surgery on the young boys to keep them from becoming sexually mature, or at least sexually potent. It was easier to control them and make them more trustworthy around the women of the house. Notice that, in this story, eunuchs take care of all the king's women.

JULIE: And they function as messengers. They are the agents that move between the world of the men and the world of the women in the story. They're the ones that know everything that's going on everywhere. That's the main thing. They keep the plot going. This is the part Marlena will play.

(*MARLENA looks down at her crotch and casts a sidelong look at JULIE.*)

SOPHIE (*ignoring this "mechanical" explanation*): This—surgery— would happen against their will?

JESSICA: Duh! Do you think they would've volunteered? You know how proud boys are of their equipment!

SOPHIE: I don't think it's funny. I've heard that in some places, they do something kind of like that to girls. They cut off parts of their bodies so they can't feel anything when they're having sex. And they sew them up so they can't have sex with anyone but their husbands.[18] (*The girls fall silent.*) I wouldn't want anybody doing that to me. (*She looks at JESSICA.*) Would you?

(*MARLENA shudders and shakes her head.*)

JESSICA: No, of course not.

SOPHIE: These boys couldn't ever be dads?

---

18. See Walker and Parmar 1993.

JULIE: No, they could never be dads. You're right, Sophie. We shouldn't make light of it. Surgical violation is a pretty horrific thing to have happen whether it's done to boys or girls. Being separated from your family and enslaved is bad enough in and of itself, but procedures like these generate even more losses—the loss of pleasure, the loss of your body's natural functions, the loss of a certain kind of future. Sometimes it means infection, even death. And in the case of eunuchs, it means never having a family of one's own.

VENESIA: My great-great grandparents were slaves in this country. Slavery's a bad thing, even if you get to work in a palace. Slaves here weren't turned into eunuchs. Just the opposite. Their masters wanted them to have lots of children so they would have more slaves to work and sell. Children got sold away lots of times, so their parents never saw them again.
(*MARLENA nods sadly.*)

R. ROSEN: Children who were turned into eunuchs often never saw their parents again, either.

ADELA: So . . . we have a few dirty little secrets in the happy kingdom.[19] I guess somebody's got to pay for the party.

---

19. On narrative secrets, Frank Kermode (1980: 83-84) writes:

> Secrets . . . are at odds with sequence, which is considered as an aspect of propriety; and a passion for sequence may result in the suppression of the secret. But it is there, and one way we can find the secret is to look out for evidence of suppression, which will sometimes tell us where the suppressed secret is located. It must be admitted that we rarely read in this way, for it seems unnatural; and when we do we are uncomfortably aware of the difference between what we are doing and what the *ordinary reader* not only does but seems to have been meant to do. To read a novel expecting the satisfactions of closure and the receipt of a message is what most people find enough to do; they are easier with this method because it resembles the one that works for ordinary acts of communication. . . . Authors, indeed, however keenly aware of other possibilities, are often anxious to help readers behave as they wish to; they "foreground" sequence and message. This cannot be done without backgrounding something, and indeed it is not uncommon for large parts of a novel to go virtually unread; the less manifest portions of its text (its secrets) remain secret, resisting all but abnormally attentive scrutiny, reading so minute, intense, and slow that it seems to run counter to one's "natural" sense of what a novel is.

While the youth minister is encouraging a "reading for sequence and message," the girls have uncovered a "secret." The simple, somewhat fantastic, story of the fairy-tale-like kingdom is haunted by the oppression upon which the kingdom is built.

> The secrets to which these words and ideas are an index have no direct relation to the main business of the plot; as some analysts would say, they are not kernels but

VENESIA: And somebody's got to clean up after the party. Can you imagine the mess that many drunk men would make? Not enough Lysol in all of Persia I bet.

ANNIE: You got that right.

R. ROSEN: OK, where were we?

ANNIE: The eunuchs were going to get Vashti so the king can show her off to everybody.

R. ROSEN: Yes: "But Queen Vashti refused to come at the king's command . . . "

ADELA (*jumping up*): That's my cue!

JESSICA: Well, "just say no!"

ADELA: NO! Not gonna do it, don't want to do it, can't make me do it, no way, no how, no matter! (*strutting and overdramatizing*) No ifs! No ands! No buts! No crown! No gown! No rule! No drool! No strutting! No slutting! No dancing! No prancing! No ro-mancing! No show! No go! No! No! No!

THE GIRLS (*laughing and clapping*): The girl says no! Don't hold back! Tell us how you really feel! Girls rule!

JULIE (*laughing*): Are you quite through?

ADELA: NO! (*revving up again*) Tell the king he's on his own. *Entertainment Tonight* is not being broadcast because I refuse to be cast as a broad! Women of Persia unite! You are more than boy bait! More than boys' toys! Just say no!

---

catalysts or, as Seymour Chatman calls them, "satellites." But they form associations of their own, nonsequential, secret invitations to interpretation rather than appeals to a consensus. They inhabit a misty world in which relationships are not arranged according to some agreed system but remain occult or of questionable shape. (Kermode 1980: 89)

The physical violation of the boys who are turned into eunuchs becomes part of the web of sexual violation that is seen in the king's treatment of Vashti and his co-opting the sexual services of all the attractive young virgins in the kingdom. The "secret" of the eunuch also connects to the plot of Esther as well as the play in which it is presently embedded.

EVERYONE: NO!

R. ROSEN (*to JULIE*): Where was she when we were trying to get the ERA passed?

JULIE: Still in the womb, my dear!

R. ROSEN (*to the girls*): Shall I continue?

GIRLS (*laughing, still caught up in the moment*): NO!

R. ROSEN: "The king was very angry, absolutely enraged."

ANNIE: Yeah, he's *drunk* and he's not getting his way.

R. ROSEN: "He turned to his advisors and asked 'What, according to the law, should be done to Queen Vashti for not obeying the king's command?'"

JESSICA: He's consulting lawyers already? Why doesn't he just go deal with her himself?

ANNIE: He's drunk, *confused*, and not getting his way.

NINA: He's clueless! He can't make a decision about anything by himself.

R. ROSEN: "Thereupon Memucan spoke up . . . "

ADELA: *Memucan!* Now *there's* a name for your firstborn!

R. ROSEN: "Memucan spoke up and said to the king and the ministers, 'It is not against you only that Queen Vashti has committed an offense, but against all the officials and all the peoples in all the provinces of the kingdom. For this deed will be become known to all women causing them to treat their husbands with disrespect. For they will say, 'The king himself ordered Queen Vashti to appear before him and she would not come.' This very day the noblewomen who have heard of the queen's behavior will be citing it to all Your Majesty's officials and there will be no end to the disrespect and fury!'"

JESSICA: Ooo, talk about taking it personally! She really upset the apple cart![20]

ADELA: Never underestimate the power of "no." It can scare every man in the kingdom.

VENESIA: Yeah, but they'll have to make an example of her, won't they? Put her in her place. Isn't that the way some men deal with uppity women?[21]

ANNIE: Especially drunk men who aren't getting their way.

R. ROSEN: You're right, Venesia, that's exactly what Memucan proposes: "If it please Your Majesty, let a royal edict be written into

---

20. This episode in the book of Esther depicts a classic social drama. Victor Turner (1980: 146) describes a social drama thusly:

> (A) social drama first manifests itself as the breach of a norm, the infraction of a rule of morality, law, custom, or etiquette, in some public arena. This breach is seen as the expression of a deeper division of interests and loyalties than appears on the surface. The incident of breach may be deliberately, even calculatedly, contrived by the person or party disposed to demonstrate or challenge entrenched authority . . . or emerge from a scene of heated feelings. Once visible, it can hardly be revoked. Whatever may be the case, a mounting crisis follows, a momentous juncture or turning point in the relations between components of a social field—at which seeming peace becomes overt conflict and covert antagonisms become visible. Sides are taken, factions are formed, and unless the conflict can be sealed off quickly within a limited area of social interaction, there is a tendency for the breach to widen and spread until it coincides with some dominant cleavage in the widest set of relevant social relations to which the parties in conflict belong.

See also Turner 1974.

21. Cf. Turner (1980:147):

> In order to limit the contagious spread of breach, certain adjustive and redressive mechanisms, informal and formal, are brought into operation by leading members of the disturbed group. These mechanisms vary in character with such factors as the depth and significance of the breach, the social inclusiveness of the crisis, the nature of the social group within which the breach took place, and the group's degree of autonomy in regard to wider systems of social relations. The mechanisms may range from personal advice and informal arbitration to formal juridical and legal machinery and, to resolve certain kinds of crises, to the performance of public ritual. Such ritual involves a literal or moral "sacrifice," that is, a victim as scapegoat is offered for the group's "sin" of redressive violence.

the laws of Persia so that it can never be rescinded, that Vashti is never again to come into the king's presence.

NINA: I bet she was really heartbroken about that! She didn't want to be with him in the first place.

JESSICA: But isn't that just like a boy? You say you don't want to go out with him and, next thing you know, he's telling everybody he wouldn't ask you out if you were the last girl on earth.

ADELA: It's called saving face.

R. ROSEN: "And let her royal position be given to another better than she. Then when Your Majesty's edict is heard throughout the kingdom, all women will treat their husbands with respect."

VENESIA: Sounds like Memucan's got a problem with his own wife, if you ask me. (*MARLENA nudges VENESIA and whispers in her ear.*) Yeah (*giving voice to MARLENA*), why *do* men think they have to "lay down the law" to get women's respect? If they really deserved respect, they wouldn't have to force the women to respect them. They're just trying to keep the women down.[22]

ADELA: You'd think that being honest about the way you feel might be a sign of respect!

NINA: Who are you kidding? This isn't about honesty—it's about conformity. These guys want nice girls who follow the rules. Not girls who are "honest about the way they feel!"

R. ROSEN: That's the end of the first part of the story.

SOPHIE: I don't get it. When are we gonna get to Esther?

---

22. "The final phase" of a social drama, writes Turner (1980: 147),

consists either in the reintegration of the disturbed social group—though the scope and range of its relational field will have altered, the number of its parts will be different, and their size and influence will have changed—or the social recognition of irreparable breach between the contesting parties, sometimes leading to their spatial separation. . . . This phase, too, may be registered by a public ceremony or ritual, indicating reconciliation or permanent cleavage between the involved parties.

JULIE: She's coming. The point of the first part of the story is to get rid of Vashti to make room for Esther.

ADELA: Hey! I resent that! Vashti's more than just a foil for Esther!

JULIE: You think?

ADELA: Yeah, I do think. *She thinks, too.* She thinks she's tired of living at the beck and call of the king. She says *no.*

JESSICA: And she gets canned for it. Some statement *she* makes.

NINA. Yeah, but look at what her action exposes. It throws all the men into a tizzy at the thought that their own wives might also say no. That tells you right there how fragile this patriarchal stuff is. One woman says no and the whole Persian Empire starts to tremble. (*She bites her nails in mock fear.*)

ANNIE: It also shows how insecure and indecisive the king is. There's no way to predict what he'll do when things don't go his way.

SOPHIE: That doesn't make things very easy for Esther and Mordecai.

VENESIA: No, they'll have to learn to wear the mask. (*MARLENA moves her hand across her face as though donning a mask.*)

JESSICA: What do you mean, "wear the mask"?

MARLENA (*stepping forward, her hands over her face, peering through her outstretched fingers, and taking on a completely different persona*):

We wear the mask that grins and lies,
It hides our cheeks and shades our eyes,—
This debt we pay to human guile;
With torn and bleeding hearts we smile,
And mouth with myriad subtleties.

Why should the world be overwise,
In counting all our tears and sighs?
Nay, let them only see us, while
We wear the mask.[23]

(*The girls are both surprised and delighted by this impromptu performance from MARLENA who, once she's dropped her hands from her face,
quickly sits back down by VENESIA.*)

EVERYONE: Wow! Great poem! Well done, Marlena!

VENESIA: In other words, Esther and Mordecai will have to act like
they want to do things they don't want to do. They'll have to look
happy when they aren't happy. Be nice when they're not feeling nice.

SOPHIE: That's what my mom tells me to do all the time: "Be nice.
Think of others."[24]

ANNIE: That's what I used to *have* to do all the time, just to keep
the peace around my dad when he was on one of his binges.

JESSICA: Well, I think being nice is vastly overrated. If you want to be
Somebody instead of Nobody, you can't afford to be nice all the time.[25]

---

23. From the poem "We Wear the Mask" by Paul Laurence Dunbar (1930).

24. In her work on the spirituality of adolescent girls, Patricia H. Davis (2001)
writes about the problems of "niceness":

> Niceness requires putting away genuine feelings, avoiding conflict, swallowing
> hurts, denying pain, and being untruthful. Niceness requires self-denial and often
> self-forgetting. The nice person eventually forgets to notice how she really feels, even
> in extreme circumstances. The truly nice person doesn't even know when she"s
> angry, and wouldn't admit to being angry if questioned. The nice person would
> never fight on her own behalf. Most often, nice people are not able to feel strong pos-
> itive emotions either. Nice people are "calm, controlled, quiet."
>   . . . [I]t is a prime virtue taught to adolescent girls by mothers, teachers, and other
> adults who have internalized dominant cultural messages about "good" women:
> that they are self-sacrificing, nurturing, and never angry—that they are ultimately
> responsible for maintaining and protecting relationships. (pp. ix-x)

25. See Margaret Talbot's (2002) interview of Rosalind Wiseman, author of *Queen
Bees and Wannabes: Helping Your Daughter Survive Cliques, Gossip, Boyfriends and other
Realities of Adolescence* (Crown, 2002), in an exploration of adolescent girl clique poli-
tics. Talbot also discusses in passing other studies expected out this year: Rachel
Simmons, *Odd Girl Out: The Hidden Culture of Aggression in Girls*; Emily White, *Fast
Girls: Teenage Tribes and the Myth of the Slut*; and Phyllis Chessler, *Woman's Inhumanity
to Woman*. My thanks to Michelle Campbell for bringing this article to my attention.

ADELA: You should know.

JESSICA: What's that supposed to mean?

ADELA (*with mock "niceness"*): I was just "being nice" and agreeing with you. We all know how popular you are and we also know that you certainly didn't get that way by being nice!

JESSICA (*indignant*): You're just jealous because you're not part of my group at school.

ADELA (*sarcastically*): Oh, you've found me out! The sleepless nights I've spent worrying over that . . .

NINA: Well, I think niceness is overrated, too, but not exactly for the same reasons. I mean, there are times when you have to play the game—do things you may not want to do just to get by. But you can't do that all the time. If you did it all the time, you'd lose something of yourself. Sooner or later, you'd forget how you were supposed to feel about anything.

R. ROSEN: Well, with this topic in mind, you might find Esther's predicament rather interesting. Shall I continue with the story?

(*GIRLS respond affirmatively*): Yeah. Sure. OK.

R. ROSEN: "Some time afterward, when the anger of the king had subsided, he remembered Vashti and what she had done and what had been decreed against her."

ANNIE (*bitterly*): In other words, when he sobered up he was sorry for what he did. They always are. Only then it's too late. The damage is already done. (*MARLENA comes over to ANNIE again and puts her hand on her arm in sympathy.*)

NINA: Well, I feel for those poor advisors who steered him down this path. Notice he's not exactly blaming himself. If he's missing Vashti really bad, they're in big trouble for persuading him to get rid of her.

R. ROSEN: Hmmm. Maybe that's why the servants jump in so quickly here with a distraction. They suggest that all the beautiful young women of marriageable age be gathered in order that one might be found who pleases the king.

JESSICA: A beauty contest, you mean? You didn't tell me there was a beauty pageant in the show. *I* know how to stage that. I was in the Our Little Miss pageant three times (I won the third time). I was Miss Apple Harvest, Miss Dogwood Festival, and Miss Henderson County.

ADELA: You missed Miss Hogwash. Didn't you win that title, too?

JESSICA: Jealous again?

ADELA (*with a mock grimace*): Yeah, I've always wanted to walk up and down a runway in a swimsuit in front of a lot people I don't know, worrying if I'll get a wedgy right in front of judges' table!

JESSICA (*with a touch of superiority*): Well, for your information, you wouldn't have to worry—we use tape to keep that from happening!

NINA (*howling with laughter*): You duct-tape your swimsuit to your ass?!
(*The other girls laugh, too.*)

JULIE (*trying to stifle a laugh herself*): Girls! Language!

NINA: Sorry! Just think if you ever won Miss America, you could do commercials for duct tape! (*in a mock announcer's voice:*) Duct tape: A Girl's Best Friend! The ultimate protection against wedgies! It holds your tummy in, your boobs up, and how do you think we get those perpetual smiles? A little duct tape before bedtime . . .
(*Even JESSICA is laughing with the girls now.*)

SOPHIE: But still, I think pageants are fun. Kind of magical. Somebody gets to be a princess.

R. ROSEN: Yes, and in this case, it was Esther. "It so happened that in the capital city there lived a certain Jew by the name of Mordecai. He was descended from the tribe of Benjamin. His family had been carried into exile by King Nebuchadnezzar of Babylon. He took care of Hadassah—that is, Esther—his uncle's daughter. The young woman was shapely and nice to look at and, when her father and mother died, Mordecai took her to himself as a daughter."

VENESIA: That's kind of weird the way they say that.

JULIE: Say what?

VENESIA: That she was beautiful so that when her parents died, Mordecai took her in. Like maybe he wouldn't have if she'd been ugly.

JULIE (*frowning*): Well, I don't think that's necessarily the implication . . .

VENESIA: How do you know? There're lots of kids who don't get adopted because they're not cute enough. Or because they're the wrong color.[26] Or they're too old. Or they have something wrong with them. Kids don't get adopted just because they need parents. Usually it's the parents who need the kid. And most of the time, they need for the kid to be perfect.

R. ROSEN: Well, whatever motivated Mordecai to adopt Esther, she doesn't get to stay there very long. Like the other young women being rounded up, she's taken to the palace and put into a year-long beauty school.

SOPHIE: You mean she learns to cut hair and do nails and stuff like that?

---

26. Cf. this statement from the Sixth Circuit Federal Court of Appeals: "Were baby prices quoted as prices of soybean futures are quoted, a racial ranking of these prices would be evident, with white baby prices higher than nonwhite baby prices." Judge Richard Posner and Professor Elizabeth Landes, "The Economics of the Baby Market." Quoted in Williams (1994: 55).

R. ROSEN: Not exactly. She undergoes an extensive beauty treatment herself.

JULIE: It's probably more like an old-fashioned charm school. She probably learns how make herself look beautiful, how to pick out attractive clothes, how to behave in public . . .

NINA: Do you think she learns the trick about duct tape?

(*More laughter*)

JESSICA: Duh! They probably didn't even have tape back then. She probably learned all the other pageant tricks though.

ANNIE: What makes you think so?

JESSICA: She *won*, didn't she?

R. ROSEN: Well, as a matter of fact, she did. She became the favorite of the eunuch who took care of the girls. He gave her advice about what the king liked. And when it came time for her to be introduced to the king, she did everything the eunuch advised her to do.

JESSICA: See, it's no wonder she won. She had the advice of a seasoned pageant director.

ADELA: Well, she learned a few more things than just pageant tricks, I imagine.

NINA: Yeah, doesn't she have to have sex with the king? If she's just a kid, somebody better teach her a thing or two. The king's gonna need more to impress him than just a pretty smile and a desire to work for world peace.

ADELA: Brings new meaning to the term "talent contest," doesn't it?[27]

SOPHIE: But it's not just having sex, is it? They're supposed to be married, aren't they? That's how she gets to be queen.

ADELA: Sort of. But he marries her after she's proven she knows how to "make him *happy*," if you know what I mean. And, there are all those other "contestants" in the king's harem still in the picture.

SOPHIE: What's a harem?

ADELA: The king's collection of women—his wives and concubines. He doesn't just let the others go home, you know, now that he's found Esther.

SOPHIE: Well what are all those girls supposed to do?

JESSICA: Lie around on silk couches, eating grapes, and getting fanned with palm branches.

NINA: Ya think?

JESSICA: That's how it is in the movies.

SOPHIE: If I wasn't going to get to be queen, I'd want to go home and live with my family.

NINA: Well, that's not exactly how it works. Once in the king's harem, always in the king's harem. There's a queen bee and a lot of wannabes. You just take a number and wait your turn.

---

27. Alter (1992: 32) describes the king as a "man with a shaky scepter" and speculates that the king may face certain sexual challenges:

> The young women are all equally fragrant and lubricated, and being virgins, none has any sexual expertise by which she might plausibly offer the king some unexpected pleasure. Ahasuerus himself, hardly an energetic or assertive man, seems an unlikely figure to be up to this strenuous regimen of nightly erotic exercises. Is it conceivable that the reason he is said to "love" Esther above all the other women and choose her as queen is that with her alone he is able to perform the act? (The subsequent narrative, after all, shows that Esther is not only beautiful and loyal but also patient and quietly reassuring.)

SOPHIE: What if the king dies?

NINA: Then the next king inherits the harem.

VENESIA: So basically they're slaves. (*MARLENA whispers in her ear.*) Like the eunuchs. The king decides who has to have sex and who can't have sex at all.[28]

NINA: Pretty much. But even though the girls are enslaved, so to speak, they probably don't have to work very hard—not during the day anyway! It's hard to charm a king with dish-pan hands!

VENESIA: But they don't get to have families of their own, do they?

NINA: Not unless they have a kid by the king.

VENESIA: What are the chances of that, if you're only one of a thousand women? Unless you can do some really interesting tricks, the king won't even remember you're there!

ADELA: Judging from the character of this king, I bet some women counted on that! They probably would just as soon keep each other company as to have to deal with the king. So, while some of them were trying to move up the line, others were just laying low, doing nothing to draw attention to themselves, just hoping they wouldn't be noticed.

VENESIA: You got that right. (*She looks at MARLENA.*) Sometimes just laying low is the best thing to do. Besides, I know plenty of families made up only of women and they seem to be doing just fine.

JULIE: I guess the thing to remember is that, in the ancient world, life wasn't necessarily fair or easy. People did what they had to in order to survive.

---

28. One might profitably compare Foucault's (1976, 1984, 1984) classic study of the institutional rituals, social hierarchies, and moral discriminations that have regulated sexual behavior in Western culture.

VENESIA (*looking again at MARLENA*): Just like nowadays.

JULIE (*sensing there might be some underlying referent*): Yes. Just like nowadays. In fact, Esther herself has to "lay low" about at least one thing.

VENESIA: What's that?

JULIE: Mordecai tells her not to tell anyone that she's a Jew.

SOPHIE: Why couldn't she tell anybody that?

JULIE: The story doesn't say. But clearly Mordecai thought Esther should keep her background a secret.

NINA: Maybe he suspected early on that there were people in the palace who didn't like Jews.

VENESIA: In my community, we call that "passing." You know—like black people passing for white, so they get treated better. Sometimes it even saves their lives.

(*MARLENA whispers to VENESIA.*)

VENESIA (*to MARLENA*): Yeah, I think that's the point—If Esther tells her secret, she might get hurt.

R. ROSEN (*looking thoughtfully from VENESIA to MARLENA*): Perhaps. The palace is certainly not without its dangers. It just goes to show that a beautiful home is not necessarily a safe one. (*MARLENA stiffens and VENESIA takes her arm. R. ROSEN continues, pretending not to notice.*) In fact, after Esther is made queen, Mordecai uncovers a conspiracy within the palace to assassinate the king.

NINA (*sarcastically*): What? In the happy kingdom? Someone wants to do away with our model leader? What on earth for?

R. ROSEN: All it says is that two eunuchs who are members of the royal guard become angry and plot to lay hands on the king.

JESSICA: Ah. Two *eunuchs*. That explains it. I'd want to kill him, too, if he'd cut off my—

R. ROSEN (*jumping in*): ANYWAY, Mordecai relays the information to Esther who reports it to the king in Mordecai's name. (*She says casually to VENESIA and MARLENA*) Some secrets need to be told when someone's life is at stake. (*VENESIA and MARLENA exchange glances, but otherwise sit very still.*) The incident is written in the king's annals, but nothing more is done about it. (*Again, for VENESIA and MARLENA's benefit:*) I suppose that's always the risk in telling a secret: What if you tell and no one does anything about it? (*She turns to the others.*) In fact, just when you think Mordecai is sure to be promoted for saving the king's life, the king promotes someone we've never heard of—Haman the Agagite.

JESSICA: Haman. That's me. But what exactly am I gagging at?

NINA: Mordecai!

R. ROSEN: Haman is identified as an Agagite. The Agagites were bitter enemies of the Jews, especially of the tribe of Benjamin to which Mordecai belongs.

SOPHIE: Oh, so not only is Mordecai not rewarded, but one of his worst enemies is promoted ahead of him?

JULIE: You got it.

SOPHIE: I'm starting to see what you mean about nothing happening in this story exactly the way it's supposed to.

JULIE: That's right. And this creates the next problem in the story.

R. ROSEN: Haman is now the big shot on the scene and Mordecai is the only one of the king's courtiers who won't bow down to him.

ANNIE: Why is that?

R. ROSEN: Well the story isn't clear on that point. It may have something to do with the fact that he's a Jew and Jews despise Agagites.

SOPHIE: Or he may be jealous because he got passed over for a promotion.

ADELA (*raising an eyebrow toward JESSICA*): Or maybe he just thinks Haman is a jerk and he's refusing to bow out of spite.

NINA: I'm Mordecai. I'll answer that. The answer is "D"—all of the above and more, too. I do carry a grudge against Agagites because they oppressed my people in the past.[29] *And* I'm pissed off because I've been pissed on—

JULIE: Nina! Watch your language!

NINA: *and* I think Haman is a jerk, *and* I want to see if I can *really* get under his skin. *AND* I'd *really like* to be treated like a *human being*, not a second-class citizen!

VENESIA: But it sort of backfires, doesn't it? Defending one's "personhood" doesn't seem to get you very far in this kingdom. Didn't we just see what happened to uppity women in the episode about Vashti? What makes Mordecai think uppity men are going to be treated any differently?

ADELA: Because he's a *guy* and he thinks he's *special*!

NINA: *BECAUSE* it's a matter of honor and principle. (*She pauses.*) And besides, I saved the king's life and I'm banking on some extra privilege. (*She throws her shoulders back and sticks her chin in the air.*) Damn the torpedoes, full speed ahead!

SOPHIE: What torpedoes?

R. ROSEN (*amused*): It's just an expression from an old movie. It describes someone who doesn't think about the consequences of

---

29. See Exod 17:14-16; Deut 25:17-19; and 1 Samuel 15.

his or her actions. In this case the torpedoes turn out to be a little more than what Mordecai bargains for. Mordecai's disdain infuriates Haman. He is so angry that he plots to destroy not just Mordecai, but Mordecai's entire people.

JESSICA: That seems a little excessive!

R. ROSEN: Indeed. But it points to the fact that Haman's hatred of Jews is already in place. He is angry with Mordecai before he ever knows he's a Jew. But when the other servants tell him of Mordecai's ethnicity, his vengeance then spreads to the entire Jewish population.

JESSICA: So Mordecai becomes an excuse.

R. ROSEN: That's the implication.

VENESIA: But Mordecai is not exactly squeaky clean in all this.

JULIE: What do you mean?

VENESIA: The *secret*. Have you forgotten about that? Making Esther keep the secret about being Jewish means that Mordecai knows there's danger for Jews in the palace. He should've been more careful about how he behaved. He makes her wear a mask, but he thinks he's above that.

NINA: Maybe he's just reached his limit. It's one thing to wear the mask when everything is at least tolerable. It's another to have to grovel to someone who hates you and wants to hurt you. In the words of that poet we studied last week in class, "there is some s—t I will not eat!"[30]

JULIE: Nina!

NINA: I was *quoting*!

JESSICA: So what happens next?

---

30. From e. e. cummings, "i sing of Olaf" (1931).

ADELA: If you'd read the book, you'd know . . .

R. ROSEN: Haman casts lots, *purim*, to determine the day upon which the Jews would be exterminated. He then goes to the king with an "indecent proposal." Let me read you what he says: "There is a certain people, scattered and dispersed among the other peoples in all the provinces of your realm. Their laws are different from those of every other people and they do not obey the king's laws. It is not in your Majesty's interests to tolerate them. If it please your Majesty, let a decree be written for their destruction and I will pay ten thousand talents of silver into the king's treasury."

JESSICA: He bribes the king?

R. ROSEN: So it appears! The king then gives Haman his royal seal and says, "The money and the people are yours to do with as you see fit."

VENESIA: Haman doesn't even mention the Jews by name, just calls them "a certain people." And the king doesn't even ask who he's talking about or what laws they're supposedly breaking. What's with this king?

NINA: He doesn't want to be bothered with unpleasant details *or* with making a decision.

ANNIE (*glumly*): He doesn't want to be bothered because it's happy hour.

R. ROSEN: Yes, as a matter of fact, it is. As soon as Haman instructs the scribes to issue the decree, Haman and the king sit down to drink together.[31]

---

31. Of this scene Spiegel writes:

When the king and Haman feast to celebrate the edict ordering the extermination of the Jews, their action hints at deeper saturnalian undercurrent in the story. The sinister complicity of their private celebration suggests the dubious moral authority of the law, shown here to be solely in the interest of the personal rather than of society at large. (1994: 200)

ANNIE: Yeah, and while they're drinking the rest of the world is going to hell in a handbasket.

(*JULIE clears her throat in response to the word "hell."*)

JESSICA: Haman thinks it's his handbasket though and that he's got it under control.

ADELA: Vashti revisited.

JESSICA: What do you mean?

ADELA: An entire group is made to pay for one person's rebellious act. The legal system is exploited in retaliation. All of a sudden, it's us versus them. In Vashti's case it's the boys against the girls. In Haman's it's all the rest of the Persian empire over against the Jews.[32]

ANNIE (*looking at her own text*): But look how concocted that is. Haman and the king may think everything's settled because a law has been passed and they've had a drink on it, but the story says the rest of the city was "dumfounded." The rest of the people don't understand this us/them thing.

NINA: Well, it's not like the rest of the Persian empire were all the same nationality with the same friends and enemies. Even Haman himself is supposedly an outsider.[33]

ADELA: All the more important for him to cozy up to the king. By depicting the Jews as people who are different and who don't obey the king's laws, he's implying that he *isn't* different and that he and the king see eye-to-eye on everything.

---

32. For a discussion of the parallels between "woman-as-other" and "Jew-as-other" in the book of Esther, see Beal (1997: 54-59; 112-15).

33. Magonet (1980: 175) writes:

> We forget that the information that he is an Agagite tells us not only that he comes from the line of Israel's enemies, but also that he, too, is an outsider in the Persian court. When he speaks of the people scattered throughout the land whose laws are different from those of every other people (3:8), he is also describing, in a projection, some aspect of his own outsider status. For Haman, too, is insecure, part of a minority group, relying on his wealth or other keys to power to maintain his position, ready to invent a scapegoat to insure the continuance of his power.

SOPHIE: You mean he's a wannabe, too.

ADELA: Yep. He's definitely a wannabe.

VENESIA (*glancing briefly toward JESSICA*): I guess we've seen his type before.

(*The girls are quiet, mulling over the politics of group identity.*)

JULIE: Well, have we covered enough for one night? Are you tired?

VENESIA: Is the time up already?

JULIE: Afraid so. It's a school night. We'd better call it quits for the evening.

R. ROSEN: The important thing is, what do you think? Is this a worthwhile enterprise? Do you want to continue working on this together?

(*The girls look at each other.*) Sure. Why not? Yeah, it was OK.

R. ROSEN: All right, then. Let's plan to gather again next week, same time.

JULIE: Why don't we meet at our sanctuary next week? (*The girls start to gather their things to depart.*) OK. Fine. See you. G'night.

ADELA (*over her shoulder as she walks out*): Hey, and Jessica, maybe by then you'll have time to read the story. (*Under her breath*) You can read, can't you?

ACT 2

Scene 1

A week later, in the church sanctuary. A large cross hangs at the front of the room. There's at least one pulpit chair on the podium and the altar has been moved to stage right. The girls and their leaders wander in from various entrances and begin to situate themselves at the front. The senior minister at the church, REVEREND RICHARDS, has stopped by the sanctuary to confer briefly with his associate minister. JULIE SPRINGER is introducing him to DEBORAH ROSEN and explaining what the girls are doing.

NINA, dressed as Mordecai, wearing torn, dark clothing, her hair mussed, and ashes on her face, enters from the back, coming up the aisle in mock "I Love Lucy" type weeping and wailing. She's also twirling a hand-held noise-maker like those used during Purim festivities. The girls turn to stare at her, first surprised and then amused.

VENESIA: Look! It's Mordecai!

ADELA: Already in character, Nina?

NINA: Well, Vashti, if you can say *no*, so can I—only I get to *whine*! (*She commences to wailing again and sounding the noise-maker.*)

REV. RICHARDS (*with marked consternation*): Excuse me, young lady, but is that any way to enter a *sanctuary*?

NINA (*a little taken aback but quickly recovering*): It's the way Mordecai tries to enter the king's sanctuary. I thought I was here to practice a play. Was I supposed to check my character at the door?

REV. RICHARDS: If your character feels the need to make that much noise and look like Pigpen from the *Peanuts* cartoon, then, yes, you should check your character at the door. Your behavior is quite disrespectful.

NINA: Disrespectful? To whom?

REV. RICHARDS (*impatiently*): To God.

NINA (*incredulously*): To God? God doesn't like noise? Or sack-cloth and ashes?

ADELA: Hmmm. God's starting to sound like the king in the story. Unpleasantries Unwelcome Here.

REV. RICHARDS (*looks disapprovingly at Adela and then back again at Nina*): You're not fooling anyone. These aren't real sackcloth and ashes. You're neither mourning nor praying. You're just acting.

NINA (*feigning innocence*): So, God doesn't like acting?

JESSICA: God doesn't like *bad* acting!

REV. RICHARDS (*unused to this kind of banter and growing more irritated by the minute*): This *is* a house of worship! Your clowning around is highly inappropriate for this context.

NINA: God doesn't like clowns? On the contrary, from the looks of things, I'm guessing God has quite a remarkable sense of humor.[34]

REV. RICHARDS (*now quite livid*): Young lady—

NINA (*raising an eyebrow*): My name is Nina.

REV. RICHARDS (*through clenched teeth*): —there is no need to create this kind of uproar in the house of God. It's not—

NINA: Nice?

---

34. Cf. Bakhtin (1973: 104):

> The *laughter* of carnival is itself deeply ambivalent. It is genetically related to the most ancient forms of ritual laughter. Ritual laughter was directed toward a higher order: the sun (the chief god), the other gods, and the highest earthly authority were disparaged and ridiculed, and thereby forced to *renew themselves*.

REV. RICHARDS (*barely controlling his anger, turns to JULIE*): Please try to keep these girls under control while they're here. (*He turns and stalks out of the sanctuary. R. ROSEN looks amused. JULIE rolls her eyes. The girls burst into giggles the minute he's left the room and express their admiration for Nina's chutzpah.*)[35]

JULIE: Sorry girls. Rev. Richards is always very concerned about—propriety.

ADELA: Definitely some control issues there.

NINA: Bad toilet training, if you ask me.

ADELA: Maybe a permanent wedgie! (*pretending to walk with some discomfort*)

NINA: Uh-oh! Get the man some duct tape!

(*The girls are giggling.*)

R. ROSEN: Actually, this is a remarkable point of entry back into the story. The dynamics are very similar to those in the next episode of Esther. There's a law stating that no one can come to the king's gate wearing sackcloth. When Mordecai hears about the decree, he puts on sackcloth and ashes and comes as far as the king's gate weeping and wailing.

JESSICA: So the fact that he's wearing sackcloth and ashes and making a lot of noise right there at the king's gate is bound to create a stir.

---

35. This interchange between Nina and Rev. Richards is reminiscent of a larger historical linguistic and literary struggle described by Bakhtin (1986: 132-33):

> All [modern languages] have been determined to a certain degree by a lengthy and complex process of expunging the other's sacred word, and expunging the sacred and authoritarian word in general, with its indisputability, unconditionality, and unequivocality. Because of its sacrosanct, impenetrable boundaries, this word is inert, and it has limited possibilities of contacts and combinations. This is the word that retards and freezes thought. The word that demands reverent repetition and not further development, corrections, and additions. The word removed from dialogue: it can only be cited amid rejoinders; it cannot itself become a rejoinder among equally privileged rejoinders. This word had spread everywhere, limiting, directing, and retarding both thought and live experience of life. It was during the process of struggling with this word and expelling it (with the help of parodic antibodies) that new languages were also formed.

R. ROSEN: Exactly. And indeed it does. Esther hears of what Mordecai is doing and jumps through herself to quiet him down. His behavior is "inappropriate" for the surroundings. She's afraid that the king—(*smiling at JULIE*) or the senior minister as the case may be—might discover what's happening and take offense.

SOPHIE: When she sends him clothes to change into, she's not just trying to make him feel better?

VENESIA: She's trying to keep him out of trouble.

ADELA: She's trying to keep him from causing trouble *for her*. He is her relative. His behavior reflects badly on her.

NINA: After all, he's not just mourning, he's protesting. He's *trying* to get attention, if not the attention of the king, at least the attention of Esther. He's making a gesture. And it's *not* a "nice" one!

ANNIE: But Esther wants him to be nice. She's worried. He's creating too big of a stink and who knows what the king would do in response? Especially if he's been drinking again. She's trying to keep the peace.

VENESIA (*looking from ANNIE to MARLENA*): Sometimes keeping the peace is not the answer. Sometimes you have to make a little noise. That's what Mordecai has to explain to Esther. When people's lives are at stake, the price of peace is too high. That's why he refuses the clothes and stays there at the gate raising Cain.

R. ROSEN: Marlena, this is where we'll need a messenger. Are you up to it?

(*MARLENA jumps to her feet and salutes.*)

R. ROSEN: There's a lot of going back and forth in this scene. (*MARLENA is listening and nodding, walking back and forth between VENESIA and NINA as the Rabbi indicates the trips between Esther and Mordecai.*) First, there's the offer of clothes, which are refused and sent back. Then Esther will send you back to Mordecai to find out what's going on. Mordecai will then entrust you with the story of what has happened and you will be responsible for explaining it all to Esther and commanding her to go to the king to intervene.

ADELA: This is where it gets interesting.

JESSICA: How so?

ADELA: Well, Little Miss Please Everybody is not going to be able to please everyone now. She's going to have to make some choices. She can't be obedient to everyone at once.

VENESIA: Hey, you gotta give Esther a break. She's a girl, she's an orphan, she's a Jew, and she's married to a jerk. She's got a lot of strikes against her and it's not like she's got lots of career options if this queen gig doesn't work out. Being obedient and pleasing everybody has served her pretty well so far. She may be smarter than you think.

ADELA: OK, OK, I'm keeping an open mind.

R. ROSEN (*to VENESIA*): Esther, what's your response to Mordecai's charge?

VENESIA (*standing with her text and turning to MARLENA*): You must tell Mordecai, "Everyone knows that any person, man or woman, who comes into the presence of the king without being summoned breaks the law under penalty of death. Only if the king extends his scepter may that person live. The problem is: I haven't been summoned to visit the king for the last thirty days."

JESSICA: Uh-oh. The boy's lost interest. Too busy hanging out with his new buddy Haman doing guy-things.

VENESIA (*pacing back and forth, continuing her message to Mordecai, but also seemingly speaking to herself*): You told me to survive—which I've been doing very nicely, thank you! Now you want me to risk my life! Well, which is it? Make up your mind!

(*VENESIA sends MARLENA over to NINA. MARLENA whispers in NINA's ear.*)

NINA: You tell this to Queen Esther: "Do not imagine that you, of all the Jews, are safe in the king's house! For if you indeed keep silent at this time, relief and deliverance will arise for the Jews from another place, but you and your father's house will perish!"

SOPHIE: That sounds kind of mean.

ANNIE: It sounds like a threat.

NINA: It *is* a threat. I'm desperate.

SOPHIE: If you really believed that deliverance would come from somewhere else, you wouldn't be so desperate.

ANNIE: When you say "relief and deliverance from another place," are you talking about God?

NINA: I'm not sure what I'm talking about. Rabbi Rosen, am I talking about God?

R. ROSEN: Perhaps, but the text doesn't say "God" or mention God anywhere else.

ADELA (*looking out at the pews*): Is there a God in the house? Hmmm . . . God doesn't seem to be attending this performance!

JULIE: What do the rest of you girls think?

VENESIA: He could be talking about God. God saved the children of Israel from the pharaoh. Maybe Mordecai's counting on some plagues or something.

ANNIE: And what about the story of Daniel in the lion's den? Or the three guys in the fiery furnace? God saved them.

JESSICA: He's telling her that she's going die if she doesn't obey him, even if all the other Jews are somehow saved. A clear case of being a bully! It's a grown-up thing. He's just trying to make her do what's in *his* best interests.

SOPHIE: But what if she really *couldn't* do anything, wouldn't God save them all anyway? Mordecai believes that, doesn't he? I would want to believe that, that God wouldn't just sit back and let them all die.

ADELA: He did during the Holocaust.

(*There's a brief silence.*)

JULIE (*to MARLENA*): Marlena, what about you? Do you have any thoughts on this?
(*The girls all turn to MARLENA who at first looks like a deer caught in the headlights. They're all expecting her to shake her head and keep quiet, but instead she swallows hard.*)

MARLENA (*quietly and slowly*): I think he's bluffing. He'd like to believe that God would come down and save him from being hurt, but he knows it's not going to happen. He probably doesn't believe anybody else is going to stand up for the Jews either. So now he's doing what he has to in order to save all the others.[36]

VENESIA (*prompting her gently*): And himself.

MARLENA: And himself.

JULIE: So, what exactly is he doing?

---

36. In her study of adolescent girls, Davis observes:

The girls who discussed (the pervasive threat of violence) revealed three different kinds of effects of violence on their lives: (1) Some express feelings of being desensitized to violence—feeling numb about it—not letting themselves feel the full extent of the fear or pain. (2) Most girls will talk about their willingness to protect others from violence, especially their younger siblings or small children. They even suggest that they might use violent means. They do not talk about protecting themselves, however. (3) Many girls wonder why God allows people to be hurt, and they think of the church as an ineffective agent of change. (2001: 108)

MARLENA: He's asking for help. He's asking someone he trusts to speak for him. He's saying it's time to tell the secret.

R. ROSEN: The secret—about being Jewish?

MARLENA: Yeah.
(*The girls are all quiet for a moment.*)

NINA (*breaking the silence with mock drama*): Well, whether I'm talking about God or not, I'm not finished with my speech! (*To MARLENA*) Say this, too, to Queen Esther: "Who knows, perhaps it was for just such a time as this that you have reached royal position!"

JESSICA: Destiny's Child!

(*MARLENA takes the message to VENESIA and whispers it in her ear.*)

VENESIA: Tell Mordecai to assemble all the Jews and hold a fast in my behalf for three days and nights. I and my attendants will do the same. Then I shall go the king, even though it is against the law and, if I perish, I perish![37]

JESSICA: Look who's giving the orders now!

ANNIE: If she's laying her life on the line, I guess she has the right to give a few orders.

ADELA: Brave speech, but she's still just doing what Mordecai tells her.

---

37. Roemer writes:

> We try to recognize the difference between things we can change and those we must accept. There are, moreover, clearly occasions when our refusal to submit to the seemingly inevitable can reverse it. It has traditionally been the task of the hero to attempt the impossible, and perhaps one reason we continue to need stories is that, despite their preclusive form, they encourage us to pit ourselves against necessity. They constitute that element in us—it used to be called the spirit—that survives and fights back even when we seem beaten. (1995: 231)

VENESIA: I don't know about that. It sounds like Mordecai would just have her march in to the king immediately, come what may. She's not willing to go without some preparation and some community support. And instead of leaving all the individual Jews to weep and wail on their own, she's pulling the community together. My daddy calls it "solidarity." This way she doesn't have to feel like she's all alone. Maybe she's not the Barbie doll we first thought.

ADELA: OK, you're starting to persuade me. Maybe Esther has something going for her after all.

R. ROSEN: After fasting for three days, Esther puts on her royal finery and goes to the king's court.

JESSICA: At least she knows what to do to get his attention—drop five pounds and get dolled up.

NINA: Hey, Esther! Don't forget the duct tape!

JULIE: Perhaps for this scene, we can put the king in a chair up on the podium and have Esther come down the aisle of the sanctuary.

VENESIA: Good idea.
(*She retreats to the back of the sanctuary to make her entrance. ANNIE takes a seat in one of the pulpit chairs on the podium. VENESIA comes halfway up the aisle. Upon noticing her, ANNIE catches her breath, as though Esther has taken the king's breath away, and then extends the scepter to Esther.*[38] *VENESIA advances as far as the steps.*)

ANNIE: Queen Esther, what a surprise! Is something troubling you? What do you need? You name it. I'll give you half of my kingdom if that's what you want!

---

38. "The golden rod, with its overt sexual innuendo, stands in for any real physical relation the king and Esther have and indicates in whose hands the true power lies" (Spiegel 1994: 198). This is a highly ambiguous statement for, though the king holds the scepter in his hand, it rises, seemingly involuntarily, at the sight of Esther.

JESSICA (*with admiration*): Wow! Half the kingdom! Must be some dress she's wearing! The girl clearly knows how to get what she wants!

ADELA: Yeah, it's just a shame she has to play that game. Wouldn't it be something if, just once, a boy was willing to listen to you because of who you are and not what you look like?

(*Some of the other girls indicate agreement.*)

JESSICA: Oh get real! That's never going to happen! So if you've got the power to drive them crazy with the way you look, then you should go for it!

VENESIA: Doesn't that get you in trouble sometimes?

JESSICA: What do you mean?

VENESIA (*glancing at MARLENA*): I mean sometimes you get attention you don't really want.

JESSICA: Well, I happen to *like* a lot of attention. (*Some of the girls roll their eyes at this.*)

ADELA: We never would have guessed.

JESSICA (*adopting a more sober tone, but still quite self-confident*): But if the guy's a real loser, pull a Vashti—just say no!

VENESIA: And what if he doesn't take no for an answer?

JESSICA: Well, you just don't put yourself in those situations to begin with.

VENESIA: What if you can't help it?

JESSICA (*growing a little exasperated with this line of interrogation*): What do you mean, what if you can't help it? You can always help it.

VENESIA (*drawing a deep breath and glancing again at MARLENA*): What if it happens in your own home?

(*MARLENA's face blanches and she lowers her eyes.*)

JULIE: Venesia, what are you talking about? Is there something you need to tell us?

VENESIA (*hesitating*): No. Never mind. I was just giving Jessica a hard time. (*JESSICA is left looking puzzled.*) What's my line?

R. ROSEN: "If it please Your Majesty . . . "

VENESIA: If it please Your Majesty, would the king and Haman care to join me for dinner? I've prepared a feast in my quarters.

ANNIE (*to VENESIA*): Excellent! (*to MARLENA*) Have Haman summoned and we'll join you immediately.

(*VENESIA, ANNIE, JESSICA, and MARLENA move to stage right. VENESIA, ANNIE, and JESSICA sit around the altar which serves as their make-shift table. MARLENA pretends to serve them food and drink and then stands in attendance behind them.*)

ADELA: That's rather anticlimactic, isn't it? You're expecting Esther to plead for the lives of her people and all she does is invite the king to dinner?

NINA: Give her time. She needs to butter him up. Haven't you ever heard, the way to man's heart is through his stomach?

ANNIE: Now tell me what you want, Queen Esther. The offer of half my kingdom still stands.

VENESIA: My wish, Your Majesty, my request—if I have found favor in Your Majesty's eyes and if Your Majesty is willing to grant my wish and do what I ask . . .

ADELA: Spit it out, girl!

VENESIA: May Your Majesty and Haman come to dinner again tomorrow night and I will do as the king has said.

(*ANNIE and JESSICA arise to go, showing signs that they are in a pleasant and tipsy mood. ANNIE goes back to the pulpit chair. JESSICA comes down the steps of the podium where NINA is sitting on the bottom step. Upon seeing NINA JESSICA scowls and hurries past. In the process, NINA sticks out her foot and trips her. JESSICA expresses her frustration with an exasperated growl.*)

ADELA: Another dinner! Esther, are you ever going to get to the point?[39]

VENESIA: Be patient! I'm laying the groundwork. You gotta remember, I haven't seen the king for a month. He needs to be reminded why he liked me so much to begin with.

NINA: Well, work a little faster! I'm dying out here, remember?

JULIE: If the suspense is killing you, then the story is working the way it's supposed to!

R. ROSEN: Yes, and now it's time for a little comic relief. This is where Haman makes plans to execute Mordecai, only to have Mordecai honored instead.

JESSICA and SOPHIE take their places at stage left (directly opposite from the previous banquet scene).

SOPHIE (*as JESSICA enters*): How are you, my husband?

---

39. Bakhtin (1990: 6) writes:

Before the countenance of the hero finally takes place as a stable and necessary whole, the hero is going to exhibit a great many grimaces, random masks, wrong gestures, and unexpected actions, depending on those emotional-volitional reactions and personal whims of the author, through the chaos of which he is compelled to work his way in order to reach an authentic valuational attitude. In order to see one we apparently know well think how many masking layers must first be removed from his face, layers that were sedimented upon his face by our own fortuitous reactions and attitudes.

JESSICA (*in an arrogant tone*): Only the most honored man in the empire—besides the king, of course. I am one of the wealthiest men I know, I have many sons, and I *am* Prime Minister of the empire.

ADELA: What? And this is supposed to be news to his wife?

JESSICA: And, on top of all that, tonight I was invited by the queen herself to attend a dinner party. The king and I were her exclusive guests. Moreover, she's invited me to another dinner party tomorrow evening. I might as well be the king himself, I've become so important in the court.

SOPHIE: That's wonderful, my dear!

JESSICA: The only problem is that that blasted Jew Mordecai ruins everything for me. Whenever I go through the king's gate, he does nothing to honor me. If he's standing, he does not bow. If he's sitting, he does not rise. He refuses to acknowledge my importance and it's driving me crazy.

SOPHIE: This calls for drastic measures. You need to make an example of him. Why don't you have a stake erected, high enough for everyone in the city to see—fifty—no, seventy-five feet high, and tomorrow ask the king to have Mordecai impaled on it.

ADELA: In other words, a pain in the ass deserves a pain in the ass!

JULIE: Adela! Please!

ADELA: Well, it's true, isn't it?

R. ROSEN: I'm glad you're getting into the spirit of Purim, Adela, but perhaps we could tone down the crudity a little for the sake of our Christian friends?

JESSICA (*feigning innocence*): Yeah, because I've never heard the word "ass" before!

ANNIE: Well, *I've* never heard it in *church*, except for Jesus sitting on his ass on Palm Sunday.

The girls howl with laughter.

ANNIE: I don't think that came out quite right!

NINA (*laughing*): And what about when Abraham ties his ass to a tree and then climbs to the top of Mount Moriah?

ADELA: Ouch! I bet that hurt!

JESSICA: I think that's a real *stretch!*[40]

JULIE (*trying to stifle her own laughter*): OK, OK. I think we'd better settle down.

R. ROSEN (*trying to get the girls back on task*): Meanwhile, back in the throne room, the king is having difficulty sleeping . . .

ANNIE starts pacing restlessly back and forth in front of the pulpit chair.

SOPHIE: Something's bothering him.

VENESIA: He's trying to figure out what Esther really wants.

ANNIE (*in a commanding voice*): Bring the royal records and have them read to me!

MARLENA comes in with a roll of toilet tissue, pretending it's a scroll. She begins to unroll it and proceeds to read from it. The girls start laughing again.

---

40. According to Bakhtin, preoccupation with the body, particularly the "lower strata" of the body, as well as bodily functions is a typical feature of carnival. This focus, with its often coarse humor and grotesque imagery, functions as a gesture of resistance against institutional abstractions and absolutes. "[T]he merry, abundant and victorious bodily element opposes the serious medieval world of fear and oppression with all its intimidating and intimidated ideology" (1984: 226).

JULIE (*in an aside to R. ROSEN*): Well, I can see the low humor is with us to stay.

MARLENA (*in a monotone*): Blah blah blah blah blah blah blah. (*She looks up at ANNIE. The king is still awake.*) Blah blah blah blah blah blah blah.

ANNIE: Oh, yes. I remember that conspiracy. Was Mordecai ever rewarded for turning in those two assassins?

MARLENA: No, Your Majesty.

ANNIE: Well, something must be done! I need advice!

NINA: As usual!

ANNIE: Who's in the outer court that I can consult?

MARLENA: Haman, Your Majesty.

ANNIE: Call him in!

MARLENA steps down from "the throne room" and motions with her finger for JESSICA to approach.

JESSICA (*entering the throne room*): Good morning, Your Majesty. I have a matter of urgent business I need to discuss with you—

ANNIE (*ignoring Haman's comment*): If I were in a mind to honor someone in particular, how should I go about it?

JESSICA (*putting her hand to her heart to indicate she thinks that the king is referring to her*): Well, Your Majesty, this is most unexpected. I suppose that, if you wanted to honor *someone in particular*, you might let that *particular someone* wear your own royal robes for a day . . .

ANNIE: Yes?

JESSICA: And ride upon your own personal horse . . .

ANNIE: Yes?

JESSICA: . . . with a crown on his head . . .

ANNIE: The horse or the person?

JESSICA: And perhaps have one of your most important officials lead him through the streets shouting, "This is what is done for the man whom the king decides to honor!"

ANNIE: Splendid idea! (*JESSICA bows to the king in anticipation of this reward.*) Have all this done for Mordecai the Jew! You lead the horse yourself! (*JESSICA leaves crestfallen.*)

ADELA (*to JESSICA*): Don't you just *hate it* when that happens?

VENESIA: This is a topsy-turvy world, for sure.

R. ROSEN: In later tradition, it became even more so. One midrash says that, when Haman led Mordecai through the streets on the king's horse, that Haman's own daughter looked out from the second story of their house and, thinking that her father was being honored and that Mordecai was leading his horse, she emptied the chamber pot on the head of the man she thought was Mordecai.

NINA: So, when the text says that Haman went home after that, mourning and with his head covered—they meant, literally!

JESSICA: Ooh, yuk! Marlena, bring that scroll! We're gonna need it!

VENESIA: Yeah, 'cause you got to get ready for my second dinner party and I don't want you showing up smelling like a chamber pot!

(*JESSICA returns stage left to where SOPHIE is waiting.*)

SOPHIE: How are you, my husband?

JESSICA: Only the most humiliated man in the empire! Mordecai the Jew was raised, all right, for all to see, but not on the stake I had put up for him. The king decided to honor him instead. And I had to parade him through the streets proclaiming his triumph. I'll never live this down.

SOPHIE (*matter-of-factly*): No, you probably won't.

JESSICA: Is that all you have to say?

SOPHIE: Yes, that's all. You're done-for.

JESSICA: Gee, with a supportive wife like you, who needs enemies like Mordecai?

SOPHIE: Well, that is something to think about.[41]

(*At this point MARLENA arrives to escort Haman to Esther's dinner party. She gestures with her finger that he follow her. ANNIE joins them as they cross the stage. VENESIA welcomes them and motions for the king and Haman to sit. As they get settled, MARLENA pretends to put out food and wine. When finished she retires to the background.*)

ANNIE: Now that we have returned, Queen Esther, you must tell me: What is it that you want? Whatever it is, it shall be yours. Even to half my kingdom.

NINA: Boy, he's really wanting to unload that real estate, isn't he?

VENESIA: If I have found favor in Your Majesty's eyes and if it pleases Your Majesty—

ADELA: Cut to the chase!

---

41. The character of Zeresh in the book of Esther demonstrates peripety (dramatic reversal) in terms of character. At first she sympathetically encourages Haman to do away with Mordecai the Jew, then, seemingly unmoved, she pronounces doom on Haman because Mordecai is Jewish and "fated" to be victorious.

VENESIA: —my request is for my life and for the lives of my people.

ANNIE: What in the world are you talking about?

VENESIA: We have been sold out, my people and I, to be destroyed, massacred, and exterminated—

SOPHIE: Like bugs!

VENESIA: Had we only been sold as slaves, I would have kept quiet, for it wouldn't be worth bothering you with, but something more terrible is happening here. There is someone . . . (*she hesitates, looking around at her friends, and then over her shoulder at MARLENA*) . . . there is someone in this house who is hurting your family and you do not even know what is happening.
(*The room gets very quiet. The rabbi and the minister look at one another and then back to the players. ANNIE and VENESIA exchange looks. ANNIE gives a slight nod, swallows hard, and resumes character.*)

ANNIE: Who would dare to do this?

VENESIA (*standing and pointing at JESSICA*): This man you brought to live with us, that you trusted—this scumbag you call a boyfriend![42]

(*ANNIE stands and leaves the table. She begins pacing back and forth at stage left. JESSICA, suddenly realizing what is happening, grabs VENESIA by the arm and starts shaking her.*)

JESSICA: You little snit! This was supposed to be our little secret! You'll be sorry you ever opened your mouth!

---

42. Behind biological fathers, the second largest group of perpetrators of incestual abuse are "social fathers" (stepfathers, foster fathers, adoptive fathers, mothers' boyfriends). Moreover, abusive nonbiological fathers are two to two-and-a-half times more likely to engage in sexual than in nonsexual abuse of children. See Gordon (1988: 210-11).

(*MARLENA slowly moves forward into the light, fixed on the action. ANNIE storms back to the table and stops in shock when he sees JESSICA and VENESIA.*)

ANNIE: You mean to tell me that he's molesting my little girl, in my own house?

MARLENA (*shouting*): YES! (*lowering her voice, but with a determined tone*) Yes, he is. And if you don't get him out, he's going to do the same to my sister, too.

(*There is a stunned silence. JULIE moves to approach MARLENA who seems to be realizing only now what she's actually said. ANNIE motions for JULIE to wait.*)

ANNIE (*gently to MARLENA*): What should be done with this . . . villain?

(*MARLENA looks around at all her friends and drops her shoulders in relief. As she considers the question, her eyes begin to glint and an odd smile appears on her lips.*)

MARLENA: A eunuch. He should be made into a eunuch.[43]

(*The girls look around at each other and begin to laugh.*)

ADELA (*dryly*): Let's hear it for the spirit of Purim. Anyone happen to have a pair of scissors?[44]

(*The laughter and chatter builds as the girls gather around MARLENA in support. JULIE and R. ROSEN look at each other in disbelief and then join the girls. The lights dim as they all escort MARLENA out through a side door of the sanctuary.*)

---

43. On "dismemberment" and carnival, Bakhtin writes:

> The scene of the scandal and discrowning of the prince—the carnival king, or more precisely, the carnival bridegroom—is carried out as a *dismemberment*, as a typical carnivalistic "sacrificial" tearing to pieces. . . . Carnivalization allows [authors of carnivalesque literature] to see and depict aspects of the character and behavior of people which in the normal course of life could not reveal themselves. (1973:135-36)

44. "Seriousness burdens us with hopeless situations, but laughter lifts us above them and delivers us from them. Laughter does not encumber [us], it liberates [us]" (Bakhtin 1986: 134).

(ACT 2)

Scene 2

Later that same evening.

(*ADELA, NINA, JESSICA, SOPHIE, and ANNIE return to the sanctuary and sit on the steps to the podium, looking subdued.*)

SOPHIE: What do you think is going to happen now?

NINA: Dunno.

JESSICA: I guess rehearsal is over for the night.

ADELA: That would be a safe bet. (*Silence. VENESIA enters and joins the others on the steps.*)

SOPHIE: How's Marlena?

VENESIA: She's OK, considering. Her mom and sister are here now. Julie and Rabbi Rosen are talking to them all about what's going on and making some phone calls.

JESSICA: Maybe the rest of us should go home.

NINA: Yeah, I guess we should. (*No one moves.*)

(*ADELA turns to VENESIA, ANNIE, and JESSICA*)

ADELA: That last scene was . . . pretty amazing. How did you know . . . how to play it?

VENESIA: I don't know. Just all of a sudden it seemed like there was a different script that needed to be played.

JESSICA: It was like a scene out of the movies. We all just morphed into something else.

ANNIE: The story was different and yet the same.[45]

SOPHIE (*suddenly shivering*): I'm cold.

(*NINA moves close to her and puts her arm around her. Silence again. R. ROSEN enters.*)

SOPHIE: Is Marlena OK?

R. ROSEN: She will be, though it may take time. Her mother and sister are here with her. We've contacted the proper authorities—

ADELA (*dryly*): I hope they're not all at a six-month drinking party!

R. ROSEN (*with a small sad smile*): Me, too. Anyway, Marlena's mother's boyfriend is being taken into custody.

ADELA: One Haman down, a million more to go.[46]

SOPHIE: The world's a really mean place.

R. ROSEN: Yes, it can be.

JESSICA: Why didn't Marlena tell anybody all this time?

R. ROSEN: That's hard to know. Venesia, did she tell you?

VENESIA: Only after I figured it out myself and started asking her about it.

ANNIE: Maybe she didn't think it would do any good to tell.

VENESIA (*agreeing*): Well, she doesn't exactly trust grown-ups much.

---

45. In a fragmented note, Bakhtin writes: "The rupture between real life and symbolic ritual. How unnatural this rupture is" (1986: 154).

46. "In the spirit of carnival, the Book of Esther is a kind of fun-house mirror to reality, whose distortions can make us laugh, but whose recognizable reflections make its contortions all the more disturbing" (Spiegel 1994: 202).

SOPHIE: Why not?

ADELA: Well, think about it. She has two main adults in her life. One is hurting her, and the other is turning a blind eye.[47] Doesn't exactly inspire much confidence, does it?

SOPHIE: No, I guess not. But here at the church, wouldn't there be someone?

NINA: Right! Can you imagine laying something like that on Rev. Richards? How very unpleasant!

ANNIE: And inappropriate for this context!

ADELA: It's hardly what "nice" girls do![48]

NINA: Besides, "men of the cloth" aren't exactly proving to be very trustworthy these days where children and sex are concerned!

---

47. In the study of incest cases done by Gordon, 78 percent of the mothers in two-parent incestuous households were substantially weakened in their child-raising authority and confidence by any of a number of factors:

> The most common was that the woman herself was the object of her husband's or lover's violence—44 percent were beaten themselves. . . . Thirty-six percent of the mothers were ill or disabled; 34 percent had other debilitating problems such as alcoholism, rejection by their own relatives, recent migration to the United States, inability to speak English, isolation as evidenced by infrequent trips outside the home. (1988: 212)

The inability of mothers to stand up to men "prevented girls from internalizing the self-esteem they needed to resist sexual exploitation themselves" (213).

48. Gordon (1988: 249) writes:

> Just as incest often occurs in families with exaggerated feminine subordination, so the girls' resistance to incest often assumed, perhaps had to assume, the form of resistance to the norms of feminine virtue, passivity, and subordination. Despite the revulsion incest has provoked, it opens a frightening but vital line of questioning about ordinary family relations. It identifies tensions between family solidarity and individual autonomy, between adult authority and children's rights, between women's status as victims and their responsibility as parents, tensions that one should not expect to resolve easily. It shows that many feminine virtues, not only those one might want to reject—obedience, quietness, obligingness—but also those one might want to preserve—discipline, responsibility, loyalty—can support victimization.

SOPHIE: What about Julie?

VENESIA: I don't think she knew her well enough. She hasn't been here very long. Maybe in time she would have told her.

SOPHIE: I bet she told God.

ADELA: Fat lot of good that did.

SOPHIE: Maybe it *did* do some good. Maybe that's how Venesia figured it out.

ANNIE: And Venesia rewrote the script.

JESSICA: Sort of like Esther.

NINA: Without the duct tape and the prom dress!

(*Everyone smiles at that, even VENESIA.*)

ADELA: That still doesn't change the fact that there are plenty of hard situations where God is nowhere to be found, where *no one* stops the play *or* rewrites the script.

ANNIE: Don't remind us. It makes me very sad. If we can't count on our parents to protect us, or public officials to care about us, or our communities to listen to us, or God to rescue us, where does that leave us?[49]

---

49. Cf. Levinas's reflections on a story written during the final hours of the Warsaw Ghetto resistance:

> The path that leads to one God must be walked in part without God. . . . The adult's God is revealed precisely through the void of the child's heaven. This is the moment when God retires from the world and hides His face. . . .
>
> The God Who hides His face and is recognized as being present and intimate . . . is this really possible? . . . [T]he link between God and man (sic) is not an emotional communion that takes place within the love of a God incarnate, but a spiritual or intellectual [*esprits*] relationship which takes place through an education in the Torah. It is precisely a word, not incarnate, from God that ensures a living God among us. (1990: 143-44)

R. ROSEN: I know you're all feeling pretty vulnerable right now. But what you've said isn't true of *all* parents or officials or members of the community. And, as for God—what other hands does God have besides ours? (*The girls reflect on this.*) Think about what's happened here tonight. You helped a friend find her voice and tell a painful secret. You created the space that allowed her to burst back into the circle of life.[50] Your presence gave her the strength to save herself and probably her sister and maybe even her mother, too. If not for you, she might have continued to suffer in meaningless, useless silence. Instead, she imagined a new ending to her story of suffering.[51] You have no idea how important that is.

(*A brief silence.*)

ADELA (*a small smile forming*): And it *was* a *wonderfully wicked* ending.

VENESIA (*agreeing*): The shoe's-on-the-other-foot-now kind of ending.

NINA: A very Esther-type ending.

JESSICA: What do you mean?

(*The other girls look at her and in unison they shout:*) IF YOU'D READ THE STORY, YOU'D KNOW!!!

JESSICA: I *did* read it. Well, most of it. OK, I didn't quite make it to the end.

---

50. Cf. Bakhtin's cryptic note: "The search for one's own (authorial) voice. . . . Not to remain tangential, to burst into the circle of life, to become one among other people" (1986:147).

51. "In postmodern times, becoming a narrator of one's own life implies an assumption of responsibility for more than the events of that life. Events are contingent, but a story can be told that binds contingent events together into a life that has a moral necessity" (Frank 1995: 176). See also Levinas (1988) who speaks of self-enclosed suffering and "the possibility of a half opening" to the other: "For pure suffering, which is intrinsically meaningless and condemned to itself without exit, a beyond takes shape in the interhuman" (158).

R. ROSEN (*rising and motioning for the girls to rise as well*): Don't worry, Jessica, there's always next year.

VENESIA (*as they are all departing*): Well, next time, somebody else can play the role of Esther. Being such a nice quiet girl who pleases everybody all the time just wears me out.

The little girl from up the street was the same age as the children of the house. She was visiting one day during story time. The children had insisted upon the story of David and Goliath. It was a story they all knew well but the little girl had never heard before.

As she listened to the story, her eyes, usually sad and somewhat vacuous, began to glow strangely, and her small jaw tightened. When the story was over, she insisted that it be told again.

After that day, every time she visited, she asked to hear the story. Always that one. Never a different one. Finally the mother, sensing some unnamable need, said one day in answer to her request, "Why don't *you* tell *me* the story instead?"

The little girl nodded and began to narrate, "Once upon a time there was a big bad guy who would come in the middle of the night to hurt the children of Israel. . . ."

CHAPTER SEVEN

Hannah's Song

(Judges 19–21; 1 Samuel 1–3)

It was a long, long time ago,
before there was a king in Israel
when the judges judged (righteously sometimes)
and heroes fought (faithfully sometimes)
and the people followed the Lord (sometimes—
when it was convenient
and they were in trouble)
and the Lord looked after Israel
(for a while—
until he felt like he was being taken for granted).
It was a long, long time ago,
when God had grown quiet,
the future became uncertain,
and the people mostly did as they pleased.[1]

---

1. Judg 18:1; 19:1; 21:25.

It was a time when people who had been living peaceably side by side
for years suddenly turned on each other with a great slaughter.
Neighbors—
even kinfolk—
began to treat each other like enemies.
And everyone who was different was an enemy.[2]

It was a time when lives were cheap,
when women were objects
to be owned and to be disposed of at will,[3]
when children were murdered simply because of where they lived
and who their parents were.[4]

A time when people were killed for their property,
when real estate was more valuable than human life.[5]

It was a time when the clergy sold their services
to the highest bidders,
when people sought to buy personal security
by building private sanctuaries
and by employing ministers with the very best pedigrees.[6]

A time when priests confiscated for themselves
the largest and best portions of the people's offerings to God.[7]

It was a time when clergymen harassed and seduced the women
who came to serve and to worship in God's house.[8]

---

2. Judges 19–21; cf. Judges 12.
3. Judges 19.
4. Judg 21:8-12.
5. Judg 18:21-31.
6. Judges 17
7. 1 Sam 2:12-17.
8. 1 Sam 2:22-25. David Jobling, who argues forcefully that Hannah's song envisions a restoration of an (ideal?) judgeship rather than a move toward monarchy, writes:

> These women are subject to the authority of the priests, so that they cannot be considered as entering voluntarily into these liaisons. The women are victims of exploitation. Their routinized rape continues the theme of rape from the end of Judges. But though their situation certainly lacks the sheer horror of the story of the Levite's wife in Judges 19 it seems more sordid than the mass abduction of women

A time when people had been oppressed for so long,
they were content to live with oppression.[9]

It was a very long time ago—
   or was it so very long ago?—
      when there was no leadership in the land
      and people did whatever they could get away with.

That was when it started[10]—
the song, that is—
when a woman named Hannah rode into Shiloh
with her husband
and her husband's other wife
and her husband's other wife's children.

           (Now Shiloh was a holy place
            where people came to worship,
        to bring their gifts and offerings to God.
          Eli had been a priest there for ages.
            He had even been there
when all those girls were rounded up for the men of Benjamin.)

               Did you read about that?[11]

Judges 21, with which it can more easily be compared. . . . The conduct of Eli's sons represents a move toward the conditions that characterize monarchy: men of hereditary privilege using women as they wish, without anyone's being able to check them. (1998: 180)

9. Israel is being oppressed by the Philistines, but not only do they not cry to YHWH for help, they chastise Samson for making trouble with the Philistines: "Do you not know that the Philistines rule over us? What is this you have done to us?" (Judg 15:9-13).

10. While the tendency for commentators is to read the story of Hannah forward as a prelude to the story of Samuel (and thus the stories of Saul and David), some have seen many connections to the preceding stories in Judges. For example, Pseudo-Philo situates Hannah's story in Israel's larger search for a leader (*Biblical Antiquities*, 49-51). In his version, the people cast lots for a leader; the lot falls on Elkanah, but he refuses. The leadership role is then extended to Elkanah's future son, Samuel. Peter Miscall (1986) has shown multiple connections between this story and those preceding in his discussion of intertextual connections and the undecidability of reading. For a critique of his reading see, Havea 2003. More recent commentators who read Hannah against Judges and preserve more of Hannah's subjectivity and moral awareness include Fewell and Gunn 1993; Jobling 1998; and Havea 2003.

11. Judges 21.

Shiloh,
a holy prison camp
for 400 young girls captured from Jabesh-Gilead.
Their families—
murdered—
so that the virgin daughters could be taken
and given to men who needed wives.
The weeping and wailing could be heard for miles.
The men of Benjamin came and took them away.
But they were not enough.
So the Benjaminites returned and abducted
two hundred more girls
while they danced at the annual festival.
It was pretty nasty episode, all right.
Community-sanctioned rape.
The screaming and sobbing could be heard for miles.
Mothers mourning the loss of their daughters.
Fathers and brothers being bullied
into letting their daughters and sisters be taken away.
Every family fractured.
God knows how the girls themselves ever learned to live with it.

But what's done was done.
There was really nothing Eli could have done about all that.
The people didn't even consult him.
Why look to a priest for leadership when it comes to
matters of life and death?
Even the people themselves had turned their heads.
Nothing was said.
Nothing was done.
After all, what's a tribe supposed to do
when you kill all their women and children?
They do what they have to in order to survive.

And besides, what could a single priest do *really*?
Especially when the people want to blame the whole thing
on God anyway.
Hadn't it been *the* L*ord* who had
"made a breach in the tribes of Israel"?[12]

---

12. Judg 21:15.

So religious life went on as usual.
Families continued to make their pilgrimages,
celebrate their feasts,
offer their sacrifices
as if nothing had happened,
as if their daughters had nothing to fear.

But their daughters had plenty to fear.
Their dances had turned to dirges,
their laughter to lamentations.
Their own community had conspired against them.
Their holy ground had become a place of holy terror.

Yes, their daughters had plenty to fear
—and so did everyone else.
Eli the Indolent, the Priest of Passivity,
had sons only too eager to abuse priestly power and position.
Molesting the women serving in the sanctuary,
threatening the men offering their sacrifices,
rapacious
ravenous
their lust for flesh was never ending.
But even though Eli knew what his sons were doing,
he couldn't bring himself to do anything about it.
A little slap on the wrist.
A wagging finger.
But in the end, what could a single priest do?
Especially when his own livelihood is at stake.

This was Shiloh,
the holy place,
where women young and not-so-young were routinely violated,
where gifts to God were forcefully taken
by men more interested in themselves
than in their people.

And one day Hannah came to be there—
Hannah and her song.

It was a sad song in the beginning.
A song born of great pain
  and frustration
    and longing.
The song of someone caught in a world not of her own making,
indeed the song of someone who,
by all rights, could never hope
even to alter,
  much less remake,
    her own world.
For, you see, Hannah was barren.
God and her body had both betrayed her,
refusing change,
refusing to let her extend life into the world beyond.[13]
From the confines of a locked womb
the song began its mournful strains—
a sorrowful echo trapped inside a body that could not change.

No one else could hear the song.

Certainly not Peninnah,
Hannah's husband's other wife.
But you can't really blame her for not hearing the song.
How would you feel if your husband took another wife?
  A younger one.
    A prettier one.
As if you weren't good enough?
How would you feel if he clearly loved her more than you?
If you were forced to watch his favoritism day after day?

---

13. On barrenness in the Hebrew Bible, Elaine Scarry writes:

Everything is at stake in the alterability of the body, for this attribute is at once inten-
sified and lifted away from the body and attributed to God. First the self-alterability
of the body is denied, for to be barren is not just to be without child but to be unalterable, unable to change from the state of without child to with child: barrenness is
absolute because it means "unalterable" except by the most radical means, unalterable except by divine intervention. This, then, is the second step, a doubling and lifting away of the power just denied in the woman; God in changing the body from
barren to fertile is not simply changing it from being unpregnant to pregnant but
changing it from being "unchangeable" to both changed and pregnant. . . . This
intensification of the body and lifting of its central attribute away from it and assignment of that attribute to the immaterial and spiritual are . . . crucial in the overall con-
version of body into belief. (1985: 194)

Knowing that, while you took care of the children,
he was taking care of *her*?[14]

No—
Peninnah was much too busy defending her own self-worth
to hear Hannah's song.
How in the world could she reach out to this other woman,
when her own storyteller had already labeled her a "rival,"
when her own husband constantly pitted the two of them against
each other?
No—
her role was already prescribed.
There was nothing else she could do.
She could only taunt Hannah with the one thing she had
that Hannah didn't:
Children.[15]

Some days, when the taunts were particularly relentless,
when Hannah's feelings of emptiness were particularly unbearable,
the song thundered[16] in her head.
But no one else could hear it.

Certainly not Elkanah,
Hannah's husband.

---

14. Other scenarios are imaginable. Fewell and Gunn explore multiple options:

> How and in what order Elkanah acquired these two women is not disclosed. We are only told that Peninnah has children while Hannah has none (1 Sam 1:2), and that Elkanah loved Hannah (1:5). We are immediately led to think of Jacob's love for Rachel, of Rachel's barrenness, and of Leah's fertility. Jacob had been tricked into his double marriage. What about Elkanah? Had Elkanah married Hannah first and, upon discovering her infertility (like Abraham), taken a second woman to bear his children? Had Elkanah married Peninnah first but, considering her less desirable after having borne his children, found a more pleasing woman in Hannah? Did he, like David, take the two women at the same time (cf. 1 Sam 25:42-43), so that it was clear to both of them from the beginning that they were partial and replaceable?
>
> Any one of these possibilities marks this a marriage of male convenience. For the women involved it is a different matter. (1993: 136)

15. In regard to this language, Lillian Klein writes, "[T]he language conveys (and thereby shapes) the expected behavior of two women who share a husband. ... Masculine mimetic desire is displaced onto the female" (82). Later she observes "There is . . . no feminine bonding depicted; Peninnah's mimetic desire obviates that possibility" (1994: 83).

16. "Her rival provoked her exceedingly to make her thunder" (1 Sam 1:6).

But you can't really blame him for not hearing the song.
As a man who had everything he wanted—
indeed his name was "God has acquired"—
he was completely bewildered by Hannah's discontent.
He was perfectly happy with his marital arrangement.
He had a wife to provide him with children
and a wife to provide him with pleasure
and the fact that he had two wives
brought him great prestige in the neighborhood.
Clearly it was a measure of God's favor.
Why couldn't Hannah be happy?
He had given her everything a woman could possibly want
—including himself!
"Am I not worth more to you than ten sons?" he used to say to her.[17]
Why can't you just be happy taking care of me?
(Don't you like ironing my shirts?)
After all, I'm a considerate, attentive husband, am I not?
I treat you with favor.
I notice when you're upset.
Do I not show concern about your feelings?
   "Why are you weeping?
         Why aren't you eating?
               What has made you so resentful?[18]
               Am I not better to you than ten sons?"
(See, I even have an inkling what the problem is.)
I do not have to wait for an answer.[19]
—Wait, where are you going?

---

17. Elkanah's effort to comfort Hannah, writes Jobling, "is not an impressive one. If you wish to assure someone of your love, the line 'Are *you* not more to *me* than. . . ?' seems much more promising than 'Am I not more to you . . . ?'!" (1998: 131)

18. An ambiguous question: literally, "Why is your heart evil?" which may mean "Why are you sick at heart?" or it may carry the accusatory connotations of the literal words.

19. Klein insightfully remarks:

> Elkanah's "consoling" of Hannah does not allow her time to answer his initial questions, which would effect communication between husband and wife, but would also draw him into involvement. That his questions are rhetorical and thus not intended to probe Hannah's situation is evident from their quick succession. While they do not allow Hannah to convey her thoughts or feelings, Elkanah's questions do relinquish some tacit information about him. His questions are typical of what psycholinguist Virginia Satir classifies as the "Blamer Mode." Such speakers "don't bother about an answer; that is unimportant. The blamer is much more interested in throwing weight around than really finding out anything." (1994: 87; [Satir 1988: 87])

No,
clearly, Elkanah would never be able to hear any song
that might displace him as the center of Hannah's life.[20]

To Hannah, the song was growing louder every day.
But no one else could hear it.

Certainly not Eli
the priest.
But you can't really blame him for not hearing the song.
Heavy, immobile Eli,
sitting at the doorpost of the house of God.
Always sitting, eyes failing.
    Unwilling to do more.
      Unable to do better.[21]

He wasn't used to seeing a woman praying in the holy place.—
His clergy sons had a way of keeping most of the women confused
about who God was
and what God demanded.
Most women didn't make it into the inner sanctuary alone
to speak to God
face-to-face.

In fact,
after years of presiding over structured liturgy,

---

20. Cf. Amit 1994: 75:

> Elkanah's words reveal him to possess the egocentricity of a child who perceives himself as the centre of his world and is disappointed when his behaviour fails to receive the attention he expects. Elkanah is revealed as one who cannot accept the fact that Hannah wants to be mother to her children and not mother to her husband. According to this interpretation, Elkanah's flow of questions is the complaint of a man who never matured, who perhaps enjoys moving back and forth between two women when one is the mother of his children and the other continues to fulfil the oedipal role of his own mother.

21. Cf. Doody's description of the relationship of Samuel to Eli: "Samuel is not a particularly resigned personality, either in childhood or later on, but he has to resign himself to the fact that Eli will do no more and can do no better" (1994: 121).

Eli may have even forgotten
what prayer from the heart really sounded like.
Involuntary, uncontrollable prayer.[22]

It's no wonder he thought she was drunk.
Hannah's song had become passionate.
Passion
makes people who have no passion
very nervous.
So nervous they won't even ask what you're praying about.
"Go in peace," says Eli.
"May the God of Israel give you
whatever it is you've asked of him."[23]
Just don't bother me with it.

Peninnah.
    Elkanah.
        Eli.
You can't really blame any of them for not hearing Hannah's song.
They were all just trying to survive in a world gone mad.

---

22. Marcia Falk (1994: 98) writes:

The social politics of this situation are at once ordinary and extraordinary. A seemingly ordinary woman, a woman immersed in longing, Hannah prays from the
depths of her heart, silently, privately. In this behavior she follows no convention—
and she becomes extraordinary. At this moment, talking to God, she does something
entirely on her own. She stands at the sanctuary—the sanctuary where priests offici-
ate as men offer up their sacrifices—and she prays, using her own words and her
own voice, without intermediaries. Her act is all the more extraordinary in that, by
all accounts, she is the first woman—indeed the first "ordinary" person—to pray in
any sanctuary, at this point in time before institutionalized prayer has replaced sacrifice as the means of public worship. In so acting, Hannah stands poised to become
a symbol for rabbinic Judaism, providing for the early rabbis—the Amoraim—a
model of authentic prayer, which is to say, "the prayer of the heart"—although all
Hannah has *meant* to do is to speak her *own* heart. We may call her intentions spiritual, but the result of her action is both spiritual and political. Hannah discovers her
own voice, and herself legitimates that voice.

23. Cf. Klein:

When his presumption proves utterly false, Eli fails to accept responsibility for his
misjudgment; instead, he utters easy platitudes that could apply to any person, any
prayer. Hannah is judged abnormal (drunken) and thereby marginalized, and this by
a man to whom she has not turned, a man who unjustly criticizes her with the
authority of his position. (1994: 90-91)

Their lives were not perfect—
and yes,
they lived in fear like everyone else—
but, for the most part, they had escaped the bad things
that were happening all around them.

Peninnah was not one of those women
who had been violated on sacred soil.
She had not been ripped
from her home and given to a stranger.
The children dying around her
were not her children.

Elkanah had lost
neither family nor property in the recent tribal wars.
Unlike the men of Benjamin,
he did not have to scramble to find a wife
or worry about how to perpetuate his lineage.
Indeed, he had not one wife,
but two
and many children
and many possessions.

And Eli,
despite the fact he no longer heard a word from the Lord
and was morally incapable of doing the right thing,
still had the choicest appointment in the conference.

They had all escaped.
        They were surviving.
                They were all taking care of themselves.
It's really no wonder they could not hear anyone else's song.

Especially a song as irrepressible as Hannah's song.

✳✳✳

So what was so urgent about Hannah's song?

Oh, we all know the story
about how barren Hannah desperately wanted a child,
how she prayed,
and how God answered her prayer by giving her her son Samuel.
We know the story.
How Hannah's faith was repaid with the ultimate reward.
We like to tell it on Mother's Day
when we're feeling generous.
On our more jaundiced days,
we say she caved in.
She succumbed to social pressure.
You ain't nothing if you ain't a mama.[24]
A mama of a boy-child.
Take that, Peninnah. I could do it, too.[25]

But, in actuality,
Hannah's song was not really about motherhood, *per se*.
Face it,
any woman willing to hand over her three-year-old son
to a man who had done such a lousy job of raising his own kids
is hardly eligible for the Mother of the Year award.
But neither was the song simply about wanting
a better seat at the social table.

No, Hannah's song was about something else.
　Something more.
　　Something other.
　　　Something different than the world in which she lived.
It was a grand imagining of Something Else.[26]

---

24. In fact, her forfeiting of Samuel have led many to think she only wanted a son to improve her own social status. See, for example, the readings of Polzin 1989: 19-24 and Eslinger 1985: 70-121.

25. Cf. the comment of Rosemary Radford Reuther (1982: 182):

> As a wife, Hannah has only one justification for her existence—to bear a son and male heir for her husband. Lacking that honor, she is accounted worthless. It is not simply that she is childless. If she had only girl children, she would still be accounted unfortunate. Only male children can redeem woman's existence. The idea that she might have a girl rather than a boy is, in fact, not even considered in the text.

26. "[T]he process of the imagination . . . begins not by man (sic) conceiving of signs separable from himself but by man conceiving of his own body as *a sign of (and substitute for) something beyond itself*, and then bringing forth other signs that can perform the work of representation in his dear body's place" (Scarry 1985: 237; italics mine).

A child, yes.
But not just any child.
Not a child to be kept and nurtured by her alone.
A child to be shared.
A child whose presence would alter not just her body,
>   not just her status,
>>   not just her purpose in life,
>>>   but the world itself.[27]

Hannah's song was certainly not about caving in.
If anything,
it is about saying *No*.
>   NO to the order around her.
>>   NO to the order imposed upon her.
In fact the first word out of Hannah's mouth is *No*.

"No, my lord," she says to Eli,
"I am not a worthless woman."
Desperate does not equal worthless.
Your stereotypes do not apply.
I am not a drunken spectacle.
No, my lord. No.
"I am a woman hard-pressed of spirit.[28]
I have been pouring out to God my deepest yearnings.[29]

---

27. Jobling proposes, "[Hannah's] vow opens up another possibility, that what she wants is a son *in the service of* YHWH, a son being prepared for a position of leadership in Israel. Perhaps this is an ambitious woman who, having little scope herself, hopes to satisfy her ambition vicariously through her son" (1994: 132). The reading that Jobling puts forward and that I am attempting to further imagine, complicates the feminist critique expressed by Reuther above (n. 25). The backdrop of Judges and the behavior of Eli's sons paints a dim existence for female children who would have a difficult time surviving, let alone achieving the position of leadership that Hannah envisions for Samuel. Hannah's desire is tempered by her reality.

28. Literally "hard of spirit," a loaded phrase with a range of possible meanings: a spirit in difficulty, a stubborn, willful spirit, a burdened spirit, a violent spirit, an unyielding spirit, a resentful, bitter spirit, etc.

29. Literally, "I have been pouring out my *nephesh* to the face of YHWH." The Hebrew word *nephesh*, usually translated "soul," is the seat of one's desires, appetites, emotions, and passions.

From my great protest and frustration[30]
I have been speaking all this time."

It's no wonder no one wanted to hear her song.
Who wants to be confronted with that kind of pain?
That much anger?
Who wants to be incriminated?
Who wants to have to respond?[31]

Only God.
Only God is willing to hear Hannah's soundless song,
words that can't even break the silence.

> "Oh, Lord of Hosts,
> Look upon the oppression of your servant—
> Remember me.
> Do not forget.
> Give your servant the seed of men,
> and I will give him to the Lord for all the days of his life."

From a god who has been
   as immobile as Eli,
      as resistant to change as Elkanah,
         as indifferent to her suffering as Peninnah,
Hannah asks for movement,
   for alteration,
      for a *seed*,
         for an opening in her womb and in her life.[32]
It's just a seed.
What difference can it make?
Despite the fact that he is being implicated in her misery,
God assents

---

30. Most translations soften the confrontational connotations of these verbs. Cf. Tanakh: "anguish and distress;" KJV: "complaint and grief"; NRSV: "anxiety and vexation."

31. "[B]y transporting pain out onto the external world, that external environment is deprived of its immunity to, unmindfulness of, and indifference toward the problems of sentience" (Scarry 1985: 285).

32. Havea describes Hannah's vow as "the string of words that break YHWH's grip over her womb."

and grants her a child.
Not just any child.
But a child that will, in his person, represent God's presence
and extend Hannah's vision into the broader world.[33]
A child that will be shared
by God and Hannah with the rest of Israel.

> "His name shall be
> 'his name is God,'
> for I sought him from the Lord."

✳✳✳

"Aren't you coming to Shiloh?" asks Elkanah after Samuel is born.

> *To give up my child so soon?* she thinks.
> *So things can go back to the way they were for you before?[34]*
> *To be part of your ritual of favoritism*
> *so that I will feel obligated to you?*
> *To be reminded again of the wrongs of Shiloh?*

---

33. Scarry writes:

The imagination is not, as has often been wrongly suggested, amoral: though she is certainly indifferent to many subjects that have in one era or another been designated "moral," *the realm of her labor is centrally bound up with the elementary moral distinction between hurting and not hurting*; she is simply, centrally, and indefatigably at work on behalf of sentience, eliminating its aversiveness and extending its acuity in forms as abundant, extravagantly variable, and startlingly unexpected as her ethical strictness is monotonous and narrowly consistent. The work of the imagination also overlaps with another interior human event that is usually articulated in a separate vocabulary, for it has become evident that at least at a certain moment in her life cycle, she is mixed up with (is in fact almost indistinguishable from) the phenomenon of *compassion*, and only differs from compassion in that in her maturer form she grows tired of the passivity of wishful thinking. (1985: 306; italics mine)

34. Cf. Jobling (1998: 133): "At the time of the next annual Shiloh festival—after Samuel is born, but when he can scarcely be more than three months old—Elkanah assumes that the whole family will be going to the festival and that they will take the baby to the shrine to fulfill Hannah's vow. Perhaps this assumption is dictated by a desire to get back as soon as possible to the way things were before Samuel arrived!"

"No," she says.
"Not while the child is nursing"

> knowing and thinking,
> *The song is in the milk.*[35]

"Once he is weaned, I will bring him," she says,
"and then he must stay there for good"

> knowing and thinking,
> *Once the song is sung in Shiloh,*
> *it will be up to Samuel to learn to sing it for himself.*

"Give my portion to Peninnah.
Give my greetings to Eli the priest.
(Tell him, Don't bother getting up.)
Excuse my absence.
God knows what I am doing."

> *The song is in the milk.*

"Do what seems right in your eyes."[36] responds Elkanah.
"Remain here until you have weaned him.
—Only may the Lord raise up his word."

---

35. Cf. these lines from Pseudo-Philo's rendition of Hannah's song in *Bib. Ant.*:

> Drip, my breasts, and tell your testimonies,
> because you have been commanded to give milk.
> For he who is milked from you will be raised up,
> and the people will be enlightened by his words,
> and he will show to the nations the statues,
> and his horn will be exalted very high.
>
> (Harrington 1985: 365)

36. A play on and a stark contrast to the refrain at the end of Judges: "In those days there was no king in Israel and every man did what was right in his own eyes." In connection with this phrase, Jobling's reading also

> posits a Hannah who understands very well what happens when "all the people," even the priests of Israel, "do what is right in their own eyes." She can respond only by doing what is right in her own eyes. Why does she want to dedicate her son to the shrine? Is it as a way of intervening in the appalling situation there, a way of protesting that what the priests are doing is "not done in Israel"? Does she go further and make a connection between the national situation and her own? Does she connect the power of a priest to use the women at the shrine in whatever way he wishes with the power of any man to marry several wives and play them off against each other as he wishes? Does she look for fundamental systemic change for the benefit of her sex? (1998: 134-35)

> *His word?*[37]
> *What word?*
> *If God had offered a word,*
> *I wouldn't have to offer my son.*

> *But until then, the song is in the milk.*

✳✳✳

The months go by.
Then the seasons.
   Two more times Elkanah asks.
   Two more times Hannah declines,
     keeping her son and her song to herself.
She watches him gradually wander
farther and farther from her reach,
becoming too interested in the world around him
to take his mother's milk.

And then one day the milk dries up.
The song is caught in Hannah's throat.
With the shadow of Shiloh chilling her bones,
she prepares for the journey from which her son will not return.
A three-year-old bull,[38]
   an ephah of flour,

---

37. LXX, 4QSam, and the Syriac read: "May YHWH raise up the word of your mouth."

38. The Masoretic text reads "three bulls," while the LXX and 4QSam read "a three-year-old bull." In verse 25 "they" sacrifice "the bull." Alternative scenarios are logically possible: (1) Three bulls were taken. One bull was sacrificed while the other two were left as part of the boy's board. (2) Only one bull was taken for the sacrifice. The fact that it is "three years old" may mirror Samuel's age and thus the sacrifice of the bull could be a symbolic representation of the dedication of the three-year-old boy. (Most children in the ancient world were weaned at the age of three to four years.) One might also speculate that, because a bull is specifically mentioned, it is being designated as a whole burnt offering (see Leviticus 1). As such, it would function to get God's attention on this special occasion and it would preclude Eli's sons from insisting on a (choice) part of the meat since, for the burnt offering, no part of the animal is designated for human consumption.

a jar of wine
suffices to celebrate and sustain her son in Shiloh.[39]

It is the same old Shiloh,
but a different Hannah.
Before,
her lack had been so deep
that she could not even bring it to pass her lips.
Now
both a son and a song
cross the bounds of her body
to bring a shareable excess into the world.[40]

No doubt Eli,
and perhaps his sons as well,
see in the young Samuel an apprentice to be taught and trained,
a child offered on account of a parent's respect
for the religious institution and priestly office.

---

39. The contrasts between this visit to Shiloh and her previous one are stark. Most obviously, she is now giving back what on the earlier visit she was praying for. Moreover, her subjectivity has completely changed. She does not simply accompany Elkanah to Shiloh as she did before. She makes the initiative to undertake the journey. She brings her own provisions and shows herself to be independent of Elkanah's apportionments. On this point Klein observes that, by bringing her own provisions, "Hannah has extricated herself from Elkanah's disruptive and isolating conduct" (1994: 90). Her agency is so pronounced that Elkanah's presence is actually left in question. He is not mentioned by name until 2:11. Only the vague "they" in verse 25 ("they brought the boy to Eli") and "he" in verse 28 ("he worshiped the Lord there"—which many translators take to be Samuel) give any hint that Elkanah is there. The most drastic contrast is the sound of Hannah's voice. Where before she had been reduced to silence by her family, and had been unable to vocalize her prayer in the temple, she now prays a long, articulate, and public prayer.

40. Scarry writes:

> [T]he imagination is large-spirited or, at least, has an inherent, incontrovertible tendency toward excess, amplitude, and abundance. Perhaps because it originally comes into being in the midst of acute deprivation, it continues to be, even long after that original "given" has disappeared, a shameless exponent of surfeit. (1985: 323)

The excessiveness of Hannah's imagination is, in Scarry's terms (1985: 324), translated into sharability. Her vision is now being distributed among a larger number of people.

Hannah, however,
sees differently.
The boy enters the service of God,
his presence becoming a service to all around him.
He is the child who will speak wisdom to the adults,
who will model a different way of being.
As a child, he will do what no adult can.[41]
As a child,[42] he is part of the upside-down world

---

41. It's hard for many of us to imagine putting our children at risk, exposing our children to violence and corruption in the name of some higher good. To conceptualize what this means, I'm reminded of Robert Coles's description of Tessie, one of the four black six-year-olds who initiated school desegregation in New Orleans in the early 1960s. Every day upon going to school she faced a barrage of taunts, obscenities, and threats from an angry mob. One morning, when she expressed hesitancy about facing school again, her grandmother gave her this word of encouragement:

> "It's no picnic, child—I know that, Tessie—going to that school. Lord Almighty, if I could just go with you, and stop there in front of that building, and call all those people to my side, and read to them from the Bible, and tell them, remind them, that He's up there, Jesus, watching over all of us—it don't matter who you are and what your skin color is. But I stay here, and you go—and your momma and your daddy, they have to leave the house so early in the morning that it's only Saturdays and Sundays that they see you before the sun hits the middle of its traveling for the day. So I'm not the one to tell you that you should go, because here I am, and I'll be watching television and eating or cleaning things up while you're walking by those folks. But I'll tell you, you're doing them a great favor; you're doing them a service, a big service." (1993: 3)

If this grandmother could have gone on behalf of Tessie, she would have. If Hannah could have brought about the needed change in Israelite society, she would have. But both women operate in a world that is dependent upon children to alter the world and they must wait in the wings with only a vision and words of encouragement while their children forge ahead to the front lines.

Later Coles reflects upon his own concerns as a pediatrician and a child-psychiatrist (and I daresay as a parent) as he engaged with Tessie and her family:

> [N]one of us was quite prepared for Tessie or her grandmother.... Tessie and her grandmother turned many of my ideas and assumptions upside down. Where I expected trouble, they saw great opportunity; where I waited for things to break down, they anticipated a breakthrough of sorts; where I saw a child bravely shouldering the burden of a divided, troubled society, they saw a blessed chance for a child to become a teacher, a healer, an instrument, maybe, of the salvation of others. (1993: 7-8)

42. Indeed, the candor and courage Samuel displays as a child loses a great deal of its charm and efficacy when he becomes an adult. As Doody observes:

> [Samuel] learns very quickly the art of telling others their faults that God teaches him. There is a certain officious quality already present in the youthful Samuel; it is part of his energy and his unaffected charm. He also has a good deal of curiosity. Curiosity and officiousness help to get him up on a dark night to go running in to the old man he thinks called out to him. Samuel the adult won't be happy unless he's managing other people's lives—not an amiable trait. (1994: 120-21)

Hannah envisions in her song
—the song
that finally finds its way
into the open air:

> My heart rejoices in the Lord;[43]
> My horn[44] is lifted high on account of the Lord.
> My mouth is open wide against those hostile to me;
> I revel in your deliverance.

> There is no one holy like the Lord;
> There is none beside you;
> There is no rock like our God.

> Speak no more arrogance;
> Nor let impetuous words come forth from your mouth.

---

43. The scholarly debate regarding the fit and authorship of Hannah's song is legendary and will not be recounted here. Joan E. Cook (1999: 40) offers a somewhat typical, but perhaps more diplomatic, assessment of the poem, trying to acknowledge both its place in the narrative and its sociological context outside the narrative frame:

> The words of the hymn do not directly address her particular situation, but rather praise the God who reverses the fortunes of all, upsets the status quo, and offers particular protection to the more vulnerable members of society. Hannah sings a carefully crafted hymn that expresses the specific concerns of an agricultural and pastoral society in the Galilean hills: the enemies are hunger, barrenness and poverty. Likewise it expresses the conviction that those who rely on the Deity will be protected and rewarded with reversals of fortune in their daily life.

The translation that follows is an attempt to take advantage of the wide semantic range of various words and phrases to present a song that does address the narrative situation presented in this reading. (The textual and grammatical problems are legion. For a detailed discussion of these, see McCarter 1980: 68-73; and Cook 1989: 61-86, 102-31.)

44. "Horn" is often translated "strength" due to its biological function in the animal kingdom. As a symbol of masculine virility, it does seem out of place in the mouth of Hannah. However, one might also imagine the horn depicted here as an instrument that signals (e.g., Josh 6:5) or makes music (Dan 3:5, 7, 10, 15 [Aramaic]) or at the very least seems to make some sort of noise that draws attention to the possessor (cf. Ps 75:5-6). The emphasis in the song would be on the freedom of sound and speech that was denied Hannah in her earlier visit to Shiloh. See also the reference to Hannah's open mouth in the next line (2:1), the arrogant speech of others in 2:3, the silencing of the wicked in 2:9, and the Lord's "thundering" (cf. Hannah's own [silent] "thundering": 1:6) in 2:10.

For the Lord is a knowing God;
He has the measure of abusive deeds.

The bows of the mighty are broken;
Those stumbling are clothed in strength.
Those once with plenty hire themselves out for bread,
The hungry hunger no more.
While the barren gives birth to seven,
The one with many sons has become despondent.
The Lord deals death and gives life,
Sends down to Sheol and raises up.
The Lord impoverishes and enriches
He casts down, he lifts high.
He lifts the lowly from the dust,
From the garbage dump he raises up the needy
And seats them among the nobility.
He gives them a seat of honor as their inheritance.
For the pillars of the earth are the Lord's;
He has set the whole world upon them.
He guards the feet of his faithful;
But the wicked will be silenced in darkness,
For not by force shall one prevail.

The opponents of the Lord will be shattered.
In the heavens he will thunder against them.
The Lord will judge the ends of the earth.
He will give strength to his king
And raise the horn of his anointed.

You were expecting a lullaby perhaps?
Hannah's song
is not for those trying to sleep through life.
Not for those safe and secure in the world as it is.
Hannah's song
is for the Others
who want and deserve to be safe
but who are never likely to be that.
Hannah's song
is a vision.
A vision of a world

Other than the one she had known in her lifetime.
A world where violators and violations
would be brought to an end,
where the arrogant speech
of greedy priests
and patronizing husbands
and rival wives
would be silenced,
where barren women might have children,
the hungry would be fed,
and all those trampled into the dust would be lifted up
and set back on their feet again.
A world where the faithful could live without fear.
A world where the bottom becomes the top.
The last becomes the first.
The margins become the center.

Is it really any wonder that no one wanted to hear this song?
If you've negotiated this world with all its evils,
if you have survived
and even succeeded
according to the rules of this world,
why would you want to hear a song like Hannah's?
It's so much easier to let things be.

Perhaps that's why
her song is met with silence.

And so with silent indulgence
young Samuel is taken into the house of God
as the answered prayer of a desperate woman,
to be a house-boy in the house of God,
an assistant,
the hands, feet, ears, and eyes of Eli.

And Hannah goes back home to re/make her life with Elkanah
and to make coats for her son,
and once a year
to follow her husband to Shiloh.

When—
and only when—
Hannah lays aside things political
to take up things domestic,
her loan of Samuel earns her a blessing from Eli.
Five more children.

(Did she ask for them?
Does she want them?
The story doesn't say.)

Five more children to attend to
and care for.
Yet Samuel is never forgotten.[45]
Thus, Hannah becomes
a traditional wife and mother,
and less of a disturbance to those around her.

And yet, she is different.
No longer barren and unchangeable,
no longer sad and silent,
she's had a vision.
She's birthed a son.
She's composed a song.
And now she makes more children
—and coats.

---

45. Doody puts it well:

> This is a profitable equation indeed: 1 child given to the Lord = 5 children. Certainly the author(s) of this book did not want us to feel that Hannah was shortchanged. Yet the text, having introduced her momentous gift, her loan, and her loss, can never quite get rid of the sense of her loss. While she may rejoice in her five new children, the very first is absent: "The child Samuel grew before the Lord"—in that clause we see that Hannah is missing even among the cluster of her five children. Samuel grows before the Lord, not in her sight. She has lost the child who might play near her, in the room or in the dooryard, who might be schooled nearby and learn a trade and marry some nice neighbor girl and come around of an evening. All the vivid home hopes and daily affections are cut off. That suppressed desire to be part of Samuel's life, to surround him with her love, emerges in the annual gift Hannah brings to her "Temple child." . . . Here is another substitution: For words of love and playfulness, for kisses and hugs, there is substituted the making of an object and then just the object. (1994: 111)

With every child,
>   she extends herself
>   and her vision into the world.
And with every coat,
>   she embraces her son
>   protecting him from the elements.[46]
With every coat
>   she reminds her son
>   to make what he can out of what he's been given.
With every coat
>   she shows her son
>   the relationship between imagination and compassion.
With every coat
>   she tells her son
>   that he is not alone.
In every coat
>   she weaves the song
>   so he can clothe himself with strength.

Once simply the recipient of Elkanah's largesse,
Hannah is now generous to the world.[47]
And unlike Elkanah's allotment of sacrificial portions,

---

46. Cf. Scarry:

> In the attempt to understand making, attention cannot stop at the object (the coat, the poem), for *the object is only a fulcrum or lever across which the force of creation moves back onto the human site* and remakes the makers. The woman making the coat, for example has no interest in making a coat per se but in making someone warm; her skilled attention to threads, materials, seams, linings are all objectifications of the fact that she is at work to remake human tissue to be free of the problem of being cold. She could do this by putting her arms around the shivering person . . . , but she instead more successfully accomplishes her goal by indirection—by making the freestanding object which then remakes the human site that is her actual object. So, too, the poet projects the private acuities of sentience into the sharable, because objectified, poem, which exists not for its own sake but to be read: its power now moves back from the object realm to the human realm where sentience itself is remade. . . . Like the coat-maker, the poet is working not to make the artifact (which is just the midpoint in the total action), but to remake human sentience; by means of the poem, he or she enters into and in some way alters the alive percipience of other persons. (1985: 307)

47. Cf. Scarry: "[W]hat originated as a wholly interior counterfactual wish has been objectified into a sharable outcome" (1985: 316).

Hannah's gifts dictate no particular response.
She doesn't insist on gratitude or reciprocity.
Her song,
   her son,
     her children,
       her coats
         are gifts of change and surplus,
gifts that disrupt
the equations and stagnations offered by those around her,
gifts that declare

                       this is not a world
            where one husband equals ten sons,
   where personal indulgences are as good as the honoring of God,[48]
         where it's just as well to let corruption continue
               as it is to do anything to stop it,
           where one thing is as good as another,
       where it is easier to let things stay as they are.
Hannah's gifts chant transformation and excess:
There is more that can be done
There is more that can be shared
There is more that can be
There is more
There is more
There is more.[49]

In time God, too, catches on.
Taking a lead from Hannah's song,
God, too, tests the divine capacity to re/create
and formulates a vision of change.
Those gorging themselves
            with the choicest portions of holy sacrifices
            will find themselves begging for bread.[50]

---

48. 1 Sam 2:29.

49. Scarry writes that one of the attributes of the imagination is "its nonimmunity from its own action. The imagination's object is not simply to alter the external world, or to alter the human being in his or her full array of capacities and needs, but also and more specifically, to alter the power of alteration itself, to act on and continually revise the nature of creating" (1985: 324).

50. 1 Sam 2:27-36.

A new priest shall rise up, (the barren woman has given birth!) one who will listen for the word of the Lord, who will speak God's will to the people, and who will be trustworthy as a leader of Israel and a prophet of God.[51]

There is more that can be.

Indeed.

✳✳✳

Samuel.

"Here I am, Eli. You called?"

"No, my son. Go lie down."

Samuel.

"I am here, Eli. I heard you call me."

"No, my son. Go back to sleep."

Samuel.

"Here I am, Eli. I know you called me."

"No, my son . . . You've heard something beyond me. Something different. Something else. Lie back down and listen."

✳

Samuel! Samuel!

---

51. Cf. Doody:

> Tradition, the fathers, the priests, and the learned need not necessarily know best. God skips over learning and tradition and the institution and the recognized authorities—looking for somewhere he can make a breakthrough. . . . [I]f God gets fed up with the holy mess created by the holy orders and skips about ignoring the hierarchies of the institutions, why, then there's no reason why the vision of God, the word of God, the truth of God might not strike suddenly the least likely person. (1994: 118)

"Speak, Lord, for your servant is listening."

I am about to do a thing in Israel, so new that the ears of all who hear of it will tingle.

"That sounds like a song my mother used to sing."

Indeed. It's a song worth knowing. And it's time you learned to sing it, too.

"Sing, Lord, for your servant is listening."

✳

"Samuel, my son?"

"Here I am, Eli."

"What did you hear?"

"A song my mother used to sing. Did you ever hear her song?"

"No. Not really."

"That's too bad. You should have listened to her song, Eli. You should have taught it to your children."

"Can you . . . sing it for me now?"

"Yes. I can. But it will make your ears tingle."[52]

---

52. "We should be frightened of Samuels," writes Doody, "for they mean a change is on the way" (1994: 122).

> Energy, persistence, openness to divine revelation, and unnerving candor—these qualities accompany a certain heartlessness on the part of children. Children understand this quite well themselves, and grown-ups don't want to know about it. Infant piety is a frightening thing. Either it is feigned . . . , in which case it is a sticky piece of hypocrisy. Or it is genuine, which means the child who is listening to God and not to us will be capable of startling revelations, and will refuse to be taken in by our show. (1994: 122)

"I really like these new books I'm reading," said the eleven-year-old.

"Oh?" said the mom. "That's good! What do you like about them?"

"Well, they're like diaries. The person telling the story is writing it in a diary, so it's like you're reading their special secret story, the things they want to remember the most. Besides that, you get the story in bits and pieces and you have to put it together yourself."

"If you like stories told like that, there's a book you'll want to read when you get older. In that book the story is told by a young woman writing letters to God."

"What happens to her?" asked the girl.

"At some point she stops writing letters to God and starts writing to her friend instead."

"Yeah. I can see why she might do that."

"Oh?" said the mom.

"Yeah. It's not as though God's ever gonna write back, is he?"

"No, I suppose not," said the mother, smiling and adding, "I see you've joined the long line of people asking questions about how God relates to us."

"Well, sometimes it seems like God is deaf—well, not exactly deaf—but you know how some deaf people have trouble talking and some don't speak at all? Isn't there a word for that?"

"You mean 'mute'?"

"Yeah, mute. Mute. I think God is mute."

"Hmmm. That's a very interesting idea."

"I know, a lot of people think God's a great big perfect guy in the sky," said the girl, making a sweeping dramatic gesture, "but I think that if we could imagine even one little thing wrong with God, everything would make a lot more sense."

"I think I see your point."

"In fact," said the girl, mulling this idea over, "you know the sign language that deaf people use to talk to each other?"

"Yes," said the mom.   "Well, I think that's probably how God talks to us—in signs. Maybe the problem is that we just don't bother to learn the language."

❧

A Prayer
(In the Spirit of Isaiah 11)

May your spirit—
    a spirit of wisdom and insight,
        a spirit of counsel and courage,
            a spirit of knowledge and reverence—
light upon us

                              and interrupt us.

Show us the difference
    between what is right and what is wrong
        because our eyes are often dim
            and our ears are sometimes untrustworthy.

May justice and faithfulness
    empower us
        and guide us
            to protect all who are vulnerable
                —especially our children.

Help us envision a world transformed,
    where our living does not require our killing,
    where the wolf might dwell with the lamb,
     and the lion with the fawn,
    where the names predator and prey are heard no more,
    where our children might live without fear
        and make their homes in peace
            among the rest of your creatures.

Help us envision a world transformed,
    a world fit for your holy dwelling,
        a world fit for our children,
    where nothing evil would ever come to pass,
        where the knowledge of God would fill the land
            as water fills the sea.

For
    once we have such a vision,
        we will know
            what must be done.

Bibliography

Books and Articles

Alter, Robert. 1992. *The World of Biblical Literature*. New York: Basic Books.

Amiran, Minda Rae. 1992. " 'She Was Wildly Clad': Orphan Girls in Earlier Children's Literature." *The Mid-Atlantic Almanac* 1: 85-92.

Amit, Yairah. 1994. " 'Am I Not More Devoted to You than Ten Sons?' (1 Samuel 1:8): Male and Female Interpretations." *A Feminist Companion to Samuel and Kings*. Ed. Athalya Brenner. Sheffield: Sheffield Academic Press. Pp. 68-76.

Bakhtin, Mikhail. 1973. *Problems of Dostoevsky's Poetics*. Trans. R. W. Rotsel. Ann Arbor, Michigan: Ardis. (First published as *Problemy tvorchestva Dostoevskogo* in 1929.)

_____. 1984. *Rabelais and His World*. Trans. Hélène Iswolsky. Bloomington: Indiana University.

_____. 1986. "From Notes Made in 1970-71." *Speech Genres and Other Late Essays*. Trans. Vern W. McGee. Eds. Caryl Emerson and Michael Holquist. Austin: University of Texas. Pp. 132-55.

_____. 1990. *Art and Answerability: Early Philosophical Essays*. Eds. Michael Holquist and Vladimir Liapunov. Austin: University of Texas.

Baldwin, Joyce. 1978. *Daniel*. Downers Grove, Illinois: InterVarsity.

Bauman, Zygmunt. 1997. *Postmodernity and Its Discontents*. New York: New York University.

Beal, Timothy K. 1997. *The Book of Hiding: Gender, Ethnicity, Annihilation, and Esther*. London: Routledge.

Bettelheim, Bruno. 1976. *The Uses of Enchantment: The Meaning and Importance of Fairy Tales*. New York: Alfred A. Knopf.

Boling, Robert G. 1975. *Judges*. New York: Doubleday.

Boyarin, Daniel. 1990. *Intertextuality and the Reading of Midrash*. Bloomington/Indianapolis: Indiana University.

Brenner, Athalya, ed. 1998. *Genesis: A Feminist Companion to the Bible (Series II)*. Sheffield: Sheffield Academic Press.

Brooks, Peter. 1985. *Reading for the Plot: Design and Intention in Narrative*. New York: Vintage.

Bruns, Gerald. 1986. "Midrash and Allegory." *The Literary Guide to the Bible*. Eds. Frank Kermode and Robert Alter. Cambridge, Mass.: Harvard University. Pp. 625-46.

Burney, C. F. 1970. *The Book of Judges*. New York: KTAV.

Carroll, Robert P. 1991. "Textual Strategies and Ideology in the Second Temple Period." *Second Temple Studies, 1: The Persian Period*. Ed. Philip R. Davies. JSOTSup. Sheffield: JSOT Press. Pp. 108-24.

Coles, Robert. 1993. *The Call of Service: A Witness to Idealism*. Boston/New York: Houghton Mifflin.

_____. 1997. *The Moral Intelligence of Children*. New York: Random House.

Cook, Joan E. 1989. *The Song of Hannah: Text and Contexts*. Ph.D. Dissertation, Vanderbilt University.

_____. 1999 *Hannah's Desire, God's Design: Early Interpretations of the Story of Hannah*. Sheffield: Sheffield Academic Press.

Cornia, Giovanni Andrea and Sheldon Danziger, eds. 1997. *Child Poverty and Deprivation in the Industrialized Countries, 1945–1995*. Oxford: Clarendon. [UNICEF copyright.]

Council of Bishops of The United Methodist Church. 1996. "Children and Poverty: An Episcopal Initiative. Biblical and Theological Foundations." Nashville: United Methodist Publishing House.

Couture, Pamela D. 2000. *Seeing Children, Seeing God: A Practical Theology of Children and Poverty*. Nashville: Abingdon Press.

Craig, Kenneth. 1995. *Reading Esther: A Case for the Literary Carnivalesque*. Louisville: Westminster/John Knox.

cummings, e. e. 1959. *Poems 1923–1954 by e. e. cummings*. New York: Harcourt, Brace Jovanovich.

Davies, Philip R. 1985. *Daniel*. Sheffield: JSOT.

_____. 1995. *In Search of "Ancient Israel."* JSOTSup 148. Sheffield: Sheffield Academic Press.

Davis, Patricia H. 2001. *Beyond Nice: The Spiritual Wisdom of Adolescent Girls*. Minneapolis: Fortress.

Delaney, Carol. 1998. *Abraham on Trial: The Social Legacy of Biblical Myth*. Princeton: Princeton University Press

Derrida, Jacques. 1991. "At This Very Moment in This Work Here I Am." Trans. Ruben Berezdivin. *Re-Reading Levinas*. Eds. Robert Bernasconi and Simon Critchley. Bloomington/Indianapolis: Indiana University. Pp. 11-48.

_____. 1995. *The Gift of Death*. Trans. David Wills. Chicago/London: University of Chicago.

Dijk-Hemmes, Fokkelien van. 1994. "The Great Woman of Shunem and the Man of God: A Dual Interpretation of 2 Kings 4:8-37." *A Feminist Companion to Samuel and Kings*. Ed. Athalya Brenner. Sheffield: Sheffield Academic Press. Pp. 218-30.

Doody, Margaret Anne. 1994. "Infant Piety and the Infant Samuel." *Out of the Garden: Women Writers on the Bible*. Eds. Christina Büchmann and Celina Spiegel. New York: Fawcett Columbine. Pp. 103-22.

Dunbar, Paul Laurence. 1930. *The Complete Works of Paul Laurence Dunbar*. New York: Dodd, Mead.

Dundes, Alan. 1991. "Bruno Bettelheim's Uses of Enchantment and Abuses of Scholarship." *Journal of American Folklore* 104: 74-83.

Edelman, Marian Wright. 1995. "Cease Fire! Stopping the Gun War Against Children in the United States." *The Chicago Theological Seminary Register.*

Eskenazi, Tamara C. and Eleanore P. Judd. 1994. "Marriage to a Stranger in Ezra 9–10." *Second Temple Studies, 2: Temple Community in the Persian Period.* Eds. Tamara C. Eskenazi and Kent H. Richards. JSOTSup 175. Sheffield: JSOT. Pp. 266-85.

Eslinger, Lyle. 1985. *Kingship of God in Crisis: A Close Reading of 1 Samuel 1–12.* Sheffield: Almond.

Exum, J. Cheryl. 1993. "On Judges 11." *A Feminist Companion to Judges.* Ed. Athalya Brenner. Sheffield: Sheffield Academic Press. Pp. 131-44.

Fackenheim, Emil L. 1970. *God's Presence in History: Jewish Affirmations and Philosophical Reflections.* New York: NYU Press; London: University of London.

Falk, Marcia. 1994. "Reflections on Hannah's Prayer." *Out of the Garden: Women Writers on the Bible.* Eds Christina Büchmann and Celina Spiegel. New York: Fawcett Columbine. Pp. 94-102.

Fewell, Danna Nolan. 1991. *Circle of Sovereignty: Plotting Politics in the Book of Daniel.* Nashville: Abingdon Press.

_____. 1992. "Judges." *The Women's Bible Commentary.* Eds. Carol Newsom and Sharon Ringe, Louisville: Westminster/John Knox. Pp. 67-77.

_____. 1997. "Imagination, Method, and Murder: Un/Framing the Face of Postexilic Israel." *Reading Bibles, Writing Bodies: Identity and the Book.* Eds. Timothy K. Beal and David M. Gunn. Biblical Limits Series. London: Routledge. Pp. 132-52.

Fewell, Danna Nolan and David M. Gunn. 1993. *Gender, Power, and Promise: The Subject of the Bible's First Story.* Nashville: Abingdon Press.

Fewell, Danna Nolan and Gary A. Phillips. 1997. "Drawn to Excess, or Reading Beyond Betrothal." *Bible and Ethics of Reading (Semeia 77).* Atlanta: Society of Biblical Literature. Pp. 23-58.

Foucault, Michel. 1976, 1984. *History of Sexuality.* New York: Vintage.

Fox, Michael. 1991. *Character and Ideology in the Book of Esther.* University of South Carolina Press.

Frank, Arthur W. 1995. *The Wounded Storyteller: Body, Illness, and Ethics.* Chicago/London: University of Chicago.

Fuchs, Esther. 1985. "The Literary Characterization of Mothers and Sexual Politics in the Hebrew Bible." *Feminist Perspectives on Biblical Scholarship.* Ed. Adele Yarbro Collins. Chico, Calif.: Scholars. Pp. 117-36.

_____. 1993. "Marginalization, Ambiguity, Silencing. The Story of Jephthah's Daughter." *A Feminist Companion to Judges.* Ed. Athalya Brenner. Sheffield: Sheffield Academic Press. Pp. 116-30.

Ginsberg, H. L. 1954. "The Composition of the Book of Daniel." *Vetus Testamentum* 4:246-75.

Ginzberg, Louis. 1998. *The Legends of the Jews. Volume One: From the Creation to Jacob.* Trans. Henrietta Szold. Baltimore/London: Johns Hopkins University. 1st ed: 1909.

Gordon, Linda. 1988. *Heroes of Their Own Lives: The Politics and History of Family Violence.* New York: Penguin.

Gray, John. 1967. *Joshua, Judges and Ruth.* London: Nelson.

_____. 1964/1970. *I & II Kings. A Commentary* OTL. Philadelphia: Westminster.

Gunn, David, and Danna Nolan Fewell. 1993. *Narrative in the Hebrew Bible*. Oxford: Oxford University.

Hamilton, Mark W. 1995. "Who Was a Jew? Jewish Ethnicity During the Achaemenid Period." *RQ* 37:102-17.

Harrington, D. J. 1985. "Pseudo-Philo." *The Old Testament Pseudepigrapha*. Vol 2. Ed. J. H. Charlesworth. New York: Doubleday.

Harris, Irving B. 1996. *Children in Jeopardy. Can We Break the Cycle of Poverty?* (The Yale Child Study Center Monograph Series on Child Psychiatry, Child Development, and Social Policy) New Haven: Yale University.

Harvey, Pharis J. 1995. "Where Children Work: Child Servitude in the Global Economy." *The Christian Century*. April 5: 362-65.

Hatley, James. 2000. *Suffering Witness: The Quandary of Responsibility After the Irreparable*. New York: State University of New York.

Havea, Jione. 2003. *Elusions of Control: Biblical Law on the Words of Women*. Semeia Studies. Atlanta: SBL.

Heard, R. Christopher. 2001. *Dynamics of Diselection: Ambiguity in Genesis 12–36 and Ethnic Boundaries in Post-Exilic Judah*. Semeia Studies. Atlanta: SBL.

Hoglund, Kenneth G. 1992. *Achaemenid Imperial Administration in Syria-Palestine and the Missions of Ezra and Nehemiah*. SBLDS 125. Atlanta: Scholars.

Jabès, Edmond. 1983. *The Book of Questions, Volume VI*. Trans. Rosemarie Waldrop. Middletown, Conn.: Wesleyan University Press.

Jobling, David. 1998. *1 Samuel*. Collegeville, Minn.: The Liturgical Press.

Johnson, Willa Mathis. 1999. *Interethnic Marriage in Persian Yehud*. Dissertation, Vanderbilt University.

Josipovici, Gabriel. 1988. *The Book of God*. New Haven/London: Yale University.

Kermode, Frank. 1980. "Secrets and Narrative Sequence." *On Narrative*. Ed. W. J. T. Mitchell. Chicago/London: University of Chicago. Pp. 79-97.

Klein, Lillian. 1994. "Hannah: Marginalized Victim and Social Redeemer." *A Feminist Companion to Samuel and Kings*. Ed. Athalya Brenner. Sheffield: Sheffield Academic Press. Pp. 77-92.

Kristeva, Julia. 1980 (Fr. 1969). *Desire in Language: A Semiotic Approach to Literature and Art*. Trans. Thomas Gora, Alice Jardine, and Leon S. Roudiez. Ed. Leon S. Roudiez. New York: Columbia University.

_____. 1982. *The Powers of Horror: An Essay on Abjection*. New York: Columbia University Press.

_____. 1989. *Black Sun: Depression and Melancholia*. Trans. Leon S. Roudiez. New York: Columbia University.

_____. 1991. *Strangers to Ourselves*. Trans. Leon S. Roudiez. New York: Columbia University Press.

_____. 1995. *New Maladies of the Soul*. Trans. R. Guberman. New York: Columbia University.

Landy, Francis. 1997. "Do We Want Our Children to Read This Book?" *Bible and Ethics of Reading* (*Semeia* 77). Eds. Danna Nolan Fewell and Gary A. Phillips. Atlanta: Society of Biblical Literature. Pp. 157-76.

Levinas, Emmanuel. 1969. *Totality and Infinity: An Essay on Exteriority*. Duquesne Studies Philosophical Series 24. Trans. Alphonso Lingis. Pittsburgh: Duquesne University. [*Totaité et Infini*. The Hague, Netherlands: Marinus Nijhoff. 1961].

_____. 1976. *Noms propres*. Montpellier: Fata Morgana.

_____. 1985. *Ethics and Infinity. Conversations with Philippe Nemo*. Trans. Richard A. Cohen. Pittsburgh: Duquesne University. [*Ethique et infini*. Librairie Arthème Fayard et Radio France. 1982.]

_____. 1986. "The Trace of the Other." Trans. A. Lingis. *Deconstruction in Context*. Ed. Mark Taylor. Chicago: University of Chicago. Pp. 345-59.

_____.1988. "Useless Suffering." Trans. Richard A. Cohen. *The Provocation of Levinas: Rethinking the Other*. Eds. Robert Bernasconi and David Wood. London/New York: Routledge. Pp. 156-67. [1st appeared "La Souffrance inutile," *Giornale di Metafisica* 4 (1982): 13-26.]

_____. 1989. "Revelation in Jewish Tradition." Trans. Sarah Richmond. *The Levinas Reader*. Ed. Seán Hand. Oxford/Cambridge: Blackwell. Pp. 190-210.

_____. 1990. *Difficult Freedom: Essays on Judaism*. Trans. Seán Hand. Baltimore: Johns Hopkins University.

_____. 1994. "Revelation in the Jewish Tradition." *Beyond the Verse: Talmudic Readings and Lectures*. Trans. Gary D. Mole. Bloomington: Indiana University. Pp. 129-50.

_____. 1998. *Otherwise Than Being or Beyond Essence*. Trans. Alphonso Lingis. Pittsburgh: Duquesne University Press. [*Autrement qu'être ou au-delà de l'Essence*. Dordrecht: Martinus Nijhoff, 1974]

Levinas, Emmanuel, and Richard Kearney. 1986. "Dialogue with Emmanuel Levinas." *Face-to-Face with Levinas*. Ed. Richard Cohen. New York: State University of New York.

Long, Burke. 1988. "A Figure at the Gate: Readers, Reading, and Biblical Theologians." *Canon, Theology, and Old Testament Interpretation: Essays in Honor of Brevard S. Childs*. Eds. Gene M. Tucker, David L. Petersen, and Robert R. Wilson. Philadelphia: Fortress. Pp. 166-86.

_____. 1991. "The Shunammite Woman: In the Shadow of the Prophet?" *Bible Review* 7: 12-19, 42.

Magonet, Jonathan. 1980. "The Liberal and the Lady: Esther Revisited." *Judaism* 29: 167-76.

_____. 1991. *A Rabbi's Bible*. London: SCM.

McAfee, Noëlle. 1993. "Abject Strangers: Toward an Ethics of Respect." *Ethics, Politics, and Difference in Julia Kristeva's Writing*. Ed. Kelly Oliver. New York/London: Routledge.

McCarter, P. Kyle Jr. 1980. *1 Samuel: A New Translation with Introduction, Notes, and Commentary*. Garden City, N.Y.: Doubleday.

Miscall, Peter. 1983. *The Workings of Old Testament Narrative*. Semeia Studies. Chico, Calif.: Scholars; and Philadelphia: Fortress.

_____. 1986. *1 Samuel: A Literary Reading*. Bloomington: University of Indiana.

Mullen, E. Theodore, Jr. 1997. *Ethnic Myths and Pentateuchal Foundations: A New Approach to the Formation of the Pentateuch*. Semeia Studies. Atlanta: Scholars.

Müller, Hans-Peter. 1972. "Mantische Weisheit und Apokalyptic," *VTSup* 22: 268-93.

Meyers, Carol. 1988. *Discovering Eve: Ancient Israelite Women in Context*. New York/Oxford: Oxford University.

Newton, Adam Zachary. 1995. *Narrative Ethics*. Cambridge/London: Harvard University.

Nicholsburg, George W. E. 1981. *Jewish Literature Between the Bible and the Mishnah*. Philadelphia: Fortress.

Ochs, Peter. 1996. "Postcritical Scriptural Interpretation in Judaism." *Interpreting Judaism in a Postmodern Age*. Ed. Steven Kepnes. New York/London: New York University. Pp. 55-81.

Ostriker, Alicia Suskin. 1993. *Feminist Revision and the Bible*. Oxford, U.K./Cambridge, USA: Blackwell.

Patte, Daniel. 1995. *Ethics of Biblical Interpretation: A Reevaluation*. Louisville: Westminster/John Knox.

Phillips, Gary A. 1999. "The Killing Fields of Matthew's Gospel." *The Labour of Reading: Desire, Alienation, and Biblical Interpretation*. Eds. Fiona C. Black, Roland Boer, and Erin Runions. Semeia Studies 36. Atlanta: Society of Biblical Literature. Pp. 249-65.

Polzin, Robert. 1989. *Samuel and the Deuteronomist: A Literary Study of the Deuteronomic History. Part Two: 1 Samuel*. San Francisco: Harper & Row.

Porteous, Norman. 1965. *Daniel*. London: SCM.

Rashkow, Ilona N. 1992. "Intertextuality, Transference, and the Reader in/of Genesis 12 and 20." *Reading Between Texts: Intertextuality and the Hebrew Bible*. Ed. Danna Nolan Fewell. Louisville: Westminster/John Knox. Pp. 57-73.

Reinhartz, Adele. 1994. "Anonymous Women and the Collapse of the Monarchy: A Study in Narrative Technique." *A Feminist Companion to Samuel and Kings*. Ed. Athalya Brenner, Sheffield: Sheffield Academic Press. Pp. 43-65.

Reuther, Rosemary Radford. 1982. "Woman as Oppressed; Woman as Liberated in Scriptures." *Spinning a Sacred Yarn: Women Speak from the Pulpit*. New York: Pilgrim. Pp. 181-86.

Roemer, Michael. 1995. *Telling Stories: Postmodernism and the Invalidation of Traditional Narrative*. Lanham, Md.: Rowman & Littlefield.

Sartre, Jean-Paul. 1965. *What Is Literature?* Trans. Bernard Frechtman. New York: Harper & Row. Cambridge: Harvard University Press.

Satir, Virginia. 1988. *The New Peoplemaking*. Mountain View, Calif.: Science and Behavior Books.

Scarry, Elaine. 1985. *The Body in Pain: The Making and Unmaking of the World*. New York/Oxford: Oxford University.

Schwartz, Howard. 1998. *Reimagining the Bible: The Storytelling of the Rabbis*. New York/ Oxford: Oxford University.

Scott, James C. 1990. *Domination and the Arts of Resistance: Hidden Transcripts*. New Haven, Conn.: Yale University.

Shields, Mary E. 1993. "Subverting a Man of God, Elevating a Woman: Role and Power Reversals in 2 Kings 4." *JSOT* 58: 59-69.

Smith-Christopher, Daniel. 1991. "The Mixed Marriage Crisis in Ezra." *Second Temple Studies: 2. Temple Community in the Persian Period*. Eds. Tamara Eskenazi and Kent Richards. JSOTSup 175. Sheffield: JSOT. Pp. 243-65.

Spiegel, Celina. 1994. "The World Remade: The Book of Esther." *Out of the Garden: Women Writers on the Bible*. Eds. Christina Büchmann and Celina Spiegel. New York: Fawcett Columbine. Pp. 191-203.

Talbot, Margaret. 2002. "Girls Just Want to Be Mean." *The New York Times Magazine*. February 24; Section 6.

Tamez, Elsa. 1986. "The Woman Who Complicated Salvation History." *New Eyes for Reading: Biblical and Theological Reflections by Women from the Third World*. Eds. John S. Pobee and Bärbel von Wartenberg-Potter. Geneva: World Council of Churches; Bloomington, Ind.: Meyer·Stone Books. Pp. 5-17.

Todorov, Tzvetan. 1984. *Mikhail Bakhtin: The Dialogical Principle*. Minneapolis: University of Minnesota Press.

Trible, Phyllis. 1984. *Texts of Terror: Literary-Feminist Readings of Biblical Narratives*. Philadelphia: Fortress.

Turner, Victor. 1974. *Dramas, Fields, and Metaphors: Symbolic Action in Human Society*. Ithaca, N.Y.

_____. 1980. "Social Dramas and Stories About Them." *On Narrative*. Ed. W. J. T. Mitchell. Chicago/London: University of Chicago.

Walker, Alice, and Pratibha Parmar. 1993. *Warrior Marks: Female Genital Mutilation and the Sexual Blinding of Women*. New York: Harcourt Brace.

Warren, Carol, and Barbara Laslett. 1980. "Privacy and Secrecy: A Conceptual Comparison." *Secrecy: A Cross-Cultural Perspective*. Ed. Stanton K. Tefft. New York/London: Human Sciences Press. Pp. 25-34.

Waters, John. 1991. "Who Was Hagar?" *Stony the Road We Trod: African American Biblical Interpretation*. Ed. Cain Hope Felder. Minneapolis: Fortress. Pp. 187-205.

Webb, Barry. 1987. *The Book of Judges: An Integrated Reading*. Sheffield: JSOT.

Weems, Renita J. 1988. "A Mistress, a Maid, and No Mercy." *Just a Sister Away: A Womanist Vision of Women's Relationships in the Bible*. San Diego: LuraMedia. Pp. 1-19.

Wiesel, Elie. 1979. *The Trial of God (as it was held on February 25, 1649, in Shamgorod)*. Trans. Marion Wiesel. New York: Schocken.

Williams, Patricia J. 1992 "In Search of Pharaoh's Daughter." *Out of the Garden: Women Writers on the Bible*. Eds. Christina Büchmann and Celina Spiegel. New York: Fawcett Columbine. Pp. 54-71.

Wray, Naomi. 1993. *Frank Wesley: Exploring Faith with a Brush*. Auckland, New Zealand: Pace Publishing.

Ziarek, Ewa. 1993. "Kristeva and Levinas: Mourning, Ethics, and the Feminine." *Ethics, Politics, and Difference in Julia Kristeva's Writing*. Ed. Kelly Oliver. New York/London: Routledge. Pp. 62-78.

Zipes, Jack. 1979. "On the Use and Abuse of Folk and Fairy Tales with Children: Bruno Bettelheim's Moralistic Magic Wand." *Breaking the Magic Spell: Radical Theories of Folk and Folk Tales*. Ed. Jack Zipes. Austin: University of Texas. Pp. 160-82.

Online Sources

The Annie E. Casey Foundation. 2001. *Kids Count Census Data Online*. Baltimore: Annie E. Casey Foundation. http://www.aecf.org/cgi-bin/aeccensus2.cgi?action=profileresults&area=1.

The Annie E. Casey Foundation. 2001. *Kids Count Data Book Online*. Baltimore: Annie E. Casey Foundation. http://www.aecf.org/kidscount/kc2001/.

The Annie E. Casey Foundation. 2002. *Children at Risk: State Trends 1990–2000*. Baltimore: Annie E. Casey Foundation. http://www.aecf.org/kidscount/c2ss.

Kids Count. 2002. *Kids Count International Data Sheet*. Washington, D.C.: Population Reference Bureau and Child Trends. htp://www.aecf.org/kidscount/

The United Nations Annual Reports of the High Commission: Report(s) of the Special Rapporteur on the Sale of Children, Child Prostitution and Child. http://www.unhchr.ch/huridocda/huridoca.nsf.

United Nations Children's Fund (UNICEF). 2001. *UNICEF End Decade Databases*. New York: UNICEF. http://www.childinfo.org/eddb/.

United Nations Children's Fund (UNICEF). 1996. *The State of the World's Children*. New York: UNICEF. http://www.unicef.org/voy/meeting/war/war-exp2.html.

The U.S. Department of Heath and Human Services, Administration on Children, Youth and Families. 2001. *Child Maltreatment 1999*. Washington, D.C.: U.S. Government Printing Office. http://www.acf.dhhs.gov/programs/cb/publications/cm99/index.htm.

The World Health Organization. 1997. *Fact Sheet No. 180. Reducing Mortality from Major Childhood Killer Diseases.* http://www.who.int/child-adolescent-health/New_Publications/IMCI/fs_180.htm.

The World Health Organization. 1999. *Report of the Consultation on Child Abuse Prevention.* Violence and Injury Prevention Team, Geneva, March 29-31, 1999. http://www.who.ch.

The World Health Organization Press Release. April 8, 1999. *Who Recognizes Child Abuse As A Major Public Health Problem.* http://www.who.int/.

The World Health Organization. *Africa Malaria Day 2002: Facts and Figures.* http://www.who.int/home-page/.

Index

Scripture Citations and Other Ancient Writers

Hebrew Bible

Subjects